A DIARY OF
The Lady

By the same author

The Mummy Diaries
Notting Hell
Shire Hell

A DIARY OF The Lady

My First Year as Editor

RACHEL JOHNSON

FIG TREE
an imprint of
PENGUIN BOOKS

FIG TREE

Published by the Penguin Group
Penguin Books Ltd, 80 Strand, London WC2R 0RL, England
Penguin Group (USA) Inc., 375 Hudson Street, New York, New York 10014, USA
Penguin Group (Canada), 90 Eglinton Avenue East, Suite 700, Toronto, Ontario, Canada M4P 2Y3
(a division of Pearson Penguin Canada Inc.)
Penguin Ireland, 25 St Stephen's Green, Dublin 2, Ireland (a division of Penguin Books Ltd)
Penguin Group (Australia), 250 Camberwell Road,
Camberwell, Victoria 3124, Australia (a division of Pearson Australia Group Pty Ltd)
Penguin Books India Pvt Ltd, 11 Community Centre,
Panchsheel Park, New Delhi – 110 017, India
Penguin Group (NZ), 67 Apollo Drive, Rosedale, North Shore 0632, New Zealand
(a division of Pearson New Zealand Ltd)
Penguin Books (South Africa) (Pty) Ltd, 24 Sturdee Avenue,
Rosebank, Johannesburg 2196, South Africa

Penguin Books Ltd, Registered Offices: 80 Strand, London WC2R 0RL, England

www.penguin.com

First published 2010
1

Set in 11/14 pt Adobe Minion
Typeset by TexTech International
Printed in Great Britain by Clays Ltd, St Ives plc

A CIP catalogue record for this book is available from the British Library

ISBN: 978–1–905–49067–7

www.greenpenguin.co.uk

Penguin Books is committed to a sustainable future
for our business, our readers and our planet.
The book in your hands is made from paper
certified by the Forest Stewardship Council.

To all readers of The Lady *– may our tribe increase*

'If you ask me what was more terrifying, putting a helicopter down in a 25m² clearing in the Florida Everglades or running a genteel ladies' magazine in the centre of London, I'd say the latter.'

Ben Budworth, *Sunday Express*, 12 April 2009

Acknowledgements

I would like to thank everyone in Bedford Street from the bottom of my heart – and, um, most importantly, *in advance*, before they read what follows – for being so sporting. I would like to single out for a gold medal Ben Budworth, who has put in and continues to put in dazzling, Olympian displays of tolerance and forbearance. I would also like to thank the Budworth family as a whole for entrusting the editorship of their beloved ancestral magazine into my hands. On the editorial and production side at Penguin, Jenny Lord and Juliet Annan, respectively my editor and publisher at Fig Tree, have been terrific in getting behind the project and seeing it through in double-quick time, especially the frighteningly efficient and steely Jenny. Sarah Day copy-edited rapidly and sympathetically in between – as one thrilling email told me – 'reading bits out' to her weary family. Penguin's Katherine Stroud and Alex Elam, thank you for all you do on the Dark Side to do with publicity, marketing, rights, etc. – you know – and finally, thanks as ever to my agent, the legendary and laconic Peter Straus.

Cast List

Cast of main characters at 39/40 Bedford Street,
job description, and dates of service:

MR BEN BUDWORTH: publisher and chief executive, 2008–
MR ADAM BUDWORTH: barrister and director of *The Lady*, 2008–
MRS JULIA BUDWORTH: matriarch and director of *The Lady*, 2008–
MRS MAUREEN GOODMAN: PA to the publisher, 1996–
MS ARLINE USDEN: eighth editor of *The Lady*, 1993–2009
MS RACHEL JOHNSON: ninth editor of *The Lady*, 2009–
MISS GILLIAN SPICKERNELL: PA to the editor, 2003–
MS LINDSAY FULCHER: assistant editor, 1993–2010
MS CLAIRE WOOD: design consultant, 2008–
MS CHRISSIE TAYLOR: chief sub-editor, 2000–
MS CAROLYN HART: editorial consultant, 2009–
MRS JUDY LAMB: production manager, 1979–
MR NIC BOIZE AKA 'B-CAL': marketing consultant, 2000–
MS JANINA POGORZELSKI: features editor, 1995–
MS EDWINA LANGLEY AKA 'BEENIE': marketing and PR, 2009–
MISS KATH HANLEY: classified ads manager, 1976–
MRS JOAN BISHOP: classified ads administrator, 1976–
MRS ROS PAPI: telephonist, 1995–
MR THOMAS BOWLES AKA 'UNCLE TOM': owner of 39/40
Bedford Street, resident proprietor of *The Lady*, 1959–2008

"THE LADY," 20th April, 1899.

The Lady

SPRING DOUBLE NUMBER

6^d

Per Post 6½d.

LONDON: "THE LADY" OFFICES, 39 & 40, BEDFORD STREET, STRAND, W.C.

Vol. XXIX.—No. 740. Registered as a Newspaper. ALL RIGHTS OF TRANSLATION AND REPRODUCTION ARE RESERVED.

JUNE

9 June 2009

Was working after a light lunch in the raw bar of Daylesford Organic on Westbourne Grove (slogan: 'A taste of the Gloucestershire countryside in Notting Hill'), i.e., was back in bed having an iNap. Those who don't go to offices will be familiar with this posture – stack of pillows behind head, MacBook on duvet, flipping between Word document, Google, the *Daily Mail* website, Facebook and email while labouring to crank out what one hopes will be bestselling novel. Then it came through, the contact that was to change my life.

It was from Penguin. From my publicist, Katherine. My husband makes a hollow noise – like a sheep with croup – when the words 'my publicist' come out of my mouth. He says that is the one position supernumerary to staffing requirements in any Johnson household. But anyway. Here it is:

From: Katherine Stroud
To: Rachel Johnson
Sent: 9 June 2009 15:33
Subject: FW: Rachel Johnson

Hello!

Hope you're very well – see below email re: *The Lady*.

Kx

From: Ben Budworth
To: Katherine Stroud
Sent: 9 June 2009 14:53
Subject: Rachel Johnson

Dear Katherine

Many thanks for agreeing to act as intermediary. As I explained on the telephone, I am the publisher of *The Lady* magazine and would be keen to have a chat with your client Rachel.

I don't however appear to be having much luck finding a telephone number for her.

All my telephone numbers are below.

Many thanks and regards
Ben

Ben Budworth
Publisher/CEO
The Lady magazine
39/40 Bedford Street
London
WC2E 9ER

The Lady?

All I knew about *The Lady* was what all middle-class mothers of a certain age and income bracket knew about *The Lady* – before, that is, the internet took over the world. It was where you got a nanny from. End of. I didn't know it was still in existence. I'd never read it, not even when I'd advertised for help in it, not even when a nice woman called Beverly came all the way from Devon to interview me in my Notting Hill habitat for a dear feature called 'My Favourite Things', which is, as you would expect, about kittens in mittens and parcels tied up with string. (I talked about Agas, Exmoor, Land Rovers, my family and my beloved dog, Coco.) I had never knowingly seen it on a shelf, nor heard anyone mention it, for a decade and a half (Ludo is sixteen, Charlotte Millicent fifteen, Oliver thirteen, and I haven't had so much as an au pair for five years). I thought, in fact, that it was extinct.

But still. Ben Budworth, 'Publisher/CEO', was keen. That meant something. For jobbing freelancers like me there is but one certainty in the digital age. We are like miners under Margaret Thatcher – guaranteed only built-in obsolescence instead of a pension. So we must take what crumbs we can. Despite my current lucrative gig with a many-sectioned Sunday newspaper, not to mention my sundry other commitments (my third novel is supposedly nearing completion and I am about to launch my first, *Notting Hell*, in France), I duly pinged off a precautionary email back to 'my publicist', Katherine, in which I asked whether she'd given Ben my number. She said no. So in an expansive way – as if taking out eggs and plopping them down in different baskets, and chucking irons into various fires – I sent B. Budworth my mobile number.

Now, I gave him my mobile number because I didn't want to talk on the telephone by my bed (where I fully intended to stay until my daughter came home from school), which has a loud buzzing noise on the line. And I didn't want to have to go downstairs to take the call. I was too comfortable where I was. It was then that I remembered.

When I was a thrusting young reporter on the *Financial Times*, spending my working day writing about bond markets and the coupon on the 2013 gilt, I'd left a gripping press conference at the Institution of Mechanical Engineers (or Association of Accounting Actuaries – can't remember) about the reweighting of the Retail Price Index or something, and had been dawdling past an imposing six-storey Georgian building in Bedford Street. It reared over Covent Garden in a smart livery of pinkish cream and gold and had the elegant title '*The Lady*' and the claim 'Rebuilt in 1861' picked out in gold paint on the façade, as if a Merchant Ivory film set had been plonked and forgotten amid the coffee shops and burger bars and bland retailers of twentieth-century tat.

As I passed, I'd thought to myself, my goodness, what a magnificence of an edifice. I'd paused in front of a double glass door saying 'General Enquiries' on one side and 'Classified Ads' on the other, also picked out in gold on the smart, polished glass. I'd gazed at the covers of *The Lady* magazine mounted for display inside glass cases that passers-by passed by without a glance, and read some of the cover lines. This week was, I noted, a 'You and Your Health' special:

> What to do about watery eyes?
> Do you have ovarian cancer? The tell-tale signs

. . . along with:

> Autumn colour
> Tasty treats – moist cakes the grandchildren will love

Enchanted, as if guided by some unseen, gloved hand, I entered. Within, it looked like an Irish funeral parlour *circa* 1948, with a sad vase of flowers on a side table to the left, and straight ahead, my passage was barred by a sort of pub entrance with a wooden counter containing a flap you had to flip up to pass through. There was no one in sight. Telephones buzzed, and I heard genteel voices answer out of shot, as if they had all the time in the world, 'Good afternoon. *The Lady* magazine.' No one came.

There was a white button on the counter with a bell, and a sign propped up alongside it, which said, 'Please ring.'

I stood there wondering what to do. An *Alice in Wonderland* moment. I had decided already that this would make an amusing featurette in the Saturday paper, which would allow me to show my range beyond bonds and gilts. I could already see my piece about *The Lady* in the *FT*'s weekend section, the arch headline. I therefore determined to make a general enquiry forthwith.

And so I'd pressed the button. Eventually, a woman wearing a long tweed skirt beneath which – I peered closely to confirm – a pair of greying fluffy slippers peeked out shuffled to the counter, and regarded me with suspicion. With her assistance, I arranged to interview the editor, a woman of indeterminate age called Arline Usden, at a date several weeks hence.

Fast-forward to the appointed day. In my smartest suit, I'd turned up again. As far as I remember (i.e. not very far), another middle-aged woman took notes, for an unspecified reason. I was given a cup of tea on a saucer, shortbread, and – a strange but nonetheless welcome touch, this – a freshly laundered, striped blue and white tea-towel, as if I would need to dry myself off afterwards.

I was absolutely charmed by the whole experience. The piece duly appeared in the Weekend *FT*. All I can remember is a phrase about 'teacups rattling in the Home Counties' because – shock, horror – Arline Usden was shifting the small ads and classifieds from the front to the back of the magazine, and the editorial from the back to the front. Apart from that, my mind is blank. That was the sum total of my previous experience and knowledge of *The Lady*: I once hired a nanny through its pages. And I once interviewed the previous editor.

And now a Ben Budworth was after me. It sounded like a made-up name, very Gilbert and Sullivan. I wondered what he wanted. Whether it was a wind-up. I hadn't – cough – edited a magazine since 1986, and that was a student magazine. But I had been writing for nationals continuously since then, and how hard could doing a weekly be, anyway? So I whizzed off my mobile number.

Please ring, I thought.

10 June 2009

Was in bed iNapping – it was after all mid-afternoon – and my BlackBerry vibrated.

'Ben Budworth here,' came a bouncy public-school voice. 'Thank you for your email. Did you give me a mobile number with one digit wrong on purpose?' He read out my number, one digit awry, in a staccato Alpha-Bravo-Delta voice. I wondered whether he'd ever been in the army. 'I got a builder instead of you. Twice. I had to go back to Penguin. Are you trying to make it difficult for me on purpose?'

'No, no,' I protested, apologizing. When I started out in journalism, I was forced to undergo an expensive, six-month residential training course paid for by my future employers at some outpost of the Westminster Press in Hastings. This was a precondition to my becoming a graduate trainee on the *FT*. In those palmy days of the trade, a stint in the provinces on a local paper, or failing that an accredited training course, was a union requirement before bylined Oxbridge graduates could be wafted on to national newspapers. Despite my six months on the south coast, I have no Pitman shorthand and a scanty recollection of media law, but I am horrified if I get a name or date wrong in print. Giving out a duff mobile number was the sort of thing girls did at discos to losers, and reeked of smugness. I felt very much on the back foot.

'Anyway, I've got you now,' he said. And then he came straight to the point within seconds. 'I'm looking for a new editor for *The Lady* magazine,' he said, a note of pride entering his voice.

At this point, for some reason, previous covers I'd viewed in disbelief, featuring vases of daffodils, kittens and owls, or fishing boats bobbing in Mousehole Harbour, swum into my consciousness. I was a national columnist, for goodness' sake, of many years' standing! A novelist, with two novels already published, and another due in by Christmas – less than six months hence. The proposition could not have been more out of the question, for any number of compelling reasons. I hated wearing tights and heels. During office hours, I prowled Notting Hill in unattractive sweat-pants, dipping into eye-wateringly expensive designer boutiques to try on jeans and picking up 'pan-roasted' salmon and griddled aubergine scattered with pine-nuts and pomegranate seeds for dinner from Ottolenghi, before filing the occasional article.

Never mind that the sum total of my editing experience had been, to date:

1. editing four issues of *Isis*, the Oxford University mag, in the Trinity term of my second year;
2. editing a book called *The Oxford Myth* as a student, which was greeted with a Royal Flush of vicious reviews by notables such as Alan Rusbridger (now editor of the *Guardian*), Joanna Coles (now editor of *Marie Claire* US) and William Boyd (now and then bestselling novelist); and
3. one viewing of *The September Issue* – a documentary about the effort and expense that went into producing one month's edition of US *Vogue* – on DVD.

As a result of the above, I assumed that editing was a piece of cake. No, the last thing I wanted was a . . . day job, something I'd successfully avoided having since 1996!

So I said, 'It's awfully sweet of you to think of me. But it doesn't fit my timeframe. But listen, good luck, why don't you . . .' Then, feeling charitable, I mentioned the name of an ex-*Telegraph* senior editor who had written a book about housework and I thought would fit the bill admirably. How nice of me to plug her for this job, I told myself. She will definitely owe me one.

But Ben didn't seem to pick up the signals at all.

'Never mind all that,' he said. I could hear him Googling the name 'Rachel Simhon', the person who I thought would be just the ticket, as he spoke. 'Just come in and have tea and a nose around. And then decide.'

I put his name into Google too. It came up in a nanosecond. Helicopter pilot, forty-five, who'd been working in Florida. Had also run radio stations. I clicked on a picture and a man with a decided expression, dark buzz-cut hair and sharp little blue eyes clarified on my screen. He looked like a woodland creature from *The Wind in the Willows*, slightly vole-like, but kind. And he sounded nice.

'OK,' I conceded. 'I'll come and have tea next week.' We made a date: '1700 hours,' he said; 'BST,' he added. Then he explained that BST was British Summer Time.

I knew I would cancel it – I mean, why would I spend over an hour getting to Covent Garden, and an hour getting back, not including getting-ready time, just to have tea at an old-lady magazine I had never read and didn't want to edit? But I had to get Ben – I could already picture him wearing a pilot's short-sleeved shirt with epaulettes and in a peaked cap – off the phone.

'Great. We'll get everything squared away then,' he said, as I wondered what he meant.

'Goodbye, sausage,' he chirped.

'Goodbye,' I said.

I was in slight shock.

Did a man just call me 'sausage'? My boss at the Sunday newspaper, a very tall and famously clever woman who has had issues with me since the start, only ever spoke to me in a raised voice, as if I were a very small, unruly, disobedient toddler who has emptied my potty on her desk.

I didn't know then, but Ben had me at 'sausage'.

11 *June 2009*

Took Coco to Kensington Gardens after I'd dropped Milly at school. Was walking past Round Pond, listening to the geese gabble and watching the Japanese tourists take endless pictures with enormous cameras of squirrels nibbling tiny nuts. George Osborne – the Shadow Chancellor – whizzed by in a neon anorak and a pair of white short shorts, schoolboy knees pumping. 'Good look!' I yelled. He smiled and gave a wave, and pistoned his way past me, fast-tracking no doubt to Number 11. Just then, my BlackBerry started ringing. I fished it out and saw the words 'Els Millsmobile' on the screen.

Accept or decline? Els Millsmobile was Eleanor Mills, the woman who had hired me for the paper. She'd left six months previously in order to edit the Saturday *Times*. That hadn't really gone to plan. And now, it had been announced in the *Guardian* Media section, she was to return to the fold of *The Sunday Times* as a writer and columnist. I had dimly wondered where her new column would go, and it had even flitted across my mind that it might be in place of mine.

However, John Witherow, the handsome, boyish, tennis-playing, virile, etc., editor of *The Sunday Times* had taken me out to lunch not so long ago at Shoreditch House, and had promised not to sack me. That was in February. Ivo, my husband, who is a glass-half-empty person, said that this meant nothing. But I, very much in the glass-half-full camp, sort of hoped that John Witherow's word was his bond, although I knew it was possible – especially in the current climate, with journalists leaving papers in sackfuls – that it was nothing of the kind. But still. We played tennis together. Mixed doubles. No one sacks their tennis partner!

So, feeling confident, I pressed the accept button on my Black-Berry. Might as well get it over with. Nothing worse than uncertainty.

And anyway, I assumed that everything would turn out for the best eventually.

'Hey, babe,' she said, in her confident, upbeat tones. No one gives great phone like Els.

'And hey, *you*,' I said, getting in first. 'I was going to call *you*, hon! Well done on your triumphant return to base. So you're coming back to *The Sunday Times*. Which is great!' I enthused. 'And hey – I hear you're going to write *a column*! Do you know, y'know, where in the paper it's going to go?'

Brief pause.

'Remember you asked me to tell you if I ever, you know, got wind of anything?' Eleanor began. 'Well, babes, I'm just giving you the heads-up, as a friend . . .'

'Oh yes?' I asked, striding on, keeping an eye on Coco, who had darted into the Round Pond by the sign that said 'Dogs Must be Kept on a Lead in this Area' and were forbidden to enter the water, my heart, by now, in my boots. People only used the phrase 'as a friend' as a prelude to delivering a cosh blow that the recipient was unlikely to recover from, even unto their deathbed.

'What I mean is, you might need to put out feelers,' said Els. 'To other papers. You know. Maybe give your chum Will Lewis on the *Telegraph* a bell.'

The sun bounced off the pond and straight into my eyes. I wanted to sit down, but couldn't, as Coco had disappeared. I couldn't call Will Lewis. The last time I'd seen him, it was to resign in order to join *The Sunday Times*. At this brief meeting, he'd predicted (only too accurately) that I'd last two years and then come crawling back, tail down, to the *Telegraph* fold.

'So you're going to write my column?' I asked directly, stopping to drink at a water fountain, my mouth dry, keeping things very light. *The Sunday Times* was my day job. My main source of income. And I was for the chop. If this wasn't the case, why would Els suggest I reverted back to the *Daily Telegraph*, from whence I came?

'Listen, babes, I don't know for sure,' she said, wavering. But of course she did. I knew without any doubt that I was being whacked by *The Sunday Times* by the very tall woman who found me annoying, in order to make way for the shorter one who had been so good as to hire me in the first place.

'Well done, Eleanor,' I managed to say. 'You deserve it.' The weird thing was – I meant it. I really liked Els. It was, as we say, Her Time. She had small girls, while my children were now hitting teenagerdom, so I'd had my time with them, and I would always be super-grateful for that. I did sports days and plays and endless ten-week summer holidays without breaking sweat, let alone my contract. But as I spoke, my golden years of being able to work from home, earning a salary from writing one column a week, passed before my eyes as if I were drowning.

I knew I'd never get a gig like it again. It was all over for people like me. We were, as I said, the miners of the third millennium. Columnists were thick on the ground, fighting for survival as the aftershocks of the digital earthquake just kept coming and coming, and dying in droves. Those that remained would write anything for anyone, and all were after the same golden ticket that I'd just this second lost as I circumnavigated the Round Pond: a well-paid weekly column on a national they could knock off in their pyjamas in a few hours.

I said goodbye to Eleanor, thanking her profusely for having me sacked so she could get my slot in *The Sunday Times*.

Then I dialled Ivo. When one of the children spills their Coke in a restaurant or we miss a train, he goes off the reservation, but when the shit really hits the fan – a child intubated in hospital, either of us getting sacked – he is utterly magnificent.

'Darling, all columns come to an end,' he said. 'You knew it couldn't last for ever.' Then he said in a strategic-toned voice: 'When are you seeing that nutty Ben chap at *The Lady*?'

'I don't know,' I whimpered. 'I sort of put him off.'

'Well, how about this for a scheme? I've got to go to some ghastly thing in a trendy hotel in Covent Garden for Kevin McCloud – you know, the *Grand Designs* bloke off the telly – tonight. Why don't we both go, and see him en route – there's a Tube strike, so we might as well kill two birds with one stone,' he suggested with a trace of swagger, 'and take a minicab.'

On Ivo's instructions, the next call I made was to Ben Budworth. I liked the sound of him. Plus, my only hope, I could see, as I was being dispensed with by the thundering juggernaut of *The Sunday Times*, was to somehow secure the corner office in *The Lady*, the oldest women's weekly magazine in the world (which only survived at all because its readers were too old and scared and digitally excluded to do anything – their shopping, reading, hiring – on the internet), a mag that, if it hadn't been around for 124 years, no one in a million years would even dream of inventing now . . . not *even to give it away.*

By this time I was near the Serpentine Gallery, and walking fast in the direction of the future.

'Hey, Ben,' I said. 'I have to come into Covent Garden tomorrow, so I might pop in and have tea with you after all, if it's convenient.' I made it sound like a favour, but in fact the boot was on t'other foot, though Ben didn't know this yet, and I wanted to keep it from him for as long as possible.

The Lady was in want of an editor.

And I needed a job.

12 *June* 2009

Having dwelt on Eleanor's call, I screwed up the courage to call my supreme commander, John Witherow, editor of *The Sunday Times*, i.e., one of the biggest cheeses in newspapers, and ask WTF was going on. After all, I only had I was being fired on Eleanor's say-so – maybe she was trying to panic me into resigning? Though I somehow doubted it. Everything she said sounded eminently plausible to me. I got put through not to John but to his secretary. 'Can I come in for ten minutes to see John?' I asked.

A kind note entered her voice when she heard my name, so I knew the rumour was true. I was being cleansed. 'He's very busy this week,' she said. 'Rupert Murdoch's in town.' There is also a Tube strike, so I am calculating as she speaks how long it will take to get a minicab to Wapping if I do get an audience with Witherow and how much it will cost. £30? Then she came back on the line. 'John says can you put whatever it is you want in an email?' she said.

So then I called the tall woman, Susannah Herbert, my section editor, who finds me annoying. I told her everything Eleanor Mills had said during the Round Pond exchange.

'Just wondered, y'know, what's going on,' I said. 'The thing is, if I do have to sell my house and send my children to Holland Park Comprehensive – which is very good, I hear, and I'd be lucky to get them in – it would be nice to know at some point.' I did not say that, in the course of the year, as newspapers tanked and circulation dived and readers went online, and magazines and newspapers cut freelance contracts left, right and centre, I had lost the following gigs:

- a weekly column on the *Evening Standard*;
- a monthly column on *Easy Living*;
- a monthly column on *Esquire*; and
- a monthly column on *She* magazine.

Nor did I spell out that the only remaining regular income I had left – excluding bits and bobs of freelance work (mostly *verboten* by my exclusive *Sunday Times* contract) – was my column . . . *for her.*

To her credit, she rose to the occasion, drew herself up (I imagined) to her full height of nine feet eight inches, and agreed it was outrageous that my contract was being terminated, plus it was appalling that I had heard via the person who is going to replace me. So hey ho. The grim facts of the situation are pretty much as Els Mills outlined.

I had gone from a grand total of twelve columns a month at the beginning of the year to . . . a big fat zero by the middle of 2009. It was awful. I was going from earning more than my husband (a fact he crowed about regularly) to being a *non-laying hen* in the course of a few months!

Well, at least things were clear. There was no possible way, with our spending commitments (with three children in private school, two boarding, about a trillion pounds a term), that I could join the ranks of the so-called 'economically inactive'. I had to act. And FAST.

Later, Ivo and I shared a cab to Covent Garden, en route to the Kevin McCloud thing, via tea at *The Lady*. As we bowled down Chandos Place, I gazed up at the pinky-cream façade of the magazine building, girdled by sash windows. Then I saw that the man I'd viewed online with the buzz-cut dark hair was leaning out of the window, over a box of violent-red geraniums. 'I'll let you in,' Ben called, as Ivo paid the taxi. 'Everyone's gone home.'

We went through a side door, to the left of the main Irish undertaker's entrance that I had penetrated before. Ben opened the heavy, metalled double doors edged in bronze with a small Yale Key. He pushed the right-hand door with a shoulder, stood and held it open for us to pass through, and we stepped back in time sixty years. It was like clapping eyes on my first boarding school back in 1975 – the interior was both strange, yet completely familiar at the same time. The cream and eau-de-nil paintwork inside was as proudly chipped as on my last visit. The same mail sacks with labels for 1st and 2nd Class and Overseas delivery still hung dejectedly in the passageway. The strange felty floor tiles were just as sticky.

It felt like home.

We charged past an ancient cream noticeboard with the words 'Lady Editorial', 'Lady Classified' and 'Lady Advertising' picked out in elegant black paint, and arrows pointing to different parts of the building. 'That sign's completely misleading,' said Ben. He explained that upstairs was where his 'Uncle Tom' lived, in a sprawling nineteen-room apartment fitted out like an old people's home, and pointed down to a scary-looking basement where odd-job men lurked, where the presses that used to print out many thousands of the 'Journal for Gentlewomen', at one time a power in the land of publishing, once thundered.

'Lovely,' I say. The whole place seemed completely bonkers: dusty, tatty, disorganized and impossibly old-fashioned, set in an age of doilies and flag-waving patriotism and jam still for tea, some sunny day.

I was hooked.

I didn't even think about the money. I assumed the money was crap. It was the sense of possibility – there's nothing so genuinely satisfying as the prospect of setting a nice old lady back on her feet – that had me and Ivo tailing after Ben around the warren of the ground floor.

'This way.' There seemed to be many doors and staircases to choose from. We passed stairs that plunged into dank Fred West-style declivities. We weaved past desks piled with papers, a huge open safe with a golden seal on it. Within sat open packets of cereal and bags of Tate & Lyle sugar, Fray Bentos pies, Huntley & Palmers biscuit tins, mugs; all mixed in, it appeared, with lever-arch files and paperwork. It looked like a time capsule of another, safer but shabbier age.

'I like the paintwork,' I said to Ben, running my hand over a panel in cream and pale green. 'When did you last have it done?'

'Very recently,' he replied. 'In time for the Coronation, in 1953.'

Ben showed me and Ivo into a strange mirrored corridor with a side table with a telephone sitting on it, and a room which had Dralon sofas, standard lamps with fringed shades, and a rattan coffee table. There were no windows but there was a depressing mural of a spaniel in front of an Arcadian landscape on one wall. '*The Lady*'s smoking room,' he said, shutting the door. 'I think I'll leave the third floor and the Thora Hird-stroke-Alan Bennett room to another time.'

We went upstairs via a fine central staircase that wound itself up and up to a top-floor flat that Ben, with a wave of his arm, called the Anne Frank annexe. 'My Uncle Tom lives up there,' he said. 'He handed the magazine to me last year.' We processed past several doors marked 'Private', with little keys in the locks, and prim, curtained smoked-glass windows. I learnt later that these were the loos that only the management and editor can use. I also learnt that the editor of *The Lady* has her own private lavatory, tiled in avocado with a peach WC, and every day receives two freshly laundered tea-towels. I hoped that these customs would persist in perpetuity if I was offered the job, which I assumed I would be within the hour.

Ben, the new proprietor, clad in belted black Levis and a checked shirt, pushed open a door, and we entered into a large dark room dominated by a mahogany table covered by a blue baize cloth. As we entered, he swept an invisible speck off the table with his hand (one of his tics, I was to learn – he even keeps a Dyson dustbuster on standby if someone so much as *mentions* a biscuit in there) and asked us to wait. He disappeared through another door then returned. I went to one of the two sash windows, shaded with blinds, and looked down on to Chandos Place. It seemed rude to ask to open the blinds, so we sat down in the dark and a sweet-faced woman in her sixties came in, staggering under the weight of a tea tray – cups, jug, teapot and biccies. 'Thank you, Ros,' said Ben politely. He had, I noticed, impeccable manners. Ros had put the tray in front of me.

'Shall I be mother?' I said.

We sipped our tea and I stared around the room. The chandelier was not lit. Paintings – good paintings of men in waistcoats or in uniform – were dotted sparsely on the walls. Ben pointed out a picture of his great-grandfather Thomas Gibson Bowles with quill pen poised over parchment and told me he'd founded both *The Lady* and *Vanity Fair*, sold *VF* for £20,000 while he was a Member of Parliament, but retained *The Lady* because it was a nice little earner.

'Yes,' I said, nibbling a biscuit. 'Who on earth needs piddling little *Vanity Fair* when they could have *The Lady*?'

We spoke – well, Ben spoke, with huge, sleeves-rolled-up energy and infectious zeal – about *The Lady,* and how, despite the downturn, it remained a great title with a golden future. He revealed that in its heyday back in the seventies it was selling 70,000 copies or so a week, but was now down on its heel ('It lost its way') and bobbing between 25,000 and about 30,000. Uncle Tom – he pointed to the ceiling to denote he was still in residence – had, he explained, 'raped' the old girl for years, failed to invest, and allowed the managers to write their own rolling contracts while starving Editorial of funds, and until only November 2008, when B. Budworth arrived from Florida, basically, the place was run on steam-powered typewriters on a shoestring.

I digested this in silence. He also explained that the magazine was part of publishing history, and well positioned to benefit from the demographic, which is that, soon, everyone in UK will be fed up with *Heat* and *Hello!*, not to mention deeply antique and wearing those cords with buzzers round their necks that ring the social services when they fall over (as in the famous ad picturing a Mrs Hope, outstretched on the lino, who's had a Nasty Fall but knows that Help is Coming).

Ben was most amusing and chatty. As we drank tea, he revealed (he was very indiscreet, thank God, because so am I) that Graydon Carter, the editor of *Vanity Fair*, had written to Uncle Tom Bowles while Uncle Tom was ruling the roost, asking to come and see the old place, for old times' sake.

Ben pointed to the *bergère* chair with a baize board in which Spy drew his original cartoons in a dark corner, and told how Tom Bowles, proprietor of *The Lady*, had written back to the editor of *Vanity Fair*: 'I quite see why you would want to come and see us. But why would we want to see you?'

Then he launched into a seamless spiel I sensed he had delivered many times before. About how he wanted to bring the mag into the modern age. Double the circulation to 65,000 (I gulped) and restore the lustre the title once had, when it graced the shelves as the UK's first and finest women's weekly (a boast that still resided on the cover). Oh yes, and almost halve the average age of the reader from seventy-eight to anyone over forty-five. (I gulped even harder.) He explained how the old editor, Arline Usden, had finally gone in March, that they'd had a mini-relaunch, followed by an interim editor in May (Sarah Kennedy) and that they needed a new one in September. 'So, Rach, will you do it?' he asked me directly.

I tried to look diffident. As if the editorship was neither here nor there. But I felt my pulse quicken.

I still hadn't been formally whacked by my paper, but that was only, I knew, because no one from News International could be bothered to pick up the phone to tell me and confirm what I'd already been told by Eleanor Mills ('the short one') and my commissioning editor, Susannah Herbert ('the tall one').

'Hold on,' I parried, sipping my tea and nibbling a luxury biscuit from the M&S assortment on a plate. Some were wrapped in foil, I noticed. The chocolate was nice and thick.

'Are you offering me the job without seeing anyone else?' I smelt rat, a big one, that you could see from space. 'Who else have you seen? Tell me!'

An opaque expression crossed Ben's face, and he muttered a couple of names. Then he covered the moment by mentioning a salary that was reasonably attractive given my income had plummeted, but was between a half and a third of what I earned in a good year. But this was June 2009: these were, as we all knew, not good years for journalists, and this was proving to be a particularly crap year money-wise for me.

As I clattered down yet another dusty staircase out into Covent Garden, I graciously told Ben I would think about it.

It was only as the heavy door shut behind me that it dawned on me.

Not only did I totally need the old-lady-mag gig, I really wanted it too.

30 June 2009

Got the call from the paper formally whacking me today. Richard Caseby (the managing editor) concluded the very perfunctory kitten-drowning session by asking me if I wanted, despite my contract being terminated at the end of June, to continue to file my weekly column for the News Review all the way through July and August until mid-September – i.e., work all through the summer so that my replacement, one Miss Eleanor Mills (surprise!) could have the summer off to romp carefree on sunny beaches with her children. I admit at that point my good humour momentarily deserted me. It's impossible to find people to write in July and August and I was buggered if I was going to be a stand-in for my own slot.

'Mmm . . . no thanks,' I told Caseby in a lordly way, as if money was no object. So that's it. As of now, I have no income, three children at private school, two houses to run, a dog to feed, and a summer holiday to get through on tick.

I immediately got on the blower to Ben, and threw my hat back into the ring with a vengeance.

I recanted on my previous position that editing a magazine 'doesn't fit my timeframe'. I am going for the job hell for leather. I have even gone out and bought and read a copy of the magazine for the first time ever. And it is immediately clear to me why no one's buying it apart from those who always have. It's full of random articles, about seasonal flowers and furry animals. It has its charms – if I was stuck in a dentist's waiting room for two hours it would be marginally better than reading nothing – but *The Lady* bears absolutely no relationship, so far as I can tell, to the modern universe, or the news cycle, let alone the third millennium.

In turn, Ben has asked me to come up with my manifesto for change and uplift. So what I immediately did was what I always do. I called Ivo.

'Is there anyone at the National Trust who could help me produce a dummy issue of *The Lady*?' I asked. I've been writing for the nationals since I was in short trousers, but still have no idea, you see, how a photograph or a Word document makes it from my screen on to the printed page. How it fits. How you add headlines, and pictures, and page numbers, picture credits, and make it look glossy and appetizing. Even at *Isis*, I had a designer and teams of pushy freshers to do the *actual work*.

'Sure,' Ivo said. 'I'll call Sue Herdman.' Sue Herdman edits the *National Trust* magazine, which has a circulation of – oh – several million. So within minutes I'd whistled up a professional freelance designer called Caroline de Peyer, who agreed to come to my house the next day. I rubbed my hands. Bingo! I knew it was in the bag.

When Caroline arrived, she quickly mocked up a dummy of *The Lady* while I gazed on with awe. On the inside pages of the PDF, she laid out my 'manifesto', which was basically a list of me dropping every name I could think of and offering them up as potential contributors, from Boris to Paxo via Jilly Cooper and Kirstie Allsopp.

I came up with a list of cover girls and my mission statement for the magazine. This is basically that it must be a portal product for any woman over forty-five who is fed up to the back teeth with staple weekly women's fare: mags in the hairdresser all about Posh, Britney's knickerlessness, Kerry Katona's coke habit or Demi Moore's plastic surgery on her knees. I said *The Lady* had to become a must-read for anyone who thinks that there is more to life than telly, celebrity baby-weight, Hollywood and gossip. I think my dummy – which has a winsome pic of a grinning Dame Cath Kidston of the Floral Oven Gloves on the front – is a winner. On page two ran my pitch:

The Lady is looking younger. She's definitely mislaid her Zimmer. The pastel-hued relaunch of spring 2009 is a small and sprightly step in the right direction. But she still needs someone to turn the clock back a few decades to enhance the title's appeal to vigorous, busy women in middle age as well as those in their twilight years. Someone to establish the revered *Lady* brand once more as a title on crowded shelves; to market the magazine tirelessly via television and radio appearances and authored pieces; and also to commission copy that is going to be picked up, and reprinted in the nationals.

It goes on:

Like a crumbling stately home in need of a new roof, our Lady of Bedford Street needs a facelift. She needs freshness (not in the feminine-hygiene sense, I hasten to add), confidence and humour. *The Lady* will become more hip, less hip replacement.

This was a shameless filch from Emma Soames, who applied the same claim to her *Saga* magazine with spectacular results.

More sunny-side-up, less sunset home. I can even put the fun into funeral, as Dafydd Jones, London's top society photographer, will attend the smartest memorial services and parties across town and bring you exclusive photographs of the *vieillesse dorée* in their finery for a new feature.

My pitch ends:

Under my editorship, we will together lift *The Lady* up to where she belongs, and take the title to these new readers, and give them what they want. *The Lady* can never be a Bitch or a Slut, and she is never going to be that interested in gossip or celebrity news. She will always be fragrant; she will always be *The Lady*.

I fired off the PDFs of the cover and my manifesto, feeling superconfident, with a covering email that said:

Dear Ben

I have pleasure in submitting for your perusal my early thoughts and suggestions to titivate your gracious title.

With all good wishes
Rachel

I didn't in all honesty see how Ben could resist.

After I'd sent it, I went for a walk. As I strode along, thinking about my 'manifesto', I had a wobble. However zippy I made *The Lady*, I still couldn't see why, in all honesty, my friends would buy it when they got the *Telegraph* mag on Saturday and *Style* magazine on Sunday for free with their papers, and the internet all day every day for nothing. Even if I did edit it – even if I did get scoops and interviews and fantastic writers. The problem was, however killer my manifesto, however good my feature ideas, and however bulging my Rolodex, *The Lady* – a hand-held glossy magazine for women of a certain age – was a printed media format, and therefore a product for the second millennium, not the third. And nothing was ever going to change that.

My BlackBerry vibrated. I fished it out of my pocket, hoping for something nice. After all, I had just been fired, and needed cheering up.

It was from someone I didn't know. Who'd found my email address.

From: Jimmy Burke
To: Rachel Johnson
Sent: 1 June 2009 17:57
Subject: Hmmm

I wouldn't usually do this – in fact, I've never done this – but I just feel compelled to let you know that I think it's a real shame that the media is clogged with people like you. Your essays in *The Sunday Times* are simply terrible. Badly structured, dreary and lacking any sense of purpose. No gusto, no insight, nothing but cliché. I can't detect even the faintest whiff of talent. Clearly, your career owes everything to your good fortune in being born to whom you were. And this is why I used the word 'shame': there are genuinely talented writers and journalists out there, and people such as you are keeping them from working, and us from reading them.

I stared at this for a while, thinking, WHY ME? Then I pinged mine back to him, knowing it was a mistake to rise to the fly of one of the green-ink brigade. It contained one word – 'Chippy!' – as if I didn't care. But I did.

Bad day.

THE LADY

Weekly.—Yearly subscription at this rate: 31s 2d

AN ECHOES OF EDUCATION AND DISCUSSION AND THOUGHT

Received at the New York Post Office as second-class matter.
The Postage in Outside at the thought Magazine Rate

VOL. L.—No. 1765.

The Lady

6d
Per Post, 6½d.

Christmas Number

LONDON: "THE LADY" OFFICES, 39 & 40, BEDFORD STREET, STRAND, W.C.

JULY

2 July 2009

Went to *Spectator* party. Now back home feeling even more crushed.

Not only did everyone ask me without fail, 'Is Boris here/coming?' while looking past me, as if my brother and I are joined at hip and communicate telepathically, and it was the usual crush of Piers Morgan and David Cameron and runts who work for the Tories, but A. A. Gill and Rod Liddle, now former colleagues and fellow scribes, teased me about being sacked, and when I asked Rod how he knew, he said, 'Kid, the sackee is always the last to know,' and blew smoke at me. A. A. Gill merely laughed. Then I bumped into Rowan Pelling. Rowan has a column in the *Telegraph*, and used to edit *The Erotic Review*. We stood jammed together holding glasses of champagne, and she told me that she'd been 'basically offered' the job of editing *The Lady*. And that so had X and Y and Z.

'Hey, hold on!' I cried, spilling my champagne down my cleavage in shock. 'So have I!'

We stared at each other, then laughed. Then we rapidly established that we were both going to the beauty contest at *The Lady* in Bedford Street on Saturday. I'd been asked to Meet The Budworths (four Budworth sons and their mother), all of whom were directors. When Ben told me about this event, I assumed this would be my coronation – all that remained was that Ma Budworth and the Budworth boys, all four of them, were going to see if the crown fitted.

Hah! Then Rowan rattled off a list of other hackettes/authors she knew were up for the job too: many of whom I knew. Daisy

Waugh. Imo Lycett-Green. Molly Watson, and about a dozen more from the *Standard*, *Mail*, etc. The list went on and on.

So I was up against the steely granddaughters of Evelyn Waugh and John Betjeman, two of the greatest and most entertaining men of letters England has ever sired. I would have to run against women I not only knew but had worked with, played tennis with, bitched with and counted as my friends. We gazed at each other in horror. I loved Rowan! And Daisy! And Molly! But I was going to have to grind them under my heel, like cockroaches! And Rowan was clearly thinking the same. So we both agreed. If she got the gig, she would do it as a jobshare with me, and vice versa. 'I'm totally not bothered,' I lied. 'It would be great if you got it!' We parted on the best of terms, thinking that at least we had said the right things and had not committed the cardinal error of being seen to have tried too hard, or actually *cared*.

That night I had a terrible nightmare and woke up with champagne head and heart hammering. I'd dreamt that A. A. Gill and Rod Liddle had danced around me at the *Spectator* party, and instead of being nice to me because I was a contributing editor and sister-of-Boris had jeered and taunted me, 'You've been sacked, you've been sacked.'

Then I remembered. It wasn't a dream at all. It had really happened.

4 July 2009

The day of the beauty contest has dawned. I went by cab to Bedford Street and was then taken through the mirrored corridor and made to sit by a wiry woman with a German Expressionist face and shingled hair in the airless *Lady*'s smoking room amid the rattan furniture, the unforgettable mural of the spaniel at Versailles, and copies of the magazine. I declined tea. The woman who showed me in told me that her name was Maureen and she was a belly dancer. This seemed highly improbable – the fact that she was a belly dancer, that is, not her name being Maureen. Then Ben bounced down to fetch me. He had a swift cigarette on the stoop; 'Only my forty-fifth,' he said. Then I followed him as he ran upstairs, and went back into the 'boardroom' where I'd been before. This time, cafetières of weak coffee took the place of the tea trolley, and I was too nervous even to eat a biscuit.

I settled into a chair at the head of the table, around which sat Mrs Julia Budworth (handsome, grandmotherly), and the four remaining Budworth boys, Adam (barrister, aquiline, floppy dark hair), Ben (as before, cheery and smiling), Richard (lawyer, grey hair and specs) and Willie (Worzel Gummidge). They were all incredibly kind. I particularly liked Mrs Budworth, who had the spirit of the Blitz and a cosy no-nonsense approach but also a definite touch of the Aunt Agathas about her. She was very direct and did not mince words, a sure sign that, sooner or later, as P. G. Wodehouse would say, out would pop the cloven hoof. I felt the interview went like a train. But then I always feel that.

Then I went to Cornwall with my oldest child, Ludo, as he had finished his GCSEs and that is the sort of thing that mothers like me must do. We go to Rock with our teenage sons and wear fleeces on beaches. We do not enter cut-throat contests with friends and fellow freelancers to edit female and frowsty weekly magazines.

15 July 2009

Still, I have heard nothing. No puff of white smoke from Bedford Street. Only news I've had is a snippet from a diary which quotes Ben, saying, 'I was expecting applicants from *Crochet Today* and *Jam Tomorrow*. It's a hard decision – I wish we could have had them all.'

I text Daisy Waugh. I feel she is the opposition.

'Are you her Ladyship yet?' I asked.

'Yes,' she texted back.

'Well done,' I replied. 'I'd love to write for you.'

I tried to get through the evening – Sue Crewe, the editor of *House & Garden*, came to supper, and I'd made delicious watermelon and feta and red onion thing from the Ottolenghi cookbook – but inside I had died. I felt incredibly sad that I'd failed.

16 July 2009

Daisy texted again. 'Only kidding,' she confessed.

19 July 2009

My triumph – I have been appointed the ninth editor of *The Lady* magazine in 124 years – is announced in a grisly spread in the *Mail on Sunday* with a hideous photograph of me lounging in a frock and Uggs, looking like the lost lovechild of Myra Hindley and Björn Borg. I immediately receive gracious emails from Rowan Pelling, Molly Watson and Imo Lycett-Green. Nothing from Daisy Waugh, who I later learn is convinced I have secured the job via 'foul means'. (I wish I knew what she means – I would have defo used them if I could.) I am off to America with the children to a ranch called Mountain Sky in Montana. I can only afford this because I am writing it up for a picture-spread for lovely Sarah Miller at *Condé Nast Traveller*. Ben is off, he tells me, to Butlins, Minehead, for the inside of a week, with some mates. 'I am still awaiting my commission from *Condé Nast Traveller*,' he added.

The die is cast. In September I will renounce my existence of shopping and coffee in chi-chi Notting Hill and take up an office job for the first time in fourteen years, a job which I happen never to have done before, and in which I am almost guaranteed to fail (show me a mag where the circulation is rising). And that's not even the catch! No, the catch is – there's a plan to film a fly-on-the-wall reality documentary for Channel 4 as I do it. They – i.e., the crew from an independent production company – are going to come in and start filming a trailer the day I start work, apparently. The company is called Optomen. So here's the deal. I don't just get to screw up, and kill off the first and finest women's weekly mag in the world. I get to screw it all up on national TV!

THE LADY.

The Lady

SPRING NUMBER 6d

LONDON: "THE LADY" OFFICES, 39 & 40, BEDFORD STREET, STRAND, W.C.

SEPTEMBER

1 September 2009

Woke up at 7.30; the curtains were wide open. Something felt wrong. I experienced a feeling of dread as the realization dawned that it was my first day as editor of a national magazine. Average age of reader, seventy-eight. Circulation – around 28,000. My new job? To lower the age of the reader to forty-five plus, despite rapidly ageing national population, and double the circulation, despite the fact that all advertisers and readers have vanished to go online. My chances of succeeding? Vanishingly small.

I got up and put on one of my eight identical West Village dresses then decided it was too clingy. Took it off. Put on my pink tweed Rachel Riley dress, i.e., Carla Bruni meets the Duke of Edinburgh: demure and ladylike *ma non troppo*. As threatened, the crew filming the trailer from Optomen arrived at 8 a.m. As all this went on, Ivo grumpily stomped about with two bags of laundry and left without saying goodbye. We'd had a torrid fight day before in which he said everything I did was done to 'bolster my massive ego'. He has a point there, of course.

'Goodbye, love,' I said, wanting to make nice, as he barged past me while the C4 crew unloaded their gear from taxis and mini-vans prior to filming me 'getting ready' for work at home.

I waited for him to say, 'Good luck, darling.' It was my first day as editor of *The Lady*, the oldest and finest weekly in the world, the journal for gentlewomen, founded 1885. I stood on the doorstep. He drove off in his battered green VW Passat without a glance.

I threw open the front door to admit the crew, dressed identically in the uniform of ironic seventies rock T-shirts and Diesel jeans. 'Coffee, anyone?' I cried, heading down to the kitchen followed by Mollie (director), Claire (VT), Derek (sound) and George (cameraman). 'We're all caffeined up,' said Mollie. 'But we can film you making a cup of tea for cutaways, can't we, Derek?'

After half an hour of the delightful crew being in my kitchen I was already exhausted by the strain of being interesting and lively and trying not to show my broken nose on my bad (i.e., right) side. They asked me to leaf through a recent issue of the magazine. I do so and find a whole article about cucumbers. I also point to the cover – which has a pretty photograph in pinks of blowsy blooms – and sneer. I say to camera that the cover makes me think that 'someone has died'. The crew snorts with laughter. They clearly want me to knock my own product. The part of me that wants to please is only too happy to oblige them, but this is breaking the first rule of PR (never piss in your own pool). So even though it's the Budworths who have gunned for this documentary to be made, more than me, I cannot see what I am getting out of this filming project apart from adding to my already well-established reputation as a publicity-prone irritant.

We cab into Covent Garden in order to film my 'surprise' arrival at *The Lady*. I have to get out of the cab three times. This means poor Kath in Classified (though I don't remember her name when I see her – have managed to delete the names and faces of everyone I've met on previous visits in my panic) has to come and answer my ring on the bell three times. There is the same sign in the entrance, the same sad vase of flowers hanging limply, and it all feels so mournful that one expects an undertaker to glide out and intone, 'We are deeply sorry for your loss.'

Instead, Ben comes out and we embrace. We are made to do this twice. I was waiting for him to call me 'sausage', but he said, 'We've waited a long time for you.' It sounded like a rehearsed line, but I liked it anyway. At my age, you have to take whatever you can get.

I go up to my new freshly painted in grey-green Farrow & Ball office with its empty shelves and a shiny piney desk. The view from my window overlooking Maiden Lane is of a new office block atop a pub on the ground floor with a beer garden. On the side of the office block there is a blue plaque, saying that J. M. W. Turner once lived there. There is a card from the literary editor, Paul Blezard, in my in tray, welcoming me.

As I struggle to switch on my PC, Gillian Spickernell, my PA, sits outside and answers the telephone in a sweet, calm voice. Vicky Murden, who does letters and the website stuff, sits opposite. In the room beyond, there is Judy Lamb, the production manager, and in the two rooms beyond that – overlooking Bedford Street and along Chandos Place – sit the designers, and the picture desk, and round the corner there's a room with three sub-editors and a white-faced Janina Pogorzelski, thirty-seven, the treasured youngest daughter of the former editor, Arline Usden, who has been here her entire working life and whom I have inherited as my features editor and welcome-on-board bonus.

Everyone seems to know what they're doing except me.

During the next two hours, I meet all the staff again and have a session with Claire Wood, the lovely Olive Oyl-lookalike in-house designer. She gives me the deeply alarming low-down re: staff, budgets, outlook, etc. When I get back from lunch there is a note from Gillian on my desk. Gillian is a willowy, balletic woman of around my age with a sweet, toothy smile and long brown hair. She looks like the sort of person who used to wander round university towns as a slip of a girl carrying a violin in a case and wearing a long corduroy skirt and a purple floaty top. She is very graceful and, like many ballerinas, carries herself beautifully and stands in second position.

'Janet called from Ipswich. Returning your call. She's at work till

1.15 p.m.' I go through to where Gillian sits in my outer office, hero-ically dealing with endless readers who ring up to complain. They ring up not just to complain, I sense, but to talk to someone – anyone. Gillian is endlessly patient as they bang on about the trouble they've had finding *The Lady* at WHSmith between *Chat* and *Take a Break*, or ask Gillian how to lay their hands on a back issue from 1973.

'Sorry, Gillian,' I say. 'I don't know anyone called Janet, and I don't know anyone in Ipswich.' There was no surname or number on the message. 'And I haven't rung anyone,' I say, as a parting shot. Then I say, 'BTW, did any mail come for me over the summer?'

I was, after all, announced as the new editor in July, and had been working pro bono for two months, commissioning copy, dreaming up columns, planning a redesign, etc. To this end, I had written in mid-July to the artist David Gentleman asking him to conjure up a figure to incarnate *The Lady*, just as *The New Yorker* has the dandy with the monocle and *Tatler* has the Bystander chap in a frock-coat peering into a spyglass.

'Yes, there was some mail for you,' she says, handing me a few letters from time-wasters. I glance through. 'Are you sure there wasn't any more?' I query. 'I have been expecting, in particular, a letter from the artist David Gentleman.' I don't explain at this point that I was surprised by his lack of response, as his daughter is mar-ried to my younger brother, Jo, and I know him quite well and admire him greatly.

'No, sorry, Rachel,' she replies. 'Nothing at all.'

Then I have a one-on-one with Lindsay, the assistant editor. Lindsay is a handsome woman of a certain age, with shoulder-length white-blonde hair. In the course of our chat, she tells me she wants to be my right-hand woman and will do whatever I like. That she wanted me to get the job. That she had dealt with two editors before me. Then she tells me that the problem with *The Lady* is that the magazine is done and dusted two weeks before publication, and that this is very inconvenient, and that she would prefer any given week's edition to be made ready to go eight weeks before. I stare at her dumbly. Surely the point of a weekly is that you can change things the week before? On *The Spectator*, I would often write something on a Tuesday that appeared in the magazine on Thursday that same week. But at least Lindsay's remark explained why *The Lady* looks as if it has been produced at any random point in time in the last 124 years (this week's edition has features on garden gnomes and woodland walks) and bears no relationship to anything in the modern world. Because it has! As she leaves, she reveals – as if on a need-to-know basis – that she lives in the next-door street to me in Notting Hill and that we both go to the same newsagent. I digest this in silence.

I have lunch with Ben and try to get him to give me 1. gym membership, 2. a car and 3. a sofa for my office. This is, after all, our honeymoon period. He will get fed up with me, only too soon.

The *Daily Mail* rings.

Could I write three hundred words on the mini-skirt, i.e., when should you stop wearing one; and do I agree with the results of the survey that say forty is the outer limit for mini-skirt wearing, commenting on the fact that, ten years ago, the survey said age thirty was. Does that mean women are getting more attractive/ glamorous?

I have to get in copy from Charlie Glass – have commissioned a seminal piece I hope about the dos and don'ts of bedding the nanny.

So first I called Charlie re: his copy, then called the *Mail* back re: mini-skirts. You bet I could! Finally – something I know how to do, which is write almost any amount of words on any given subject for a pound a word.

I rattle it off – then the picture desk rings. Can I supply a pic of me in a mini-skirt? 'I'm at work at *The Lady*,' I swanked. 'It's my first day, actually.'

Then, of course, I agree to their request for a photograph of me wearing a mini. I have to leave the building, go to Topshop on the

Strand, buy a mini-skirt, and be photographed wearing it. I stand in the middle of Covent Garden on a sunny summer day wearing a horrid skirt and tight T-shirt as crowds of tourists check me out in dismay.

'Your breasts are . . . majestic,' says the photographer, showing me a picture in the viewfinder on his digital camera. Whenever I put on weight, it goes straight on to my boobs, and I have put on half a stone in America in the summer. I recoil in horror, and spend the rest of the shoot with my arms crossed against my chest.

I leave the office with Mollie, who is directing the trailer, for the Ivy Club, to meet Pat Llewellyn, aka 'the most powerful woman in TV' (according to the *Guardian*). Pat is head of Optomen, the company that hopes to be making the doc for Channel 4. She has made Jamie Oliver, Gordon Ramsay and Valentine Warner, and I sense she is about to unmake me. She is pitching *The Lady* doc with the title 'The Devil Wears Barbour' to the Channel 4 *Bodyshock* man who commissions docs like 'Half-ton Mum' and 'My Daughter Grew Two Heads'.

'So, how was your first day?' she asks, offering me wine. It's lovely in the Ivy Club. I sink back into a sofa and mainline honey-roasted cashews. It feels so modern, after *The Lady*. Leslie Phillips is in. So is John Patten.

'Hardcore,' I say. 'Everyone I met was sectionable,' I joked. Pat glanced at Mollie, who is directing the trailer.

'Did you get her saying that?' she said. 'That line about everyone at *The Lady* being sectionable?'

'No,' admitted Mollie.

'It's a great line,' Pat enthused. I am suffused with relief that I didn't speak it to camera – phew. What a narrow escape. I am already envisaging my new staff watching me bitch them up on national prime-time TV.

'This is just the sort of thing Channel 4 wants,' said Pat, nodding meaningfully to Mollie. 'Get it taped tomorrow, OK?'

2 September 2009

Day two. Woke, and my first thought was: can't believe I have to go to an office . . . again! I went to an office yesterday, done that. Now I want to lie in bed, playing with my novel, drinking coffee, bumping into fellow loafers like my mates Shane Watson and Charlie Glass in the Tea and Coffee Plant in the Portobello Road! I opened the *Mail* and paged through to the mini-skirt and age feature. Predictably, they haven't run the picture of me muttonishly wearing the Topshop outfit so have wasted forty quid.

Belt in on Tube, as an experiment, to Tottenham Court Road. Find the experience of the Central Line in the rain in the rush hour horrid. I got to the office keenly early. No PA, no Lindsay. There was a staff meeting, and I had to make a Gettysburg Address to the troops. In the end, I introduced myself and said nice things about Ben ('He's been a delight and a bunny so far,' I said honestly.) During the staff meeting, I made the editorial staff introduce themselves, say what they did and how long they've been at *The Lady*.

It's beyond belief. Judy (the cosy den mother, production manager, aka Arkala) has been there thirty years. Capable and efficient. Janina (who is obviously bright but very nervy) refuses to disclose how long she's worked here on camera (I think it's about fifteen years . . .). Pretty, but looks awfully pale and won't make eye-contact. She must be freaked about the fact that she is now working for a new boss who hasn't given birth to her, and is being filmed by a TV crew, which is fair enough. Lindsay makes out that she basically puts the magazine out single-handed. 'I do everything really,' she says. I notice the subs and the production manager roll their eyes. Then there's Edwina, the beautiful, slender, dark-haired marketing girl, who arrived, late, with Paul Blezard, the literary editor (Paul Smith suit, red face, loud voice, flowing scarf), as I am in mid-flow of my inaugural address.

'Our readers are modern and connected,' I boomed, 'so I want *The Lady* to be modern and connected! Old folks now are more Mick Jagger than Miss Marple,' and so on. I went on about how no good magazine ever had a relaunch, they just improved, and how I wanted to make 'subtle and arousing' changes, and that a Lady never vamped, let alone revamped. This was mainly not for the benefit of the staff, who all stared at me as if I had arrived from another planet, but for the C4 crew, who filmed the whole McKinsey-esque event, and then buggered off, thank God.

Later, I asked Gillian if she'd found the letter from David Gentleman yet.

'Not so far as I know. Sorry, Rachel,' she said.

Dreary p.m., as I had a crash course in magazine editing. I went through folders of existing copy (inventory – we either have to run it, or spike it, and pay kill fees). There are endless pappy travel features, and a seemingly endless supply of articles about weekend breaks in country-house hotels written by members of staff.

So that's existing copy. As for existing staff, I've no wiggle room whatsoever. As Ben explained, for reasons of employment law, we could not sack anyone.

'Ben, all editors come in as new brooms,' I pleaded. But it was no good.

As Ben explained in words of one syllable, whatever my grand designs to spiff up the mag, I have to make do with what I've got. I can commission whoever I like to write, but in terms of staff, as opposed to freelancers, my hands are tied. And so are Ben's. If I want to get rid of anyone, and replace them, we both have to go through a long-winded process of analysing incompetence and issuing first, second and final warnings that could take months.

So it's going to be absolute agony. Editors are expected to make changes – but I can't make any. But there is one ray of sunshine. I'm smuggling in Carolyn Hart tomorrow. She is a food editor from the weekend bits of the *Telegraph*. I interviewed her in July, and liked her a lot. Not only did I like her, but she had experience of magazines which she would be able to transmit to me. Small, dark, funny, and with a wing down, as her 'partner' had buggered off, leaving her single-mothering three teenagers. For legal reasons, she is going to be called an 'editorial consultant'.

And I have to get a magazine out on this basis. So I looked through folders of copy and what is due to run on 15 September – my first issue. And what I found is – absolute cack about dormice and the ramblers and the magical properties of vinegar. Nothing there. Everyone would buy *The Lady*, and it would be the same old same old even though I'd arrived. I cast about in desperation. I had to do something, get in one piece of the type that you might possibly read in another magazine.

Then I had a brainwave. My father had written a piece for *The Spectator* about his gall-bladder op. *The Spec* hadn't had room for it, but it was bound to be better than what was available in the folders I'd scoured called 'Unused Copy' and 'Quirky Fills', 'Travel', 'Favourite Things', and so on, that I'd been shown. I called him; he whizzed it over; and I liked it. So I dropped in Dada's copy on his emergency gall-bladder operation and made it the cover story, with the line, 'They saved my life'. I also decided to launch a column called 'The Gents', a sort of antidote to 'Femail', in which we courteously give the floor to the gents and allow men to whinge about women, in revenge for all the whingeing women do in print about men. Milly, my daughter, came in for lunch and we went to Covent Garden. She looked beautiful.

Went for coffee with Blez – Paul Blezard, the literary editor. I felt bad because, in my first staff meeting, I had announced that I was dropping the short story. It turns out he had big plans for the short story. He wanted *The Lady* to be known all over the literary world for its short story, and the first thing I did was drop it.

Blez is tall, good-looking, etc., but I have noticed that he pretends he has thought of everything first, and he drops so many names in a booming voice that, according to Ben, 'There are dents in his floor.' J. K. Rowling is Jo, and Alexander McCall Smith is Sandy, and he told me on our first meeting that he has been offered a six-figure sum by both to run the Edinburgh Literary Festival on a full-time basis and is only staying at *The Lady* 'out of loyalty to Ben'. Mmmm.

In the afternoon, I picked up the phone and called various writers, on a massive copy-commissioning jag. I've asked for pieces on divorce, nannies, Agas, puppies, rose-covered cottages, crumbles, rescue ponies, etc. – all the sort of things one longs to read about. I am determined that *The Lady* will be, above all, cosy and *gemütlich*.

Lindsay came in and showed me a list of the freebies the staff had been on and all the advertorial I would have to run as a result. I love a freebie as much as the next man, but this was something else.

The inventory list of copy I have to run or spike is endless, as there seems to have been a total gravy-train when it comes to travel. There are scores of features written by freelance contributors and staff about their trips abroad (known as 'freebies'). In return for free travel, hospitality and sightseeing, the hack is expected to file a slavishly positive piece in order to please the holiday-giver's PR. I had heaps of this slurry to get through and, in theory, run. And I had to run it, in order to fulfil our side of the equation: if your hack has freebie, your paper then is honour-bound to puff her holiday. It's deeply corrupt, but that's how it works. So there were, in the folder called 'Travel Unused', endless 1,200-word pieces about Tunisia, Mexico, India, the US, the Algarve ... And there were even longer and puffier pieces about three-week cruises or press jollies taken by staff members who had then proceeded to file 3,000 words detailing how it was a wrench to leave the comfort of the hotel/ship/Nile paddle-steamer, and how they were too full for pudding.

When I gasped and protested to my publisher – some freelancers and *Lady* staffers went on a jolly a quarter – I was told by Ben that, under previous regimes, travel freebies were used – like MPs' expenses – in lieu of income, and were handed like sweeties as rewards for good behaviour to the various office pets.

3 September 2009

Day three. My birthday. Carolyn arrived. Thank God. Someone who has some magazine experience at last. We went to Caffè Nero, opposite. I took my list of ideas for new columns, and she brought with her the flatplan – basically, the flatplan is a diagram showing the run of empty pages. Editorial pages (the ones I have to fill) are in white. Advertising pages (those the display and classified-ads departments have to fill) are shaded. So what we did was fill them. Empty page one is the cover. Two is an ad. Three is the contents page. Four is a list of contributors. Then five was going to be Mary Killen on her life in a cottage (aka the 'grottage') in Wiltshire. We filled it all in (luckily, there's stacks of classifieds and quizzes and bridge cols. and gubbins at the back), all fifty pages or so until we got to the inside back cover, now 'The Gents', on page ninety.

So, in half an hour, we literally thrashed out the basic shape of the new *Lady*. After we'd played fantasy flatplan, we went over the dream review team – obviously, Nancy Banks-Smith, Lynn Barber, Julie Burchill – all the best writers we could think of.

Then we went back to the office, and we did cover lines (you know, the shouty bits on the *Cosmo* cover saying, 'Your Best Orgasm Ever', etc., only in our case, they read 'Treasure Houses of Great Britain', and 'Alan Titchmarsh's Favourite Things'). Then I read extant copy for the 15 September issue and – this seemed bizarre – chose a cover for that of the twenty-second. I have no idea what should be on the cover on 15 September let alone a week later, but then I discover it is Twiggy's sixtieth birthday and there are free images from the National Portrait Gallery, so that's easy.

I realize that being closeted with Carolyn gives a terrible impression to Lindsay, who has of course claimed that she wants to be my right-hand woman and, as officially my assistant editor, will be feeling left out. So Lindsay called me all day to relay trifles such as the fact that she is writing a list of all the men we can commission to write 'The Gents'. She says she has a hundred names. She is clearly going to try to wrest this plum role (talking to amusing men) from my grasp!

We now have a wishlist of writers, and following on from our coffee morning in Caffè Nero, Carolyn and I kick about names for agony aunt (Debo Devonshire, Georgia Coleridge, India Knight, Drusilla Beyfus), film critic (Jasper Rees, Howard Jacobson, Julie Burchill), TV reviewer (Toby Young, Giles Wood, Alexander Chancellor), and so on. Lots of other thoughts too: Merryn Somerset Webb, the *FT* columnist and editor of *Money Week*, as money honey; 'Change of Life' occasional column; Clementine Hambro to replace Carol Klein as my gardening columnist – Carol writes for the *Guardian*, is ubiquitous, snowy-haired, and I want younger blood.

I have lunch with my friend Nicola Reed at Soho House. She came from Central St Martins, where she's doing a postgrad course, me from Bedford Street. We sat on the roof terrace and froze. Delicious salad. Goat's cheese, beetroot, rye bread, cappuccinos. She is nice to take me out. She had to, I suppose, after I told her it was my birthday. And she is a member, and I'm not.

That afternoon, in desperation, I call David and Sue Gentleman at home to delve further into the mystery of the missing letter.

Sue answered. 'But David replied the next day,' she exclaimed after I falteringly explained why I was calling. 'He can't do it, he's too busy, and it's not his sort of thing, but I am absolutely sure he wrote back, straight away. To *The Lady*.'

At this point the red mist descended. I marched out to Gillian's nook and remained superhumanly calm. 'Are you sure there has been No. Other. Mail. For. Me. Since July?' I demanded.

'Well, there's that,' she said, pointing to a wire basket above a cupboard. She had to take off her shoes and clamber on a chair to hand it down. In among about a dozen letters to me was the very nice, handwritten letter of regret from David Gentleman, dated July, declining my commission. It was marked 'Personal'. It had been opened.

'Why didn't you show this to me?' I howled.

'I thought you'd be too busy,' she said.

Bolted at 5.10 p.m. to get home for birthday tea with the children and Grandma. The boys had made cards, and Milly had bought me some earrings. I love them all more than words can ever describe. They don't like me going to an office, especially Oliver, who sobbed when I kissed him goodnight. But I've been more cheerful the last two days than for any time since he was born. In fact, though I can't yet admit it to anyone, I am rather enjoying myself. I am forty-four.

4 September 2009

Day four. Arrived with latte in hand. Tired. Had to write big piece for *Mail*, had been up until 1.30 a.m. with it in order not to write it in office hours, and didn't sleep.

'Carolyn's not coming in,' said Ben. My heart sank. That's two issues to commission on my own, in about two days, i.e., fifty-odd pages of editorial; otherwise we will have to use the stuff in the folders, all about dormice and garden gnomes and woodland walks. And I still don't understand the magic process whereby people send in rubbish on email and it then appears looking marvellous accompanied by nice photographs and headlines on the right page. Chrissie, the doughty chief sub, who smells encouragingly of cigarettes, explained: the copy arrives and is put in 'Copy In'. Someone – i.e., me – reads it, edits it and shoves it in a folder called 'Copy for Subs'. Then the subs check it and correct it. Then they write headlines and make sure it's the right length and isolate 'pull quotes', i.e., the bits which are dotted about in the middle of the text to break it up. Then they send it to 'Copy for Art'.

The designers then play with it for ages and do layouts and spreads and so on. Then the subs add picture captions, and credits. Once the whole magazine has been laid out, page by page, Judy, who looks and sounds as if she should be running the Girl Guides (Ben calls her 'Matron'), presses a button, and a massive PDF is emailed to our printers. This is what Judy calls 'passing the issue', as if it were a massive gallstone.

I eventually asked Nathan, one of our brilliant designers, to write a bluffer's guide to the magical alchemy that can turn some cobblers sent in by some hack on email from his BlackBerry into a beautifully laid-out glossy page in a nationally distributed magazine. This is what Nathan sent me:

The Lady Production Process

1. Commissioned copy arrives.
2. Copy is subbed for content and/or cut to approximate length.
3. Picture desk sources low-resolution images for layouts, and suitable images are selected.
4. Layouts are created by Design and returned to subs.
5. Picture desk obtains high-resolution images for approved design layouts.
6. Copy is subbed for exact fit and removal of bad line breaks, widows, orphans, etc. (These are printer's terms for the stray single words either at the beginning or end of a paragraph.) Picture captions and credits are added. Final editorial additions, cuts and changes are made.

7. Final subbed layouts are returned to Design.
8. Design colour-corrects all images and prepares layouts for print.
9. A press-ready PDF (portable document format) file of each page is generated for submission to printer.
10. Production desk sends final layouts to printer via FTP (file transfer protocol) upload.

Additionally, a press-ready PDF of an early version of the cover is sent to the printer early in the week. We then receive a proof for colour matching. This allows us to make accurate colour edits to the cover image. Normally, we go through two or three rounds of colour edits each week, receiving a new proof each time.

I am implicated in stages 1 to 4 of this process, but Nathan left my biggest jobs off the list: I commission the whole magazine, and have to proofread it. Luckily, luckily, Carolyn came in after all, so I didn't have to do all that on my own.

Someone has pinched the bottle of champagne that Ben gave me for my birthday. I left it in my office last night. I must check to see if the card is still preserved. It's awful – now I feel I can't leave anything in my office at all, like spare Topshop tights or my Her Ladyship mug. Tried to think wildly who it could be.

Lindsay? She applied for the job, and didn't get it, so has a motive – but I don't see her sneaking in and whipping it from the bookcase. Janina? Don't think so. She knows – being the daughter of the previous editor – that she is here on sufferance, and she appears more than eager to please. Gillian? Again, no. She has other ways of destabilizing me that are more effective. I may be getting paranoid but it does seem that the people I've been coddling for months she is turning away – I hear her voice saying, 'Sorry, did you say your name was Joan Collins? Rachel's in a meeting,' and not taking a number. But time-wasters who send long articles in on spec about funny things their cat has done and then call up to see if anyone has noticed or is intending to run it (highly unlikely even under the *ancien régime*) she puts straight through.

'It's Marjorie from Snape Maltings. She says she sent in a long piece about the teazel thistle. Says she knows you. Just putting her through.'

'Tell her to go away!' I yell through to the outer office. 'She's lying!'

But she's lovely to deal with. She sends me adorable emails, and always smiles when she says hello.

Rachel,

You've been invited to afternoon tea at Temple Place on 10 Sept, for the launch of a biscuit range TLC.

Do you want to go, so I can let them know?

Thank you.
Gillian

How cosy is that?

PS: The champagne is by no means the only mystery here. There's also a ghost, apparently. When anyone goes down into the Fred West basement where the archive is, they always tell someone, as if otherwise they will be bludgeoned over the head and lie there rotting for weeks. And when I arrived, people would sometimes darkly allude to a dread matter known only as 'the unpleasantness in the ladies on the editorial floor'.

This sounded jolly. I enquired further – there is also a ladies on the ground floor where Classifieds sit – but Judy just shook her head and said that I'd have to talk to Ben. So I trotted into the boardroom.

'Ben. The ladies by my editor's loo. Tell me.'

So Ben told me in full.

'It was about 4.55 p.m. local time on a Thursday, in February 2009,' he began, like a constable reporting an incident on his beat, 'and I was going about my lawful business as publisher and chief executive of *The Lady* magazine, sitting in the boardroom with B-Cal, I think it was (B-Cal is Ben's name for Nic Boize, the pipe-smoking marketing chap, because the last company he worked for was British Caledonian). Anyway, suddenly the door of the boardroom was flung open, and Maureen' (Maureen is Ben's scrawny, belly-dancing PA) 'was silhouetted in the door frame. She was standing there, staring at me with her mouth open. She had a look on her face as if she'd just discovered a number of corpses. She said, "You don't want to be going in there. No. No. No."

'I sat and looked at her, backlit in the door. I assumed there had been a murder.

'I walked towards her, but she barred my path. She just repeated, "No, no, no. Don't."

'"It's OK, Maureen," I said. I was trying to exude calm and clinical tones. Like a pilot over the intercom when all four engines have failed. I had to push past Maureen. She was petrified. I went out and turned right out of the boardroom, and went down the corridor, through all the various doors and fire doors. I could hear Maureen still pleading with me not to go, sounding like a Hollywood starlet being strangled. I saw all the editorial staff in a group at the end, standing silently by the door marked "Ladies".

'I thought I would find a body, so I opened the door of the ladies with some force. A cursory inspection revealed nothing untoward at eye level. As my eye travelled downwards, I became aware of a familiar medieval smell.'

At this point Ben paused, as if it was too much to go on.

'Keep going,' I said, neutrally. But I was thinking – what the f*ck? What sort of place had I come to work in? Which of the, er, 'gentlewomen' I had met so far would DO a thing like that? And then I wondered – had he told the Channel 4 crew about this?

'My eye fell on what looked like a small brown puppy,' he said. 'Right in the middle of the floor in the ladies. And someone had trodden in it. And we'd only just put in that loo block; it was installed after the Silver Jubilee,' he recalled, with a misty look. 'Arline and Mum were very proud of it. It had cubicles and wash-basins and a sink for washing up . . .'

'Please just finish the story,' I said.

'I told Maureen to fetch a bucket and a scrubbing brush. But Maureen was in shock and couldn't respond to simple instructions and, as it was by now 5 p.m., she was also naturally worried about missing her train back to Eltham,' Ben continued. 'So I had to go to the cleaner's cupboard for a brush and a bucket. There weren't any gloves.' He paused at this detail. 'Everyone else had taken themselves off to as far away as they could get from the incident and had formed a cluster at the other end of the building, like passengers on a sink-ing ship. Maureen had recovered enough by this stage to act as a special constable at a crime scene, and as news of the incident spread like wildfire throughout the building, and people from other depart-ments came to rubberneck, she moved them on, saying, "There's nothing to see here, go back to your desks," while I cleared it up.

'As I was returning to the boardroom, Arline bustled past, on her way home. I said, "There's been a terrible incident in the ladies in editorial," and she said, "So I hear."

'I said, "I will be making enquiries, but I have my suspects." That was a Thursday. On Sunday night, I was at home and a strange number popped up on my mobile – an 0208 number. I answered it, and Arline's voice was on the end of the line saying, "It wasn't me, it wasn't me."'

'Arline has her own loo anyway, so it couldn't have been. Nice of her to tell you herself though,' I said. 'Did you ever find out who did it?'

'I wanted to, but apparently you can't DNA a turd,' Ben said with a look of infinite regret.

'So we'll never know.'

8 September 2009

My *Daily Mail* piece came out about what it means to be a lady today (in short 'I don't know' expanded over 1,600 words). Usual gurning, smug-looking photo of me. Awful day also because the system went very slow and then crashed, for hours. So I couldn't access email, read copy, commission copy, etc. I'm afraid the iron has entered my soul re: Lindsay, despite her being my neighbour, but I am warming to Janina, who has a dry delivery and a sense of humour. In features meetings she has mentioned Fiona Shaw, Jodie Foster, Rosie O'Donnell, Susie Orbach (twice) and Jeanette Winterson. Lindsay rang me up several times to read out emails I've sent her. I have told her not to. Then I had to send her a second chaser ordering her not to send me attachments. The system is so crap, they take hours to open.

Blez had a hissy fit in front of whole office about the fact that I teased him. He had claimed that he could get *The Lady* half an hour with Michelle when the Obamas were in town, and we simply fell about laughing. As you would.

'I work my nuts off for this magazine,' he roared, going redder, while Ben and I had to choke back our sobs of mirth all over again while he chuntered on about how he'd wrangled PRs in 'getting access to the Obamas', and so on.

Left at five. The boys go back tomorrow, and I want to be with them. Made risotto with home-made stock as a sort of penance. They guzzled it and ate a whole packet of Parmesan.

9 September 2009

Had to show Lindsay the writing was on the wall today. To her credit, she seemed aware, and said, 'I know the axe is hovering over my neck.' I kept the film crew at bay – I didn't want this going out on national TV, and nor did Lindsay. Still, it's incredible how quickly one adjusts. I have already picked my nose and changed from a tracksuit into an M&S black sleeveless shift dress and tights, forgetting that a camera filming the trailer is pointing at me throughout. I didn't disagree with Lindsay, but tried to smile as kindly as I could. She has written twenty-three 'quirky fills' since the beginning of the year, mainly about random nature subjects, and I doubt any of them would be printed anywhere but *The Lady*. Not even in an inflight magazine or contract publishing. I felt awful; didn't know where the conversation was going at all. As she left, she said to the cameras, 'Well, I'll be out of a job by Christmas.' I have also decided that the last thing we need is an in-house, full-time, staff literary editor with a very loud voice who produces one page a week.

When Lindsay had gone, the crew scuttled back in to ask how it went. I sat there. This was agony. I didn't really know Lindsay, or Blez, but I could assess their work rate, read their stuff, and I wasn't happy. But I wasn't happy about being a prize bitch to camera either. 'I think I'm going to have to do a couple of sackings,' I said.

There was a thing in the snidey Ephraim Hardcastle column in the *Mail* about how I 'decided' to be filmed taking over *The Lady*, and was that ladylike?

10 September 2009

Manic day commissioning copy, reading stuff already in, and looking at layouts. I feel bad about changing pics when the design team have already spent hours twiddling, but I find I have an aversion to generic illustrations, so have placed a fatwa on them. We are a weekly mag. Cartoons, yes. Soppy drawings of couples holding hands, fluffy hearts, flowers – God, please, no! Two-thirds of our sales come from the newsstand, one-third from subscriptions. Every week I have to come up with new gimmicks to entice new readers to pick up the blessed mag in Smith's, and heighten 'subscribability'. I must be ruthless.

I had a quick lunch with the youngest Budworth boy, Adam, at EAT (I paid). I told him I was in two minds about the C4 programme – the thing has yet to be commissioned still – and that I had everything to lose. Meanwhile, getting decent copy is like pulling teeth. Justin Webb's piece on America – well, on a little two-bit town somewhere with tumbleweed – is great. Matt d'Ancona's hasn't come in yet. Meanwhile, getting teasing emails from the gorgeous Sarah Kennedy, the interim editor, who has sensibly fled to New York.

Hullo,

If you want the vitamin D piece, I can write it, of course. Also, the recession dining is the only feature going forward that I had commissioned. Apart from: Wicker Baskets I Have Woven and a ten-parter on Funeral Florals.

Tee hee,

sx

Soon it will get to the stage when I will be actively commissioning pieces on raffia and pickling your own Christmas presents.

On the plus side, a man called Barry Fordham, a commercial-property solicitor who I bumped into in Caffè Nero, told me I was 'far too pretty to be the editor of *The Lady*' (Ha ha! My aching sides) and called me up and asked me to lunch.

Oh yes. During lunch at EAT on the corner, Adam said that *The Lady* would fold within the year. So, great! I am the rat they have hired to send the sinking ship to the bottom of the deep. I associate myself completely with a brand, become the face of *The Lady*, shake my tush at *Vogue* parties (am going to one given by editor Alex Shulman at Burberry tonight, for example) and then I am held responsible for felling the fortunes of the world's oldest and finest women's weekly. Great career move.

The *Vogue* party was fun, though. Took one of my cabs and saw massed phalanx of paps popping flashbulbs at freakishly tall models – Claudia, Stella Tennant, Eva Herzigová. They are freaks of nature (except for Stella, whose face rends my heart, for some reason).

14 September 2009

Walked Coco to Covent Garden. It took exactly fifty minutes. As she followed me in at my heels, everyone fawned over her. 'It's Take Your Dog to Work Day,' I said. Ben rushed in and said she needed a basket. If you gave me *a sofa*, she could lie on that, I pointed out. We had meeting after meeting. Production meeting, then wrote piece for *Evening Standard* on mannies, ably assisted by my ex-manny, now workie guy; then features meeting, in which Janina listed how many people she'd interviewed over the phone, from Stella Rimington to ancient showgirls whose memoirs were coming out.

Jessica Jonzen came in. Jess is a refugee from *The Sunday Times*, and has asked me to give her shifts. The answer is, yes, you bet. Jess was lovely to deal with, very efficient, and calm, and was brilliant at wrangling celebrity interviews, which is key. There's no problem writing them up, it's the getting them that's impossible. Problem is, she wants a lot of money. More than Carolyn. How will that work?

Barry Fordham (the solicitor who tried to pick me up in Caffè Nero) called twice, and emailed. Now he's pretending he's got a story. 'I'm always on for a story,' I said. His condition is this: no coffee, no story.

Lindsay – who has been merrily in charge of travel – was absent for most of the day 'at Grenada Tourist Board lunch'. I gloomily inspected cartoons to replace the 'Lady Laughs' cartoon, spoke to Sarah Langton-Lockton, a woman in her sixties who is keen to do an allotment column, wrote my editor's letter, commissioned copy, ate a Leon superfood salad with chicken at my desk, talked to Ben about La Fulcher, talked to Carolyn about Tamasin Day-Lewis, who sends me emails asking if I have given any thought to her request to write a food column (answer is yes, but Carolyn wants to do it), fielded calls from the increasingly hysterical-sounding woman who claims to be my 'long-standing theatre critic', worried about my novel, thought about my boys, and generally the day flew by. I wonder how many we will sell of my first edition – the one with my father's gall-bladder op in it?

Oh yes, also planned specially exciting Menopause Issue to coincide with World Menopause Day. Jill Shaw Ruddock, married to important hedge funder, Tory donor and supporter of the arts, has written a very positive piece in which she basically says every-thing is tip-top, life never better, etc., once tiresome periods stop and hairs start sprouting from your chin. So I have decided to go for it, make Dr James Le Fanu, our in-house doctor, do his column on The Change; Sof McVeigh, who writes about home remedies and homeopathy, tackle 'herbs for hot flushes'; and ask writer Charlie Nevin to contribute 'humorous' article about facing the change with Liv O'Hanlon, his imposing herbalist wife of Nordic extraction.

Rushed to Westminster School open day. Afterwards, I proudly mentioned my planned menopause special to Ivo, and how this would bring in advertisers.

At the words 'vaginal dryness', he blenches whiter than Ben. 'You've got 30,000 readers who love the magazine as it is,' he begs. 'Don't drive them away, or you won't get your bonus.' My bonus kicks in if I can raise circulation above 35,000 and keep it there. On current showing, even though my first figures are yet to come in, I'd say my chances of achieving this are zero.

15 *September 2009*

I have decided that we must redesign. Even though the magazine has been redesigned and relaunched and this has already been PR'd this year, in March. So I interviewed a designer called Jeremy Leslie, which meant I couldn't attend artist Sarah Graham's wedding to dealer Ivor Braka in the House of Lords. (Ivo's excuse for not going, meanwhile, was that he was 'too upset to RSVP'. He openly fancies her like mad.) Claire the Olive Oyl designer agrees we need a fresh, new, modern yet *Lady*-like look. I am desperate to make *The Lady* look like a magazine rather than a Bupa catalogue in a care home crossed with *Boots* magazine, replete with ads for dryness, runny eyes, leaky bottoms, and so on.

I liked Leslie, and told him I'd call him in a while. I have to interview another designer, this one called Stefano, and decide. Then I had to chat up a banker from Fleming's who Ben is trying to borrow serious amounts of money off to beef up editorial. He asks me three big-name writers I'd like to hire. I am a bit stumped. Then I say, Zoë Heller, Joanna Trollope, Jilly Cooper.

I go to two parties: one is design guru Stephen Bayley's at Lutyens in Fleet Street, where I try to commission blokes to write 'The Gents'; William Sitwell, the foodie writer and editor of *Waitrose Food Illustrated*, thinks me being editor of *The Lady* is a hoot, evidently. 'I think you should have a competition!' he interrupts me, shushing me as I am trying to tell a funny anecdote. 'Win a Stannah Stairlift!'

Carolyn has already asked Nick Welch for any old iron – and hurray, he is filing on having been Florence and the Machine's roadie (he is FATM's father, and it's already been in the *Mail*, but do I care? Do I hell). Sir Terence Conran is there, but I bottle out of asking him. Sir Stuart Rose, chief exec. of M&S, is very smooth again, for the second time in a week, and tells me he is looking for a girlfriend. I quite like the old silver fox. I forget to pick up my

goodie bag, which includes a pair of M&S pants. I will email Sir
Stuart and get him to send me some spares.

As I left, I realized that the cover of the 15 September issue (i.e.,
my first one as editor), with Dada's NHS piece, is a picture of three
nurses in blue scrubs running down a hospital corridor in rubber-
soled shoes towards an emergency. So, having complained loudly to
all and sundry that *The Lady* looks like a Bupa catalogue, the first
one I have had any input in producing looks like a Primary Care
Trust annual report. Hope no one notices. File memo to self that
must have women over forty on the cover almost every week, as per
my manifesto, or it will look as if I have lost my way already.

16 September 2009

Walked Coco to and from Covent Garden today, so she, at least, is
one happy puppy. Busy busy again, polishing off the 22 September
issue, doing cover lines and contributor copy, making sure that
the 29 September issue is on track, and there are some things on
the back burner for 6 and 13 October. The subs came up with
'Nanny Status' for Charlie Glass's piece – on the dos and don'ts of
nanny-bedding – which was v. encouraging. Not a bad headline.

During the day, calls came in bewailing the absence of the short
story and the fashion. And my in tray was full of plaintive letters
too, about this and that. So I composed a nice letter to Jeffrey
Archer asking him to write a short story for *The Lady*, and copied
it to Ben. He called up to say I'd referred to the venerable man of
letters as Mr instead of Lord Archer.

Meanwhile, I am madly trying to sell ads for the exciting, totally
funky menopause issue. According to my contract, if I manage to get
any advertising, above a certain unattainable threshold, I can claim a
cut. So far on my list to call: Vagisil, Menopace, Menoforce and Astroglide. I asked Lindsay if she wanted to write something, and her eyes

filled with tears. She started talking to me about the change, and I realized I wasn't up for this. 'Well, don't tell me about it,' I said briskly. 'Write about it,' and then snapped my gaze back to my screen.

17 *September 2009*

Well, going to an office certainly sorts out the problem that dares not speak its name – what on earth does a woman do with her day? No longer do I amble from Tom's Deli to Nicole Farhi to Daylesford wondering what to have for supper and spending the children's inheritance on some sourdough bread and Sicilian tomatoes on the vine, hoping to bump into mates in the Hi Street (what Ivo calls Kensington Park Road, as people wander up and down saying 'Hi' to each other), seeing how my novels *Notting* and *Shire Hell* are doing in the Travel Bookshop, and signing any copies with a flourish of biro.

No, I march from Notting Hill to Covent Garden with my iPod shuffle on, greeting casual acquaintances and passers-by, telling people, 'I'm going to *work* in *my office*,' and being too important to halt on the thoroughfare to pass the time of day.

Frenzied day, again: interviewed second possible designer for the planned relaunch, Italian Stefano Arato, in the p.m. I liked him; a smooth, white-haired, fleshy man. The best thing is, he's in love with the archive. In the Fred West basement, in a special climate-controlled room, swathed in plastic shrouds, lie copies of every issue of *The Lady* ever produced, dating back to the magazine's inception in 1885, i.e., a 'veritable wealth' of a priceless publishing resource, with line drawings, cartoons, articles about knitting foot muffs, cold cream, poultices – you name it, it's there.

'I want to go forward to the past,' I kept saying to Stefano and Ben. I worry Stefano might be a bit too chic and deluxe and cosmopolitan for us, so I kept saying our readers were ancient and out of town, but I'm not sure he believes me.

I had an extraordinary email from Julie Burchill's agent, sending me an attachment of a piece about visiting Diana's grave at
Althorp that couldn't have been more precision-engineered to
have readers cancelling subs in droves if Swiss watchmakers had
written it. It went on about how cruel and callous the Royal Family
was, and thick, i.e., wife-beaters in ermine robes, and how Fergie
was fat and only a duchess because Prince Andrew 'ejaculated
inside her' and how the only attraction of Althorp was the fact that
they had 'Diana, dead', and so on and so on. So I sent this back to
her agent:

> It is a completely brilliant piece, of course, and in its gleeful Turk-at-
> Christening way, completely unsuitable for *The Lady*. I'd love to run
> it more than anything, but I can't. Will you tell Julie that I have
> literally wet dreams at the prospect of her writing for me, and I am
> desolate I can't use it (she should offer it to *The Sunday Times*
> magazine; they pay brilliantly, and would love it).
>
> *However*, here's the thing. Would she like to be my TV critic? My film
> critic? Or my restaurant critic? She can choose, am fending off
> hordes of wannabe *Lady* columnists.
>
> Will you get on to her? I am respraying the mag now.
>
> Rachel
> (In the Ladygarden)

I have also written begging letters to the brilliant *Guardian* radio
reviewer Nancy Banks-Smith, Debo, and so on. I won't give up!
I want them. And Lynn Barber, and Posy Simmonds.

Ben has told me to concentrate on editorial after an unfortunate
incident involving a potential advertiser for lubricants in the

planned menopause issue. Her name was Elizabeth Grant. She had emailed me after I'd written a piece in the *Mail*.

I read the above article written by you in the *Daily Mail* 30 March, and although I am a previous fan and avid reader of your articles in the national newspapers and magazines, I thought you really excelled yourself with this article, which must have given many women readers a new outlook on what to look forward to and hope for a good future that lies ahead of them. It is the subject of menopause, and one of the side effects which has a most debilitating effect, and that is 'vaginal dryness'. Our company, Harlow Lubricants Ltd, are the UK distributors for Astroglide, which is recognized by women and men worldwide as probably the best personal lubricant in the marketplace. We have at the present time over 460 of the UK's leading gynaecologists recommending Astroglide, as well as the Relate organization and independent sex therapists also flying the flag. Cancer nurses are also on board, as it offers great relief to women who have had radiotherapy treatment for cervical cancer. I could go on extolling the virtues of Astroglide.

As we all could.

After that, I assumed she was in the bag, and all I would need to do was tell her about the menopause special and wait for the advertising to roll in. I also told the advertising people to get on to her. Then I got this, which slightly stopped me in my tracks.

Good Morning, Rachel,

I am astonished how both you as editor and your advertising department behave towards potential clients.

The saga started on Monday 14 September with a phone call from Bridget in your advertising department saying she had received an email from me saying that I was interested in advertising in *The Lady* magazine regarding a forthcoming issue on vaginal dryness and the menopause. As I had not emailed her, but was interested in the article with a view to advertising, I asked her to email me with both the email I had supposedly sent her, and all the information on the costs, etc., regarding the article, both of which I did not receive.

The next day I received an email from yourself telling me that I wrote to you after you had written an article in the *Daily Mail*, and you suggested that it would be an opportunity to advertise Astroglide in the issue coming out on the menopause in *The Lady* magazine in October.

I responded by asking you to telephone me to discuss the article once again with a view to advertising; you responded by emailing me, telling me you were extremely busy and that I should phone you: 'Hi Elizabeth, Will try but if I unaccountably forget, pls don't hesitate to call me at *The Lady*. It's all a bit busy. Rachel.'

Bridget then telephoned me to tell me that the email I had sent her had been deleted and she was unable to send it to me (surprise surprise) plus no email on costs, etc.

I then received a second email from you saying: 'Elizabeth – sorry, simply frantic – what do you want to discuss? Am on (my office number).'

What on earth did you think I wanted to discuss? It certainly wasn't to pass the time of day. We are also very busy and at times 'frantic' but always make time for customers with a view to future business.

I will not now be interested in advertising in *The Lady* magazine and will inform my MD of the reasons why.

Elizabeth Grant
Harlow Lubricants Ltd

Took Guy the workie to a launch party for war reporter Sam Kiley at Bloomsbury. He wants to be a war reporter. Love Sam, etc., but there's no question – I am not a party girl any more. Now I spend the entire day talking and interacting, I don't want to talk to anyone after 6 p.m. ever again. Sam tells Guy not to be a war reporter 'because it's shit'.

18 September 2009

The correspondence with Julie Burchill proceeded apace.

From: Julie Burchill
To: Rachel Johnson
Sent: 18 September 2009 16:50
Subject: FROM JULIE

Dear Rachel,

Congratulations on your job. I should very much like to become your restaurant critic.

There are three reasons why I feel this might work:

1.   I live in Brighton. I'm betting you've got a lot of readers in Sussex, and this will play well against the capital-centric tone of most restaurant columns. I am, of course, more than happy to travel to Londres and beyond, so long as Mr Raven and myself are put up at a decent hotel overnight.

2.   You remember the old saw about Jack Sprat and his missus? Mr Raven and I, though compatible in many other arenas, are comically ill-suited in the eating department. I only have to look at food and it disappears; my husband, sadly, has a narrow gullet and the appetite of a supermodel. Often, we will end up temporarily estranged as I persist in stealing food from his plate. The comic possibilities of this are endless.

3.   Finally, as you may have noticed, I'm NOT a lady. On paper, it's the last place I should be. But I'm fond of anomalies.

Yours,
Julie

PS How much?

You can get me cheap for a restaurant column (if you decide to have one) – £200, plus bill and small hotel?

HOWARD JACOBSON is my hero and heartthrob (I dreamt about him last night here in Crete), and if he's onboard, so am I!
Failing restaurants, TV good!! xx

From: Rachel Johnson
To: Julie Burchill
Sent: 18 September 2009 19:22
Subject: Re: FROM JULIE

Dear Julie

Thank you very much for this. I love the idea of you being *The Lady*'s restaurant critic, but the fee we can pay is a trifling, canapé *amuse-gueule*-type affair rather than the News Corpulent-type banquet you are used to and, of course, deserve.

We pay a bit more than *The Spec* and the *Guardian*, i.e., £250 a column (the *Indy* is now paying everybody £50 for anything), but then there would be the bill and the hotel bill and *The Lady* would fold, me having bled it dry in the first year.

I shouldn't have asked, because we can't afford you, but I thought it was worth a shot because you would see the comic value above other considerations.

What about telly? I'm shooting for Nancy Banks-Smith for radio, Howard Jacobson film . . . and may decide not to do restos at all.

Go on . . .
Rachel

I do feel Julie B. isn't for us, but I also have to show that I have pulled some big names. And Julie's definitely that. I'll also have to make sure I get Jacobson now. Blezard's copy was tripe this week – it somehow managed to be bland and gushing at the same time – and he whinged about 'how hard' he had to work in Kerala for a week and said he didn't think he should have to take any of it as holiday as he was so busy being run ragged on the press trip. Hah! Told Ben I was, despite all this, having a ball.

20 September 2009

Took Milly to London Fashion Week. It was like taking an angel to heaven. 'This is me, this is my life, this is my world,' she said as we went into the cobbled courtyard of Somerset House and stood behind Erin O'Connor and Jasper Conran at the espresso bar.

'That's Alexandra Shulman, the editor of UK *Vogue*,' I said, when we got into Betty Jackson. Alex was sitting there in a sequined top, looking bored (how many fashion shows does she have to sit through every year?). Susie Forbes, editor of *Easy Living*, in Breton top and bare brown legs, plopped down next to Alex. I texted Bill Amberg, Susie's husband, who makes beautiful slouchy leather things: 'What's Susie's mobile number? She's sitting right opposite me across the catwalk and I want attention.' Lucinda Chambers came in looking ratty-haired and scatty – Grace Coddington to Alex's Anna Wintour. Then Lisa Armstrong of *The Times*, Hilary Alexander of the *Daily Telegraph*, and Roberta Massy-Birch of *InStyle*, who offered Milly an internship. I told Lisa I would give her daughter work experience if she had Milly into the *Times* fashion department. One can see why everyone hates the middle classes so much – they divvy up the glittering prizes now even before university has already begun, in a sort of members' enclosure to which only the very privileged VIPS ever gain entry.

I leeched on to Hilary Alexander, who helped me and Milly get seats (and champagne) at the Royal Opera House for Nicole Farhi.

'This is Rachel Johnson,' she said in a loud voice. 'She's the new editor of *The Lady*.' She said it with such conviction that the velvet rope dropped and I swept through with my entourage of daughter, together with the first Mrs Rod Liddle, in her gleaming, merry slipstream.

22 *September 2009*

Jess Jonzen came in to do her first shift from *The Sunday Times*. It was nice to see her, and she brought a new sense of oomph – she's doing a 'Favourite Things' for us. She might turn into one of my favourite things. Janina looked whiter than ever, like an extra from *Corpse Bride*. Had two meetings – straightforward production meeting to go over flatplans for the issues of 29 September and 6 October, and fill holes. Still no sense of how I am doing: the readers are all writing in in droves, mainly five to one against. The post is a daily trauma – I dread opening the letters, the tide of dismay that fills my in tray, but all this is a natural process: we have to flush out the old ones before we bring new ones on board . . . I suppose. Though it would be better, I accept, if we could keep the old ones happy, or at least happier, while hooking some new ones in, but this seems to be a completely impossible brief.

Why did this not occur to me before?

Then at 2 p.m., we had a features meeting in which I asked Lindsay what she'd written since the beginning of the month, and the answer was basically zilch, apart from the 'funny and frank' piece I'd asked her to contribute to the menopause special on 13 October in which she'd described her menses in shattering detail (the words 'chopped liver' swam before my eyes). Then she went, and I got back to my emails. I've worked out that every piece I commission takes at least eight emails. This is how it proceeds, when someone 'pitches' an idea to me anyway:

Someone emails with an idea – I email back saying yes/no. If yes, they email back saying great, how many words? I email back. Then they ask how much (this is usually a bashful aside) and, finally, when do I need it. That's four emails. Then they send the piece. I usually stare at it glumly and forget to acknowledge it. A wounded period of radio silence ensues. Then they email me lightly to ask whether I received their piece. I usually answer this one. A few weeks go by, and they email me to ask when I am going to run it. Then I remember I have it, and try to schedule it. After I finally have run it, they email me to ask who to send their invoice to. And query the fee.

During all this, people keep coming and standing in my door, waiting to tell me things I don't need to know. Or they hover until I look up and then they say, 'Can I ask you a question?' I think that pretty much sums up office life at the moment.

Went to Le Café Anglais for the Portobello Trust dinner. It was huge fun but the evening was totally hijacked/ruined by drunken, tragic, aggressively self-pitying William Cash, who groped everyone and asked me things like, Did I still have a great sex life with Ivo?, and then went on about how our generation was useless and none of us had achieved anything. 'And I include you,' he slurred.

Went home and told Ivo, and he said, 'I hate those Notting Hill people.'

23 September 2009

I spent most of the day worrying about going to the Burberry show and afterparty and not being thin enough and not having waxed my legs or had mani-pedi since before the summer. HELP. Brought Fendi sample dress with cut-out panels into the office to change into, booked blow-dry, then went into a presentation with Fleming Family Bank, someone who used to be head of programming for Sky, and Emma Bridgewater, the painted-china magnate. The bank people wanted to know what I'd done to spiff up editorial before they broke open their cheque book. So I told them that I had 'Florence and the Machine's father', a piece by Michael Cockerell about Mark Thatcher's relationship with his ma, and so on, then remembered that Clemmie Hambro is going to be our gardening writer. So I mentioned at least twice that she was Princess Diana's bridesmaid, while they looked at me blankly, and then said, 'And Clemmie's going to be our *Lady*, er, Garden, er,' and the man from Sky roared with laughter and the ice was broken.

After lunch, Ben said that Emma Bridgewater talked to him for three hours about running her business. 'The good news is I now know all there is to know about running a pottery in the Midlands,' he said.

The Burberry catwalk show was WILD. Held in a marquee in Westminster. I went in with Sarah Sands, deputy editor of the *Standard*, in a state of barely controlled delirium, shrieking, 'There's Anna Wintour! And her entourage, OMG, Gwynnie with

Agyness Deyn and Emma Watson and Twiggy and Matthew Williamson,' and on and on.

Was texting Milly the whole time. I loved the venue, decked out in cream, and just before the lights went down and the music started pumping a voice came over the tannoy saying, 'Please uncross your legs.' Apparently this is because crossed legs means awful ankle-boots and high heels jutting into the middle of the picture and utterly ruining the 'purity' of the shot. I noticed that Anna didn't obey this edict but twined her legs even tighter so they looked like lean, tanned lengths of bony rope. She kept her shades on so no one could see how bored she was by the endless takes and twists on the 'classic trench'.

At the afterparty in Horseferry Road I was rammed up against Twiggy, so I said, 'Oh, hello, I just wanted to say thank you for being our cover girl this week,' and introduced myself. She looked alarmed until I mentioned which publication I was from.

'Oh – oi love *The Loidy*!' she said, moving swiftly on, with David Walliams (bigger and more good-looking in 'real life'). Flirted madly with Stuart Rose, who escorted me to my car.

Note on the Burberry afterparty. The Kooks were apparently playing live, but that passed me by. All I noticed was the music was very loud.

24 September 2009

Passing the issue day. Now I only use words that I have heard Anna Wintour saying in *The September Issue*, like 'Fix it' or 'Out of my way' or 'Make it happen, like, yesterday.'

Janina is getting even whiter of face, quieter of voice. Lindsay is trying desperately to please, which only makes me want to shout at her. Sandi Toksvig appeared suddenly at lunchtime, so I took her to Terroirs. Super-smart and dumpy, blonde hair and green eyes, she talked about documentaries and told me not to do C4. She said the head of docs had called her in, and looked concerned and said, 'We'd love you to do something for us on the difficulties you've had as a lesbian mother.'

She was furious, so said, 'I'd love to, Dawn (or Sue, or Jenni, or whoever, all BBC women are called Sue or Jenni), but there's just one slight hitch. I've never had the slightest difficulty as a lesbian mother. It's been a piece of cake.'

We ate rillettes and salami, and so on, and then Sandy Buckingham the illustrator finally arrived and showed me her work, and I fell slightly out of love with the project (they are proposing a column on Great British Women, words by Sandi with an i, illustrations by Sandy with a y), but I sense our readers will be happy. As Sandy left, she said, 'I've got to go and write jokes for the News Quiz now. Gotta go and be hilarious.'

I went through proofs excising words like 'tasty' and 'treat' and 'sweet' and 'light bite', and awful phrases like 'magic moments' or 'treasure trove'. Then I walked home through glorious sunshine thinking how lucky I am to have a job I enjoy and people to love.

That night we went to Toby Young's for supper. 'Who else is coming?' I asked as I glugged my first glass of Sauvignon Blanc.

'Susannah Herbert,' said Toby.

'Ha ha.'

'No, she really is coming,' said Caroline, Toby's wife, looking anxious. I considered leaving, but didn't. Susannah is, of course, the tall editor of the News Review who visibly found me annoying. She arrived, and all was well. No hard feelings – what's the point?

We watched the C4 documentary *When Boris Met Dave*, which I participated in, was directed by John Dower, and produced by Toby. I only did a spot in it because I was told it would be about me and my generation at Oxford, my book and Nigella. But it wasn't; it was about the rivalry between Cameron and my brother. So now people are puzzled, and my brother wounded, that I have popped up out of blue in this doc to pronounce on the Bullingdon, the Oxford Union and his university career. I thought I was being interviewed about *The Oxford Myth*, my book of juvenilia, something else entirely. Burnt fingers. My keenness to participate in the documentary on *The Lady* has dwindled further as a result of all the above.

28 September 2009

At the tennis club yesterday I saw *Sunday Times* supreme commander John Witherow. 'How's Daisy (Waugh)?' was his first question to me after sacking me in July. His second remark was, 'It's grrrreat having Eleanor (Mills) back,' grinning as if someone had given him a puppy.

First, production meeting, then hammering away at keyboard, then lunch with Jess Jonzen and Carolyn. Janina suggested a piece about alien abduction, and used the words 'anal probing' in conference, in front of Ben, for which one has to take hat off to her. I have asked her not to send me emails in the middle of the night/at the weekend. She asked Jess if she is the sort of person who 'has a glass of wine with her lunch'. Lindsay, meanwhile, has mentionitis about J. G. Ballard, whatever that means – God knows, one never ever knows these things in my view – and has stuck up pictures of Ballard and Ted Hughes in what she calls her 'Boyfriend Gallery' on her office wall.

Re: the *Lady* doc. We held a meeting with the lawyers in Bedford Street (more tea and *Family Circle* biscuits) to discuss filming, in case the trailer leads to the doc being 'greenlighted'. Conversation too boring to repeat here. Basically, as all lawyers do, they counselled excessive caution and wittered away about damaging the brand. Ben mustard-keen on doc, of course. I am detecting the feeling that my expensive appointment, coupled with the documentary, are one of the last throws of the dice. Ben arrived from Florida in November 2008, and is running the magazine like a proper business at last. But if it doesn't work, the gamble doesn't pay off and circulation falls, then it's game over. For us all.

As I was leaving at 5.40 p.m., I bumped into Ben and Adam with Uncle Tom, who lives upstairs and who had handed over control of the mag to Ben, with the five directors now being his nephews, and one sister, Julia Budworth. Tom Bowles was rheumy-eyed and had recently, one sensed, reeled out of some Pall Mall club. I said, 'How nice to meet you finally.'

He said, 'Finally?' Obviously no pushover. Talked about 'the rotten magazine'. So then I tried to smooth up to him, with limited success, by telling him I loved the building exactly as it is. He liked me more after that. Then we talked about the Mitfords, and he said that when families started to write about each other, they lost the plot. Help!

29 September 2009

Big surprise. Blez – who went AWOL last week – came back, and has been whacked by Ben. I've been asking for this since I got here, but I had nothing to do with his dismissal in the end. So the literary editor is no longer in the building. Ben told me he took it like a lamb, and handed over his key. I felt very exhilarated. In theory, that saves Ben about fifty grand a year. To pay contributors who can actually write. The page rate – i.e., the cost of producing one page of editorial and buying in images – has gone up to about £300–£400 from about £200, and now the Budworths have mortgaged 38 Bedford St (no. 38 is his mother's property, and includes a mysterious shop on street-level called Vera Trinder that sells 'Stamps & Coins, Albums & Accessories') next to *The Lady* HQ at 39/40 to pay for my editorship and relaunch. So no pressure then.

Now I need to find a literary editor. Or, maybe I don't.

On my way back to Covent Garden from the frozen-yoghurt place, I find marketing man Nic Boize standing on the stoop, puffing on his pipe with Piers, the computer guy. Boize puffs smoke at me and opens a conversation about how we are going to celebrate/commemorate *The Lady*'s 125th, which falls in February 2010. Had I any thoughts? 'Not so far,' I said. So then he tells me his. Namely, that Ben will dress up as his great-grandpa, Thomas Gibson Bowles, the quill-wielding founder of *The Lady* and *Vanity Fair*. And I will wear full eighteenth-century costume, complete with crinoline and bonnet. And then we will call a photo-opportunity with '*Heat* and *Hello!* and *Tatler*', who will all be dying to come because – 'Wait for the *pièce de résistance*, Rachel' – Boize planned to invite the mayor, my older brother, to swoop by while me and Ben are standing there like lemons in full period fig 'to unveil the plaque' while the flashbulbs popped.

I gazed at Nic Boize, stunned. At first I thought he was joking. But he clearly thought this was the wheeze of a lifetime, and watched my face for signs of early delight breaking out. I almost choked on my 99 per cent fat-free blackcurrant and gooseberry frozen yoghurt and had to restrain myself from lunging at him. 'Please will you let me into the building,' I ordered Piers. I was broken. Honestly, the man has had three months to come up with a spectacular for the 125th – in fact, he's probably had twenty-five years – and he comes up with a scheme Boris wouldn't touch with a bargepole and guaranteed to send me aka 'Boris's sister' harry bonkers.

30 September 2009

Tried to explain to Janina that the copy on a page that says 'News and Reviews' – a page she writes, which comes after the list of contributors, right at the front of the mag – has to bear some slight resemblance to, er, News and Reviews, rather than random things that people she has interviewed have told her over the telephone. There was a lead item about a 29-year-old in a boy band called Blake who was, she said, interesting because he enjoyed reading history. I said, 'That's not news.' She said, 'He's really well spoken.' I said, 'That's not news.' Then she said, 'He said "gymnasium" rather than "gym".' I said, robotically, 'Still not news.' She finally got the message and went away.

It must be weird for her, and difficult being the daughter of the woman who edited the mag, and now no longer being apple of the editor's eye, no longer the Dauphin in the Court of the Sun King (or whatever. I think a Tudor court is probably a more appropriate analogy). Plus, the fact remains: the eighth editor, though no longer in the building, is still on the masthead as editor-at-large, and is hanging on to her opera, travel and beauty gigs. Meanwhile I only have two in-house editorial staff, one is Lindsay Fulcher, and the other is my predecessor's daughter.

THE LADY
2nd APRIL, 1926.
Weekly. Yearly Subscription, Inland and Colonial, 43/-.
Allied (February Edition), 26/-.
This Foreign Edition, 34/-

ALL RIGHTS OF TRANSLATION AND REPRODUCTION ARE RESERVED.
Entered at the New York Post Office as second-class matter.
The Postage to Canada at the Canadian Magazine Rate.

REGISTERED AT THE G.P.O. AS A NEWSPAPER
VOL. LXXXI.—No. 2099.
Postage 2d.

The Lady

SPRING NUMBER   ONE SHILLING

LONDON: "THE LADY" OFFICES, 39 & 40, BEDFORD STREET, STRAND, W.C.2.

OCTOBER

1 October 2009

Oh my god, what a day. An item appears on some website saying that Janina is now books editor following Blez's sacking and the 'successful relaunch of *The Lady* under Arline Usden'.

Nigella declines my offer to be Christmas cover girl. I am not doing very well with my PA, Gillian – and know from bitter experience of having nannies and au pairs that it's more my fault than hers. She has managed to deter Sally Muir and Joanna Osborne, whom I've been fluffing for ages so I get first serial rights for their new book on knitted dogs (this is the sort of thing that I get really excited about now). On the Muir/Osborne debacle, they emailed me to say they would be in town on Friday, and could they come to see me to show me proofs of their enchanting knitted dachshunds, etc. Could they ever! I'd been after the knitted pets for *months*!

'Tell them I literally can't wait to see them,' I emailed from my BlackBerry. Gillian, unfortunately, took this to mean I was too busy to fit them in. These snafus are inevitable in the world of instant communications.

'Are you sure?' they asked. After all, my married surname is Dawnay, and this whole event had been brokered by their agent, my sister-in-law Caroline Dawnay, so they were, naturally, puzzled. 'She seemed v. keen before.'

I didn't know any of this until United Agents sent the whole correspondence to me in despair later and we revived the meeting (with the result that a pattern for a knitted reindeer helmet appeared in mid-December, just in time to turn your dog into Rudolf for Christmas).

Then it turned out that it was Gillian who had inadvertently relayed to BookBrunch that Janina would be books editor. 'Why did you say that?' I wailed. 'It's not true. Now the whole publishing industry thinks Janina is my literary editor.'

'Because I didn't know what to say when they asked,' said Gillian, looking upset. We were officially having a bad day by now. 'She did on occasion look after the short story.'

I know it will all come out in the wash, and it's impossible to be cross with someone who kindly books my taxis and is supernaturally pleasant at all times, even to the people who ring up *The Lady* editorial because they've got no one else to call. But I can see an avalanche of books and invitations to Booker dinners and literary prizes cascading on to the teetering piles on Janina's desk, where she has erected walls of press cuttings and books and notebooks to repel intruders or interest.

Later, in Holland Park Avenue, I was loitering in Daunt's when I spotted a man with a crumpled plastic bag at the counter. He withdrew a couple of copies of a fun-sized hardback book and pressed it on to one of the languid youths who mans the till. I craned my head and saw the book was *Seasonal Suicide Notes*, and deduced from the title that the Womble was the author, Roger Lewis. Whom I'd thought of as a possible replacement for the Blez! It seemed too good to be true. Lewis left Daunt's, and turned right and beetled down Holland Park Avenue, like a wind-up troll. I couldn't let him go. So I ran out and caught up with him.

'Stop!' I called. He turned around. 'Are you angry Roger Lewis who lives in Hertfordshire?' I asked. It sounded a bit great-auntish, as if I was asking if he was a Worcestershire Dalrymple. Lewis looked suspicious but admitted, *mutatis mutandis*, that he was. 'I've been trying to get hold of you,' I said, explaining that I edited *The Lady*. He looked amazed and appalled at the same time, but not uninterested.

'You can get me through Short Books. Is this the way to the Orangery?' he went on. 'I'm going to a do given by Michael Winner.'

I quite wanted him to ask me to accompany him, but he didn't. I don't think I've ever met a more unattractive writer in my life, but I liked the way he responded to my offer with the words, 'I never turn down work,' and thought me important enough, despite lack of literary cred, to show off about his Michael Winner invite.

5 October 2009

Am shattered. I doubt my ability to do this job properly and the wisdom of shoehorning the putting out of a ninety-page weekly mag into four days. It basically means: no lunches. No chatting on phone. No old life at all. It means eating salad at my desk and sending out a peon for coffee. Luckily, we are hemmed in by fast-food restaurants (the juxtaposition of *The Lady* and TGI Friday's is particularly piquant) and coffee shops. Have decided the EAT latte is streets ahead of Caffè Nero, and the porridge is good too. So Monday was manic (must stop using that awful word from Bangles song), with Carolyn away in Shetland writing about lamb and scallops, and Lindsay off, and Chrissie, chief sub, struck with flu and Judy creaking around, clutching at her stomach (she has had small op, poor love) and sighing.

Meanwhile, Janina has noticed that I have locked her out of 'Copy for Subs' and 'Art' folders after the ding-dong over her mother's cruise copy last week, so she can't get into documents and make edits. On Thursday, she finally admitted after twenty minutes' harsh interrogation (we almost ended up waterboarding her) that she *had* re-edited her mother's piece about having a two-week free cruise on Swan Hellenic, and kept putting back the same 300 words that Carolyn had kept taking out. So we have locked her out, and Lindsay, too, for good measure, as a shot across her bows.

There are daily negotiations between C4, Optomen and the Budworths re: the doc, about access, privacy, and also – they need to appoint a director.

8 October 2009

Mary Killen, who I have hired to write a column about life in the
grottage in Wiltshire with Giles Wood, her husband, came into the
office today and mungered and clettered, leaving her bags like old
tea-cosies everywhere, and spending most of her day with her face
buried in a large carry-all, looking for what she calls her 'noseguard' –
an alarmingly magnifying round mirror from Boots in which she
inspects her face for rogue hairs that might have 'marched out' overnight, and bogies and other blemishes. I spent some time gazing at
Janina's copy on Dan Cruickshank, then Mary and I rewrote her
piece on 'Bossy Women', and then Emma Tucker, editor of the *Times*
T2 section, came in to have lunch, and I showed her off – all slim and
glamorous with shiny-conker hair from the salon. Vanessa de Lisle,
a former Voguette, who is doing some fashion for us, came in to discuss the shooting spread. Penny Smith filed her copy. It's naughty,
like she is – I am thinking of calling it 'Bad Penny'. Ludo has broken
his wrist, so instead of writing my novel *Winter Games* tomorrow I
am on the train to Swindon, to the Great Western Hospital.

9 October 2009

Spent day in Great Western Hospital. When Ludo saw me, he
blushed and I cried. I am so glad I came to be with him. Then we
sat for four hours, he was anaesthetized, then we sat for another
two hours and I went home, shattered, as my BlackBerry buzzed
with Avril Groom, another of my newly appointed fashion editors,
sending me endless images for her coats copy instead of sending
them to the picture desk. Ate toast and then went to sleep even
before *Newsnight Review*.

10 October 2009

This came in from a friend in telly:

To: Adam Budworth; Rachel Johnson
Sent: 10 October 2009 17:59
Subject: C4

I don't know if C4 has come up with the TV equivalent of a puff of white smoke but I just thought you both might like to know that the director they want to do it (i.e., the doc on *The Lady*) is the one who made last week's *When Boris Met Dave*. He was their original first choice, and he turned them down, but the project he has been hanging out for has disappeared and he has told them he'd do it. I think he's called John Downer but I've been sampling sloe gin and my memory isn't what it should be.

Does that help?
Xx

So I sent back this:

John Dower is a swine – he tricked me into appearing in that doc! Said it was about my book *The Oxford Myth*, and Nigella, etc., then he Boratted me – first hour on me, my book, etc., then bam – five qus on Boris and Dave. I said, 'Why are you asking me about Cameron and the Bullingdon? . . . Bloody sting operation. I even TOLD Pat that was why I didn't trust C4 docs. Jeez.

Keep the info flowing
xx

11 *October* 2009

Went for a long walk on Richmond Park with Milly and Coco, then to Petersham Nurseries, the fashionably rural outpost of chef (Skye Gyngell's gaff) for eye-bleedingly expensive hummus sandwiches, creamy chicken salad and unexciting carrot cake, while sitting in the rain amidst wheelbarrows and trugs. Then went to see Mama. She's more unwell than usual. Wondering whether to postpone her hip operation. I lay on the floor. I love her so much it hurts. As for the children – now they're getting so big. It's reached the stage when I don't worry about me getting older – that's already happened. I worry about them getting older. My neck, as Oliver told me the other day, looks like Alan Hansen's, and my moustache – as the French call it, a *duvet* – is now, comfortably, a winter-weight tog.

12 *October* 2009

Felt ill. Tummy thing. Tottered in. Production meeting in 'the boardroom' followed by the apparition of Kimberly Quinn in demure Puritan black shift and puff-sleeved white virginal Ralph Lauren (I asked) blouse. Kimberly Quinn was publisher of *The Spectator*, and a legend at getting advertising. She was a pocket rocket. Everyone told me in words of one syllable not to let her cross the threshold, but who cares? I am open to all comers. She came out with a whole load of stuff I wish I'd thought of, and was particularly inspired about reader offers. 'Beatrix Potter boxed sets!' she squeaked. 'If something new comes out, offer them the old one again, like *Emma*, or *Brideshead*! They always hate the new one, so flog 'em the old one they like! Everyone hates change! And if all else fails, sell them Winston Churchill's speeches. Again.' I listened, open-mouthed. Complete genius. She is brilliant at this stuff. No wonder the circulation at *The Spec* climbed into the seventies.

I only came up with one good gimmick in her presence. Every time someone writes in complaining about the axing of 'The Lady Laughs' (as Ben says, it's more likely that Elvis is found on the moon than that someone raises a faint chortle at one of the 'Lady Laughs' cartoons) or the end of 'Readers' Queries' (how to get Vicks® VapoRub® out of candlewick bedspreads, etc.), I will send them a nice letter and – the sucker punch – an old copy of *The Lady*, just to remind them how 'sensationally bland' (and I quote Sathnam Sanghera, the *Financial Times*, 2002) it actually was.

Had just got rid of darling Kimberly when Jill Shaw Ruddock – who wrote a nice piece about what a blast the change is – shows up out of the blue and surges into the boardroom in her AllSaints leather shrunken jacket and gives us a PowerPoint lecture about how *The Lady* has to become *The Modern Lady* – for the new woman in you – or something. Ben handles her with aplomb. I feel red mist descending and stand up and tell her I want *The Lady* to be a readable, covetable cross between *The Spectator*, *Waitrose Food Illustrated* and another title I plucked from the air (could have been *More*). I think she is cross that we bottled out of putting the word 'menopause' on the cover. We put a bucket of apples instead, under the cover line 'Missed Fruitfulness'. WTF did she expect? 'Menopause' is basically the least sexy word in the English language.

By 3 p.m., I hadn't managed to get out of the office yet and slunk into EAT to grab a big soup. Ben joined me. No word yet on C4 and who is going to direct. But it sounds as if it might be John Dower then, the director of *When Boris Met Dave*, as my friend in telly forewarned.

The funny thing is, I do hope it's Dower – even though he tricked me. The devil you know, etc. Plus he gave the distinct impression that he had a brain and might know who Debo, Duchess of Devonshire, and the Mitfords and so forth are, as Mollie, who directed the trailer, certainly didn't. I liked him.

13 *October 2009*

Had to get up early. Breakfast award ceremony, or to give the epochal press backslapper it's full title, the Editorial Intelligence Commentariat Awards 'Champagne Breakfast', where I had to give away a gong to the Best Diary. It went to the 'Londoner's Diary'. Exhausting to have to network at 8 a.m. It didn't help that I had left behind the organizer-supplied notes about the three contenders for this prestigious award and had to riff. Ivo (known by Ben as 'Hopalong', as he has crocked his knee) came into lunch with Ben (known by Ivo as 'Dover' for the obvious smutty reason) to talk about their respective aims. Much chortling about Nic Boize and his cunning plans to have me in crinoline come the 125th anniversary in February. My position is that if anyone so much as mentions a bustle and a bonnet again I will auto-defenestrate them into Bedford Street. I slogged through the afternoon and then walked home through the dry park, passing Peter Snow in the parade-ground bit. It's sad when men who used to be so hugely energetic get old and bowed. Be me soon.

I had to break the news to Janina that I didn't really need her to come into my office to tell me every time she'd changed a comma in her copy (she showed me a change from a comma to a semicolon in the proof; am not kidding), nor did I need to know by telephone if Lindsay had placed some copy in 'Copy In'. In fact, I intimated, if they did persist in telling me, I would never get anything done at all and would go completely mad. I tried to appear reasonably threatening (again, channelling Anna Wintour in *The September Issue*).

Dada called and asked me to lunch at the Garrick, reminding me that, when he didn't answer a couple of messages yesterday, I'd had nightmares about him.

14 October 2009

The day of the *Tatler* 300th anniversary party dawns! I get into the office and am told that I have to do a Titchmarsh show on the north-south divide. North-south divide? Why me? I kick up an arsy stink. Saying I don't have to do daytime telly and it's naff and demeaning, and so on. Ben basically gives me my marching orders to the sofa, rattling off audience figures (1.3 million watch Titchmarsh). I am wrong, in other words. Daytime is our only hope.

So I rattle through the copy for the 27 October issue and look at the 3 November copy and forward-plan covers and make calls and then strip off my sweaty jogging clothes and put on a frock for my public (West Village navy with green collar). Then lovely, clean-smelling EcoLogic car arrives, and Coco and I hop in and zoom to White City where, for the first time ever, I have my own dressing room in readiness for Titchmarsh exposure. I switch on plasma and lie on the sofa sipping a Costa latte and watching *Dial M for Murder*. It is a wrench to have to go into Make-Up, where Martin Shaw is worrying about his hair and Heather Smalls from M People is warming up her voice and making noises like a Moog synthesizer, and Lynda Bellingham, fresh from being dumped from *Strictly*, is adjusting her cleavage. Then we are on for the regulation two minutes where I say nothing of note but kiss Alan Titchmarsh's pancake face at least eight times. I feel deeply ashamed of myself for doing it. Then home to Milly, and Sam Kiley comes for a drink prior to the party and I ask him, 'Why am I doing the C4 *Lady* doc, why why?' And Sam says, 'Because you're vain.'

The *Tatler* party is something. Lancaster House. Beautiful boys dressed up as Bystanderish footmen, with glasses of champagne. Tables of macaroons, pyramids of cake and champagne, delicious risotto, huge rooms, so no being pressed into a corner being sprayed with salmon-flecked canapé breath.

I love it, but the next day people complain it was déclassé and say there was 'no one there'. My brother Jo and Dada were there; enough for me. Nick Coleridge gave a speech. Catherine Ostler, who is super-smart and doesn't need to blow her own trumpet, didn't. I liked talking to two immensely tall men: Henry Wyndham and Harry Worcester. And I also liked being photographed with them in the photo booth. Told Andrew 'Radio' Roberts I'd enjoyed his piece about diary-writing (like having children, a bid for immortality). Ivo had to drag me away.

15 October 2009

Felt champagned all day.

Lots in the papers about Edwina Langley, our gorgeous in-house PR (Ivo comes in just to look at her) – reason being, she was at the theatre with the Queen. She had to actually *stand up* at the New London Theatre in order for the Queen and Dook to *squeeze past*. I had given this story to the *Tel*, but they'd buried it at the bottom of the 'Mandrake' column and then, lo! the *Standard* splashed with it. Edwina was adamant about not having her name in the press. Then I understood. The Queen had gone incognito to the theatre because she wanted to avoid any song and dance about Brenda (*Private Eye*'s name for Her Majesty the Queen) going up west. And then *The Lady* had rumbled her. Should I apologize in my ed's letter about breaching Her Majesty's privacy?

I had to eat a huge carb-loaded lunch at Leon to sop up the *Tatler* alcohol. I found out that the documentary, finally, has been green-lighted by C4, and John Dower is to direct. Liza Campbell, author of *Title Deeds*, artist, etc., came in the afternoon and we chattered away like old friends as she drank sweet tea and ate an egg sandwich and told me about her life: car-boot sales to make money, sings in a choir. She's funny and clever and beautiful (it meanly crossed my mind to wonder whether she'd had trout pout done). Ben was panting after her like a hound, but I could see she was hotter for barrister Adam, who arrived in dashing black chalkstripe, eating a Mars bar, bringing the wind from the High Court straight into the boardroom.

That evening I headed for Soho House for Emma Soames's sixtieth. I propped up the bar with Sue Crewe and Nicky Haslam, post-morteming the *Tatler* party. Nicky said the venue was too big and you lost people. But then Kim Fletcher said it had everything. I agreed. I was quoted declaring it 'obviously, the party of the year' in the *Standard* (*quelle* suck-up I am!), alongside pic of self grinning and Dada looking very drunk with mouth wide open.

Here, at Emma's do, Michael Howard, former Tory leader, very sternly told me that I had to tell Dada to *stop* trying to be an MP. I said, 'Why?' Howard said, 'He's too old.' I said, 'In what other country would sixty-something be considered too old?' It was depressing. And ironic (Soames as editor-at-large of Saga has become unofficial czar for oldies). Why should I discourage him from doing something he wants to (in the parlance, 'follow his dream') when all he has ever done, as Mama has, is encourage me?

19 October 2009

Still trying to wrangle terms with Pat Llewellyn, MD of Optomen, re: the bleeding doc. Philippa Walker, i.e., Mrs Alan Yentob – to whom I told whole *When Boris Met Dave* saga, etc., angling it most favourably to me – said I was on a 'hiding to nothing' agreeing to be on TV, which is moderately amusing, when you consider she is documentary filmmaker herself.

I got to work within fifty minutes, picked up skinny latte from David at EAT, and strode confidently in, saying hello to Kath and Joan downstairs in Classifieds. It's always so cosy to see them. Chaired the production meeting in the boardroom. Janina's ideas all left me cold, which was awful. Am longing for her to come up with something that appeals. 'I'm trying to get excited about Lulu/ Leslie Caron/Jack Dee,' I said. But I couldn't.

Then she said, 'Tattoos,' in the same sibilant way she'd said, 'Aliens,' and gone on to talk about anal probing and abductions.

'Edinburgh Tattoo: yes; tramp stamp: no,' I said. She meant the latter.

At the moment, the magazine is costing between 6k and 8k to produce, i.e., about 2.5k more than it used to when it was commissioned in-house. I think Ben is cool; however, he says that the Maggie cover has tanked somewhat. Did not go down at all well with core readership, who think Mark Thatcher is a spoilt waste of space and a mummy's boy. Won't get figures till six weeks after the cover has been out – which means the end of the month . . .

I had lunch with Susannah Herbert, to show all is forgiven. She dropped Max Hastings' name four times. Total mentionitis. On the way back, I told Ben that I'd decided about the doc. Channel 4 definitely wants it, but now it's our turn to make up our minds. I said to Ben that a one-hour one-off was high risk. So if they wanted to do it over 3x60 minutes, fine; otherwise, *nein*. I made a persuasive case. The story could unfold; they would have to show texture and context. Otherwise, the family risked 'spunking up against the wall' (to use Ben's immortal phrase) 125 years of publishing history on 48 minutes of TV (one hour minus 12 minutes of ad breaks).

Production meeting. Chrissie (who has been off for two weeks) banged on about everyone getting behind and wants copy in about six months before publication. We are chasing an interview with Liz Hurley. Jess (looking very pretty) said Liz Hurley had requested copies of the mag. Ben said a man on a bike (i.e., B. Budworth) would courier them round, although he wondered whether a penny-farthing would go down better. After the meeting, we went back to the doc, and I said again: doing a one-hour thing will do us no credit, make me look like self-publicizing bitch and insult our readers. However, a three-parter will be able to take it slowly and let things unfurl more organically, like a young fern in springtime.

20 October 2009

Clover Stroud came in, blonde with big gardener's hands. Liked her. She has a mother in a coma aged seventy. I commissioned her to write three pieces and agreed to try her out as agony aunt.

Have now told at least three people they can be agony aunt.

21 October 2009

The top people from Optomen came in. Becky Clarke (blonde, perky, Northern) and Pat (small and dark, Welsh). Adam and I told them in words of one syllable that it was a three-parter or nothing. They shook their heads and said they'd tried to get it away as a three-parter, that C4 didn't want a three-parter, it was a *Cutting Edge* or nothing. It would be a 'leap of faith' on our part, and unless we trusted them, we shouldn't do it. So then we spread our legs and begged for it, basically. I do think that if they are true to their word (OK, telly people will sell their own grandmothers downriver) then we should be fine and, on balance, the benefit just outweighs the risk. But then, it's not my family company I'm gambling centuries of unblemished respectability on for the dubious joys of being taken down on national television.

There is a Frank Johnson memorial party in the evening. A panorama of hacks drinking champagne at Christie's. I enjoyed talking to McHackie, Sarah Sands, Veronica Wadley, Mike White, Tim Razzall and Jane Bonham Carter, Norman Lamont, Amabel Lindsay, Nicky Haslam – of course (I asked Nicky if he had a picture of himself in Master of Foxhounds rig, as we were thinking of ditching our Kate

Middleton cover in favour of one of him, and his eyes glazed in a way that revealed how excited he was by the prospect of camply appearing on cover of Our *Lady* and whipped out his BlackBerry to ensure that his tame PA would email the image first thing) – Christopher Simon Sykes, Virginia Fraser, Clemmie Fraser, Rachel Billington . . . the list is endless. When I got home Ivo asked me who was there, and I said it would be quicker and easier to tell him who wasn't there.

22 October 2009

Well, we've all rolled over now and let Pat and Becky tickle our tummies. The Budworths have finally agreed terms with Optomen. So it's going to be on C4. That little Becky is impossible to say no to. The Nicky Haslam in jodhpurs image is divine but not a cover. Must remember it's not my magazine, my new baby; it belongs to the Budworths. They are the ones who are paying my salary and for the children's education and buying it, and not my smart London journalist writer friends.

Lunch with Ben in Terroirs; he is adorable and lovable, like the Andrex puppy. I have realized what was at stake: *The Lady* needed an editor, but, even more, Ben wants a wife. I must find him one – it's clearly part of my job description. I have discovered that Janina hasn't taken a single day off this year. When I asked her to, she said she couldn't, because 'something would happen while I was gone.' Stefano, who has been appointed design consultant for the relaunch, came in to show me his cover designs – I love them: colourful, playful, modern, witty. Ben will hate them, because the old clunky masthead with 'The' enfolded into 'Lady' on a white strip (to stand out on the shelf) will have to go. The cartoonist Zebedee Helm came in and I have commissioned him to do a cartoon every week. Stefano will email him images from the archive. It will all be fantastic, so long as Ben agrees to the new cover look. In the end, we run with a pap shot of Kate Middleton, and cover lines like 'Playing the Field, *The Lady*'s guide to country pursuits'. Inside, there are pieces about Norman Tebbit, who pretends that Cherie is in his sights when he's shooting; cooking wild game; and a fashion spread with a Holland & Holland jacket costing £1,000. Well, Ben did say he wanted it to be more country, less town. This issue is very gamey. I hope it does well on the newsstand. Jessica Fellowes posts this on her blog in celebration:

Tuesday 27 October 2009
The Lady

Possibly the poshest publication of all, *The Lady* has recently undergone a revamp with Rachel Johnson (sister of Boris) at the helm. For almost a thousand years, *The Lady* has been the place for posh people to find their staff. Occasionally they'd also book a villa in Tuscany or Provence through the small ads too. The rest of the pages were basically ignored, except possibly for the occasional person who ordered a pair of fleece-lined slippers or a walk-in bath. Now it's rather glossy and groovy, with top contributors – including your very own posh self. See my article on dos and don'ts for townies in the country this week. And my piece on posh foodies next week. OK, yah?

Vol. CVIII. No. 2809. 15th December 1938

The Lady

4ᵈ

LAST-
MINUTE
PRESENTS

Evening Gown by HEIM
Photo by DORVYNE

15th December 1938

November

8 November 2009

Half-term. I came in on Wednesday after a break with the children and raced into the office to see the Rosamund Pike edition being laid out and subbed. Looks good. Ding-dong over the Remembrance Sunday poppy on the cover. Claire had put an artsy, silky, blowsy one which I'd peeped at on my BlackBerry (which has since died, losing three hundred telephone numbers). Ben asks to restore the red paper and green plastic British Legion poppy one. I agree. It is a design classic and cannot be bettered, and I don't want it to look as if *The Lady* thinks it's not good enough for herself.

I have reconfigured the office. Major dramas. I have moved Vicky from my antechamber and brought in Carolyn, and removed Janina to what is called the 'cab's office' with Lindsay. So Carolyn is in, and Janina out, of main enfilade of rooms. The plan is: me; then outside me a room containing Gillian and Carolyn; then Judy the production manager and Rachel Chapman, the advertising production co-ordinator, who is now known as Little Rachel; and then a couple of big rooms with art, pictures and subs; and on another part of the same floor, through many doors and across landings, will sit Lindsay and Janina.

Janina totally freaked.

'Most journalists would be pleased to be given their own office,' I told her.

So Carolyn now sits where Vicky was and Janina has gone into the cab office with Lindsay, to the evident displeasure of both.

Ooh – this just in. *The Lady* really is SHRN. That's So Hot Right Now.

From: Lady Antonia Fraser Pinter
To: Rachel Johnson
Cc: editors@lady.co.uk
Sent: Sunday 8 November 2009 15:51
Subject: *The Lady* Killer?

Dear Rachel, I just had your French publisher – my close friend Laure de Gramont – to lunch and she brought me the wonderful edition of THE LADY with Clemmie on the cover. I read it all, as a result: amazing and enjoyable. I just had an idea that you would like a crime slot, i.e., a weekly review of a crime novel. I used to review crime for the short-lived *London News*, and I have of course written seven Jemima Shore crime novels. I thought it could be called THE LADY KILLER. Ladies read lots and lots of crime fiction (hence the leading genre on PLR [Public Lending Right]) so I thought it might be a good idea.

Ignore if inappropriate or too soon or too late. In any case, it's a deeply enjoyable periodical.

Love Antonia

Of course, the fact that she wants a column is not entirely unrelated to the fact that her newest, dewiest daughter-in-law is now *The Lady* gardener. I showed my mother on my (new) BlackBerry and she commented, 'That's the first time to my knowledge that Antonia has ever asked for anything.' The beautiful, talented, etc. Tamasin Day-Lewis is also pushing and asking if I have had 'any further thoughts' about her doing something 'regularly', but I am afraid the door is not open at 39/40 Bedford Street but firmly closed. I can't give away more prime real estate! They will have to pay me if they want to contribute. Meanwhile, strange presents from people have started to arrive, as well as ratty letters, and everyone seems to want to write for *The Lady*, as if it has become height of camp granny chic. I can't help being worried that things are going well. This is ominous. The last time I said that to myself was in 1998, and no sooner had the words formed in my mind than Ivo and I were both sacked from our *Sunday Telegraph* gigs by Dominic Lawson and had to decamp from Washington DC after only fifteen months. I had to spend the next two years on my own with three children under five in Belgium, living in a gloomy villa in the suburbs of Brussels surrounded by conifers. So scratch that.

Things are no more rubbish than usual. But then the first proper, audited circulation figures have yet to come in . . .

9 November 2009

After a hiatus, the telly people are back. It's all been very confusing, but now they are filming not the teaser/trailer, but the actual fly-on-the-wall documentary for Channel 4. The doc has been commissioned, so this is for real. So it is – bizarrely – the first day of actual filming. Am very relieved I do not work in telly. It's a total pain in the arse.

I found the crew setting up lights, etc., in my office, consisting of director John Dower in full Tour de France rig (he bicycles), plus a pretty dark-haired cameraman who looks about fifteen called Wesley, who wears Topman jeans and V-neck T-shirts. Gave them half an hour, during which they tried to get me to dish on all my staff. Dower (director of the aforementioned *When Boris Met Dave*, and an award-winning doc called *Thriller in Manila* about the prize fight between Muhammad Ali and Joe Frazier) asked me who I was going to sack.

'Piss off, John,' I groaned. It's no secret that Ben has hired me to be his attack dog. And I've already said to camera that I'm going to have to 'do a couple of sackings'. But I'm not going to spell it out. Name people. Jeez.

Ben has already warned there would be redundancies – he'd already summoned up the prospect of the P45 at the weekly Thursday meeting he's introduced. It's called the 'Strategy and Development' meeting. His PA Maureen sends round an email about it catch-lined 'Stat. (sic) & Dev'. We all sit in the boardroom, around the blue baize table. Janina lurks by the door. I usually sit at the head of the table. Classifieds, marketing, PR, distribution – all attend. Ben chairs. During the meeting Ben tells us we have to come in earlier and work later, or invites someone from the sales or marketing or distribution side to say what they do, which is to sell, market and distribute the title, so far as I can tell. We all listen respectfully. It's all getting very Power-Point. Ben has even bought a whiteboard. After the meeting, he goes over the blue baize with his dustbuster, to remove crumbs and hairs.

But back to this morning. The 10 a.m. production meeting is enlivened by Coco pushing her muzzle into Judy's crotch (she shrieked) shortly after I'd wigged chief sub Chrissie about a massive typo. Ben said something I didn't follow about a teddy bear and Mrs Budworth, and then it was Chrissie's turn to shriek while everyone covered their faces with their hands.

'What teddy bear?' I asked.

'You're not to worry about the teddy bear,' he said darkly. 'It's all under control.'

In my experience, when men say, 'It's all under control,' it never is, and there is something nasty and woodshed-sounding about the teddy bear.

11 a.m. Hugh St Clair comes in with the mood board – soft furnishings, swatches, and so on, for my office-redecoration project. My office is grim and bare, and I have persuaded Ben it needs to be cosy and elegant. Luckily, Hugh St Clair is a firm believer in 'pretty power' when it comes to office environments, and has brought mouthwatering wares. I picked out a Cole and Son wallpaper with hummingbirds against a duck-egg background and orange velvet to cover the sofa or *chaise longue* that I have demanded. Want it now!

1 p.m. Clemmie comes in for lunch and squeals with joy when she sees herself on the cover in the window of *The Lady*.

2 p.m. Brother Leo, who is easily most successful yet modest sibling to date in that he has actually made money by selling a company he created himself, Sustainable Finance, to PriceWater-houseCoopers, joins me and Clemmie for coffee at Wahaca. They bond. They both have daughters called Ruby, the same age.

2.30 p.m. Late features meeting. Janina – who I can't fault for industry or application – pitches her NASA idea about the Old Harrovian astronaut for the nth week running. I slump back in my chair in the boardroom and roll my eyes – remembering too late that the cameras are also rolling. Pretty blonde Vicky – who does our letters page and coordinates editorial for the website – is very bushy-tailed and keen to write, which is good. Am keen to encourage youthful talent! I get her to write a piece about keeping chickens – again, it's SHRN (So Hot Right Now).

4 p.m. Stefano comes in to talk about the redesign of the mag. I want him to strip it down to its elegant nineteenth-century origins, when people actually bought *The Lady* for its editorial, and the title was celebrated for its illustrations by well-known artists rather than for stairlifts/sprigged cotton nightgowns with four-way stretch/jolly-hockey-sticks ads for under-matrons to pair boys' socks at prep schools. He sits in my boudoir and reveals his new cover design on his huge silver MacBook. I love it – it's elegant and refined, with a double frame of violet and another colour each week – yellow, or pink, for example – and 'The Lady' in a font dating from 1885. It is modern and funky as well as being timeless, but I can see that Ben doesn't think it looks enough like the *Boots* magazine for our current readers, average age seventy-eight. He says the redesign isn't developed enough yet for him to 'piss away the family business on'. He may have a point there. I tell him it's a work in progress and tell Stefano to keep going. If we're going to make *The Lady* more hip than hip-replacement and as successful as *Saga*, we have to change the way it looks as well as how it reads.

7.30 p.m. Walk home via Tesco to get food and Ivo shouts at me when I am making supper at 8 p.m.

10 *November* 2009

Worked like an indentured slave from 8.30 a.m. until 7 p.m., when I got in a cab to go to the *Evening Standard* Influentials party to celebrate publication of the list of 1,000 London Influentials. Boris was number 1 most influential and I was, I think, bottom, at number 1,000. But much, much worse: am not included in the Meeja section, but in frisky, bubbly, blonde, fun-loving 'Most Invited' category, which makes me think: I must get out less. Andrew Roberts – the well-known historian, diarist and name-dropper – arrived and said, 'I can't stay here, I have to go and see Kissinger,' i.e., someone much more influential. Suzy Menkes, the fashion writer from the *International Herald Tribune* and living legend, is present, with her hair arranged in a dark Nanki-Poo coil on the top of her head. She saw me and demanded, 'Where's Christopher?', i.e., Bailey, the Burberry designer. I was carrying the Remembrance Day edition of the mag with Rosamund Pike and the British Legion poppy on the cover throughout, in the hope of being photographed for product-placement purposes.

I have found out that our menopause special – with apples on the front and the cover line 'Missed Fruitfulness', my brilliant (though I say so) reworking of Keats – tanked. Only 27,000 copies, I fear – way short of my bonus-triggering weekly sale of 35,000 copies a week, let alone the 80,000 figure that Adam on occasion mentions. When he first let slip that he thought I should aim for a circulation of 80,000 in my first year – i.e., almost trebling circulation during a savage print-media recession – I looked around for the men in white coats, but none came.

11 November 2009

Masses of Remembrance Day action in Trafalgar Square. Stephen Fry, inevitably, in the thick of it, probably tweeting during the two minutes' silence. Watched Oliver play rugby against Colet Court. It was nice pretending for one afternoon that life was back to normal, that I was a jobbing freelancer and didn't have on my plate the mountainous challenge of trebling circulation of a magazine that people had forgotten existed, or face the sack for failing to do so. So had lovely time standing in my wellies eating cake and egg sandwiches, and chatting up other Dragon School mummies at post-match tea. Having said that, it was still to some degree *work*. Becoming editor means that every time I meet anyone, I either have to 1. listen to their pitch for a column about their life in a thatched cottage in a Hampshire village keeping saddleback pigs and growing their own veg, or 2. try to get them to write something. Often the only way to get out of 1. is to offer them 2. Ergo, line between work and play has become fatally blurred. At various prep-school touchlines this term I have so far signed up fellow Dragon mums Lady Helen Taylor and models Saffron Aldridge and India Hicks to be three forthcoming cover girls, deals struck between cries of 'Come on The Dragon!' and 'Well tackled, darling!'

Our sons are in the same dorm; frankly, they can all take one for the team.

I have just received an email from Janina asking if we want to interview Joan Ruddock MP. I desperately want to give her a fair crack of the whip, but I felt my heart sink somewhat. I said it didn't do it for me. So she said she was chasing Jane Asher. 'That's more like it. Think Cotswold cottages, crumbles, puppies, rambling roses, bonfires, cupcakes, pink-cheeked children in red mittens, at all times,' I instructed. There is no room in the magazine, sadly, for the kind of searing reportage I mentally file under the category 'Clitorectomy in the Congo'.

Found out later we have already interviewed Jane Asher this year.

12 *November* 2009

Speccie lunch at Claridges. Sat between Sebastian Shakespeare (my ex-boyfriend from Oxford, editor of 'Londoner's Diary') and *Observer* columnist and scourge of New Labour Andrew Rawnsley, but only by dint of leaping up when two comparative dullards in suits sat on either side of me, one an ill-favoured MP and the other from the sponsors (dread word), Threadneedle. 'I must go and tell the "Londoner's Diary" something,' I said. I had blissful two-hour flirt with Rawnsley. Boris made hog-stamping speech in which he said that MPs had taken the bullet for the bankers. Mandelson in glistening good form, saying that he and Boris had something in common: '1. Brussels, and 2. the desire to undermine Cameron at every opportunity.' Everyone roared as they slugged claret. Mandy caressed boyish *Speccie* editor Fraser Nelson's hair in front of assembled gathering, i.e., the entire Westminster Village, at one point.

Back in the office, the issue had been passed and the *Mail* was on the phone. Would I write a piece about which frontbencher I fancied? This was apropos Miriam Gross writing a *Spectator* 'Diary' in which she argued that women secretly found Brown attractive. I was only too happy to oblige, for my usual fee. And sent them this:

I agree with Miriam. I think Gordon Brown is appealing in a primitive, Cro-Magnon way – like a bull mastodon with a secret sorrow. He is big yet vulnerable (the wonky eye, the working jaw) and has that brooding quality which hints at profundity rather than the usual hidden shallows of most public figures. His tortured jowls tell me he thinks deeply about credit swaps, etc., but is much too masculine and modest to copy a mere flibbertigibbet like me into his innermost thoughts. He would prefer to battle on, saving the world alone. Unlike Bill Clinton, Brown doesn't just say he feels our pain, he looks as if he is actually in the grip of a violent gastroenteric upset most of the time. I can't help finding that terribly attractive. I long to rush to his side, clutching a tube of Tums.

Having said that, if pushed to choose, I would go diplomatically for either Dave or George. Brown is dark and rumpled and harassed-looking, which has the curious effect of making David Cameron look extra smooth and pink, and George about twelve. But both are nice and tall with great hair and seem to like women and know how to talk to them, which always helps . . .

And so on. The *Mail*, which always commissions three times as much copy as it can use, never ran it.

Butch Stewart, the owner of Beaches, Sandals, and so on, the richest man in the Caribbean, and a good friend, cancelled coming in for tea, but totally came through on ads. Apparently he's booked about £10k worth. So a course of ads for Sandals (a resort for couples where 'all you need is love') and Beaches (for families) will be appearing in *The Lady* – a mag currently read by the over-75s. Result! Especially for us!

I went into the boardroom to ask something. Ben was on the phone: 'No, Mum. We are not going to run a half-page picture of the teddy bear.'

I raised my eyebrows. He is refusing to explain and just says it is a hangover from the previous regime and that I 'don't need to do anything'.

It all sounds very sinister.

13 *November 2009*

Called Debo, the Dowager Duchess of Devonshire, and invited myself up to Chatsworth, where I intend to go down on bended knee to ask her to be a columnist. She sounded very charmed when I called. I do think she's marvellous. She asked for a sample question over the telephone. So I came up with: A grandmother writes in despair to ask, 'What is to be done if grandchildren arrive for lunch and persist in eating with their mouths open?'

'Oh,' she cried, happily. 'Beat them! You must beat them!' She then complained about my father's dirty tricks during the Heywood Hill bookshop's recent P. G. Wodehouse competition. Different persons of differing note, i.e., Debo, my father, Daphne Guinness, members of posherati, had to nominate PGW's funniest line, and everyone had to vote online. She told me that a friend had warned her, 'Give up, Debo. As soon as a Johnson wants to win, it's all over.' I was tempted to repeat Ann Leslie's line about Johnsons, which is that they are 'like Hungarians – they enter a revolving door behind you but always come out in front' – but thought better of it.

14 *November 2009*

Drove to Tisbury for *Harper's Bazaar* travel editor, the superluscious Catherine Fairweather's birthday dins in the Beckford Arms. Sat next to the photographer Don McCullin, who is married to Catherine. Susie Forbes, the toweringly Nordic editor of *Easy Living*, told me *The Lady* would fold whatever. 'No one cares, no one's going to read it, it's all over,' the Long Blonde told me helpfully. 'Just get what you can out of it.'

16 November 2009

Got home, ate supper, and as we were watching *Curb* (Your Enthusiasm) felt ill. Will pass over volcanic details. Two days in bed.

18 November 2009

Huge hoo-ha over Christmas party. Between them, the office (without my input) has managed to invite pretty much every single maddening time-waster who has ever filed for publication a 2,000-word article about cucumbers and the magical properties of horse chestnuts (usually downloaded from the internet) to our staff, Christmas, three-course, sit-down lunch at Browns in St Martin's Lane.

I cover my eyes with horror. All invitees – and there appear to be hundreds of them – will now naturally assume they are part of my new-look, going-forward modernizing team! I don't care whose fault it is. Or that lots of perfectly nice people are coming. It's a disaster. I am furious. Between the three of them, they've invited every single living person who has ever published a piece in *The Lady* over the past forty years rather than 1. the regulars who have written weekly for yonks and 2. my new roster of columnists, none of whom has ever so much been offered a Kettle Chip at Bedford Street.

Massive inquest ensues. I march into the boardroom saying, 'This is so cocked up!' I tell Ben it's not normal to ask mere contributors to a lunch, only regulars and columnists. Mere occasional contributors count themselves lucky to be offered a glass of warm white wine once a year, if that. I keep making this point, and keep trying to explain the distinction between a generic Christmas knees-up for hundreds and a sit-down lunch. He tore a strip off

Gillian for the guest-list crisis and then summoned down Maureen
and Lindsay for interrogation in the boardroom. Under conditions
that would not have shamed the Spanish Inquisition, it was my PA
Gillian who rather magnificently fought back, a mole against a
lawnmower.

I have borrowed black sparkly sleeveless frock from Moschino
embroidered with safety-pins for the *Spectator* readers' dinner, an
annual ordeal in a marquee on the Embankment (black tie).
Talked to ex-*Spec* editors Charles Moore and Alexander Chancellor, who are civilized and amusing. Andrew Neil – editor-in-chief,
telly personage, etc. – told me I talked too much (coming from
him!). I retreated to a knot of hacks, i.e., Fraser Nelson, Dylan
Jones (editor of *GQ*), Toby Young and the event's star attraction,
magician David Blaine. I murmured to Blaine, I couldn't help
myself, 'You're hot,' and he stared at me meltingly, like a spaniel
on Night Nurse, as he did card tricks for us. Neil kept shouting,
'She's still talking!' No one was talking to *The Spectator* Readers,
needless to say. Neil's hair was looking particularly ginger and
bristly and well thatched. Dinner was the usual nightmare. Super-
ficial conversations with eight readers who all wanted to know
what it was like being Boris's little sister.

19 November 2009

Camilla Long, the super-foxy, geek-spectacled, blonde *Sunday
Times* interviewer, came in, to inspect my new premises; Avril
Groom came in, to talk fashion; Lady Antonia came in, to be crime
critic. Coco nosed up to her. 'This is the office bitch,' I told her.

'One of many, I expect,' she flung back. We had delicious pic-
nicky lunch of terrine and cornichons, and so on, in Terroirs. She
held back on the bread. 'I don't do wheat,' she said, like a Notting
Hill yummy mummy, but managed to put away three large glasses

of house white. I do like Antonia. She is dry as sawdust and super-smart and has kept her sensuous Marianne Faithfulness as she approaches her ninth decade. I love the way she always introduces my husband, Ivo (Dawnay; communications director for the National Trust), to people as 'Ivor Gurney' (sensitive war poet).

Went to Rigby & Peller for a crash course in corsetry as it's their seventieth anniversary. The whole thing was filmed by the crew from Channel 4. With hindsight, taking C4 to my bra-fitting might have been a mistake. I was thrilled to be told that I was not, as I thought, 36C, but a somewhat breathtaking 32E, and my excitement got the better of me. Having asked the fitter if R&P visually assessed Her Majesty (the company is corsetiere to the Queen) and received the correct answer, 'We treat all our customers exactly the same, Ma'am,' I forgot the cameras were there and emerged from my curtained cubicle in a padded balconette in a colour called 'smoke' and couldn't resist cheeping, 'Hello, boys!'

'That was really nice,' John said, perking up for the first time since filming started. 'Can you do that again?'

Then I rushed back to the office, where the entire staff of thirty or forty was in the boardroom and had to give a short address about the future of *The Lady*. I told them my line about trying to keep older readers and bringing in new ones. I did not reference the fact that we are in perfect shitstorm of negative conditions, in which old readers think I have done the equivalent of dressing the Queen in hotpants on Remembrance Sunday and krumping her down the Mall because I have got rid of the theatre review/short story/endless interviews with bearded actors, and are dying in droves. The cold facts remain. Women my age are used to getting their content free with weekend papers; younger readers think *The Lady* is for old people or where you get a nanny; and readers as yet unborn will have no use for the written word at all.

When I went into the subs' room they were checking a half-page with a picture of a blue teddy on it. It was made out of felt stitched together, and very sweet. The teddy had – as teddies do – eyes made of glass buttons. 'Reader Alert!' shouted the accompanying text. 'In July *The Lady* ran a picture of this teddy in a feature on knitted toys. *The Lady* would like to warn readers that the teddy featured has dangerous buttons that small children could pull off and swallow. Please be very careful.'

I studied all this carefully. At last. This was the teddy bear they were all trying to keep from me.

'Did we run the pattern for this teddy?' I asked.

'No,' said Chrissie. 'Just used this picture as an illustration for some feature about crafty careers or the rage for knit-your-own presents or something. I can't remember now offhand.'

'So, why, in that case, are we running this massive consumer alert then?' I asked. Chrissie sighed, deeply. 'I think you'd better take it up with Ben,' she said, without meeting my gaze. 'This is on publisher's orders.'

I made mental note to do so as a matter of urgency, then filed 1,000 words on brassieres.

20 *November 2009*

Went up to Chesterfield with director John Dower and cameraman Wesley formally to ask Debo, Dowager Duchess of Devonshire, to be the agony aunt for *The Lady*. As we tucked into our first-class seats on the 9.55 a.m. from St Pancras to Chesterfield, who walked in and sat down a few rows ahead of us but Nick Clegg. So we are alone in the compartment, apart from the Leader of the Lib Dems. He kissed me hello and then, when he opened his mouth to speak an awful croak came out, instead of the voice of compassionate Middle England. 'I'm very fluey, I'm afraid,' he said. At which point I thought – revenge at last.

It's a long story, and in a previous millennium now, but here's

why: in 1999 we both went to a New Year's Eve millennium party
at the British Embassy in Paris. It was lovely and much enjoyed by
all but, unfortunately (for Clegg), I then wrote up a garish account
of this revel in the *FT*. In my account I implied that a guest by the
name of 'Nick' had stayed out all night. There was more than one
Nick at the party, but Miriam González Durántez – Nick Clegg's
then fiancée – assumed this was Nick Clegg and called off their
engagement. I had to crawl on my belly to apologize formally to
her. This was when we all lived in Brussels, a lifetime ago. All I can
tell you is that Miriam is one hell of a woman. And Nick a lucky
man. And this was the first time I'd seen him since I'd almost
ruined his life with her. 'Lovely to see you, I do hope you don't
give me your nasty flu,' I said, sitting out of range of germs.

We chatted the whole way, and as I hopped off he gave me his
mobile number and was so charming – and water-under-bridgey –
that I almost came across. To the Lib Dems, I mean.

We picked up a taxi and drove to Chatsworth, where the land-
scaped water meadows lay, reflecting the blue sky like silvered
mirrors, and hikers hiked across footpaths, and the golden-stoned
façade with about thirty-six windows gazed proudly towards the
spire of Edensor and the high hills of the Peak District. I've only
been once, and I found it overdone – too much gilt, too rich, too
ornate. The Dowager Duchess seems very happy slumming it in
the eight-bedroomed vicarage with her devoted butler, Henry,
and darling factotum, Helen.

I handed over the flowers to 'Her Grace', as everyone refers to
her (as I predicted, coals to Newcastle: the vicarage is bursting
with blooms from her cutting garden, including white, spindly
roses which she showed me with a true countrywoman's pride).
I complimented her on the brilliant, billiard-table-green paint in
the hall, and gazed about. Predictably, all is perfection: smell of
flowers and log fires; dogs padding around; Norman Parkinson
photos of Debo and children draped about Chatsworth; in the

study-dining room, where work on her memoir is underway, a huge full-length photo of Nancy *en valeur* in a long gown, very sweet expression, with dimples and thoughtful eyes. A round table had been set for two.

Butler Henry served pheasant casserole, three veg, garlicky *pommes dauphinoise*, then the most marvellous tangy blackcurrant crumble. She refused to be filmed during lunch, when she talked about Eton being full of Asians and Hong Kong Chinese, as well as family. She is living history. After lunch we did a little interview. I asked her the sample agony-aunt question again – 'What does one do if one's grandchildren eat with their mouths open?'

'You bash them,' she pealed. 'You bash them, and then you put something huge and uncomfortable in their mouths.' I noticed she didn't exactly sign up on the spot to the offer of doing a weekly col., but I was so enchanted I didn't press it. After the fireside chat for the cameras, she put on wellies – she wore very unfashionable short green ones lined with downy fluff which she swore by – and went out to the henhouse. She also wore a lurid high-visibility jacket. She says she gets most of her clothes at 'game fairs'. She still looks marvellous.

The greatest thrill of all came at the end. When I needed to go to the loo she showed me into her *own bathroom*, a sunny, light, big, carpeted room upstairs. White monogrammed linen napkins had been spread out to hide her toiletries; her hanging cupboards were concealed by curtains of white toile. When I came down I gazed into her very blue eyes, sticky with macular degeneration, and held her hands to say goodbye and thank you. 'Can you see faces?' I asked, having made a great effort with my own toilette and maquillage for the excursion, worn my trusty pink-tweed shift dress, etc.

'No, not at all,' she told me. 'Yours looks like a sponge.'

When I pressed my suit upon departure, she sort of agreed to be an agony aunt, but is quite slippery about being nailed down until after her memoir, *Wait For Me*, is finished.

22 November 2009

Lunch at Al/Boris's with many children, and siblings. Marina in India on Bar Council trip. I am late because of rain, filthy traffic, roadworks. 'Every day in every way London is getting better and better all the time,' Boris intones, as he does whenever anyone complains about roadworks or the Tube. Delicious roast beef, *pommes boulangère*, roast potatoes, roast parsnips, boiled carrots, so every sort of root vegetable really. Champagne, good wine, all the cousins on form. We walk down Regents Canal. 'Good job, Mr Johnson,' everyone says respectfully. This time a year ago, they used to shout, 'Oi, Boris.'

25 November 2009

Joan Collins, the superglam seventy-something, came in for tea. I had invited her after I'd received an email from a mutual friend claiming she was 'throbbing' to write for us. She was wearing a curious grey woollen beret that looked like a mushroom. She never removed it, but kept patting the beret so it rustled, as if it were packed with tissue paper. She also kept combing out her hair extensions/wig. Having said all that, she looked fantastic, even alongside Percy, her husband-cum-business manager, forty-four. They arrived hot from the accountant in a very ill temper. At first they seemed unaware C4 was in doing the doc and would be filming them (even though I had very correctly forewarned them in writing). They made as if to leave soon after they'd been ushered into the boudoir, faces dark at the sight of Dower and Wesley.

'But I emailed Percy,' I wailed. He then started checking his BlackBerry and found the email from me warning them in advance about the filming. 'Did I show you this?' Percy asked Joan. She glanced down. 'Yes,' she admitted. So I took them through and showed Joan to the subs and the layout teams, and they took it all in their stride. I showed her the cover and asked her what she thought. She peered at it. 'Not bad,' she said in a flat voice. Then we went through to the boardroom for a slap-up tea of cake out of a packet from Tesco in Bedford Street brought in by Ros, our telephonist. Joan spooned sugar into her tea and laid about the walnut cake as if she hadn't eaten for weeks. 'This is absolutely delicious – where is it from?' asked Joan, and sent the crew packing. 'I will not be filmed eating!' she said. Her make-up was at least an inch thick, and she kept reapplying Clinique pancake and lipstick.

Then we chatted about what she could do, and I dropped Debo's name furiously and soon she was on her knees virtually begging to write for free.

'I had to chip her make-up off the teacup before I could wash it,' said Ros after.

'The teacup's now for sale on eBay,' added Ben.

I allowed the reader alert about the killer teddy-bear buttons to run, once: but apparently Mrs Budworth is in a complete tizzy about it, and wants us to run it – big – three more times, which is utter madness. I will put my foot down.

Have set-to with Lindsay about work-rate and send her stinker email. She sends me one back simply saying, 'We need to talk.'

26 November 2009

I get up at 6 a.m. to do Nick Ferrari show in a deserted LBC studio in Leicester Square. He kicks off by referring to my organ as '*Lady* Magazine'. I hold up a warning hand. 'Steady on, you're making it sound like *Nuts* or *Razzle*,' I interrupted. 'It's *The Lady*.' Coco is in attendance, and he talks about how his dog has just died and keeps stroking her intensely and telling her what a good girl she is.

Emma Soames, editor-at-large of super-successful *Saga*, comes in, and I take her to lunch at Terroirs. The canteen. She tells me lots of good things, and how we should go fortnightly. That sounds very good to me. Ben joins, and he dismisses her suggestion out of hand. She is very friendly and sparky – I do like her – especially after she tells me that *The Lady* will not be the first thing I edit, but is kind of *starter-mag* for self. I fear she is being too kind. Unless things pick up *a lot*, there won't be a *Lady* to edit this time next year, let alone any sort of second act for me.

30 *November 2009*

Usual manic Monday, in which I feel ill and grumpy. We have to publish five issues this month, because of the Christmas holiday: we have to sub, lay out, and so on, all the issues up to the Christmas double issue and the 5 January issue, and do all this before 23 December, when the office closes for two weeks. On top of this, Stefano wants to launch the new design for the Christmas double issue. So do I. I find an email from Claire Wood, the designer, which she sent on Friday when I was 'working from home' telling him there's no way they can do the redesign before 2010. I stared at this. Why not? It's not as if there's ever a good time to have a baby. She took my point. 'But this redesign for the Christmas edition is a stonking 15-pounder, delivered without drugs,' she observed.

Vol. CXV. · No. 2967. 1st January, 1942.

The Lady

4^d

KNITTED WOOL
JUMPER WITH
BECOMING
DIAGONAL
STRIPES

□

DIRECTIONS ON
BACK COVER

1st January, 1942

DECEMBER

1 December 2009

Phoebs (Fiona Mates, wife of ITN's James Mates, a great friend) came in for lunch and we went to Terroirs. They know me by name by now. '*Bonjour*, Rachel,' they say pleasantly as they see me hoving into sight with a fragrant guest, ready to eat the pork and pistachio terrine, the rillettes, etc. The most delicious boy behind the bar – tall and dark with a shortish beard – told us he would sneak us the recipe for the pork and pistachio terrine. Tried to look like a MILF.

After lunch, endless meetings: first, PR chap James Herring. Ben is trying to get me on TV to put the word out about the new-look *Lady*, and is splashing out on PR firms, one called Primal PR and now this new one, called Taylor Herring, not counting, of course, our in-house marketing PRs and 'consultants' Edwina, Nic Boize and Nicola Borton. My mouth gaped in dismay at the prospect.

'But I'm already over-exposed,' I whined.

'As Rachel Johnson you are, as editor of *The Lady*, you're not,' he flashed back. Point there.

But I still gazed at them stonily as they outlined plans to have my bum superglued to sofas on all available mumsy daytime chat shows and channels.

Called Mrs Budworth to tell her the good news that we have run the reader alert of the teddy bear as a quarter page. Then I took a deep breath to deliver the bad news. 'I'm not running the reader alert about the teddy again, Mrs Budworth,' I said. 'Our readers are sensible people. We can't assume they're imbeciles. They know about glass eyes on soft toys. I've run the thing once, and that's it. They don't need to be told four times in words of one syllable that small children can choke on buttons.'

'Yes they do!' pealed Mrs Budworth. 'I will not rest until we run the warning again. You say once is enough? Tish! What if someone didn't buy a copy of *The Lady* that week? And then they missed the warning? All over the country, small children could be pulling the buttons off that teddy and choking to death, and it would be All Our Fault! How can you sleep at night?'

'Mrs Budworth,' I said, 'my decision is final. We have already run a large item on the killer buttons on the teddy. That's quite enough. We have made our point. The editor's decision is final.'

'Not on *The Lady* it's not!' she told me in tones of decided crispness, reminding me that while I merely edit the magazine, her family owns it, and has done for a century and a quarter.

2 December 2009

I got a panic call from Lady Helen Taylor as I was walking in the rain from Embankment Tube via Pret a Manger on the Strand to the office. It was about my cover interview with her. She's already seen the photos – we did a shoot at the Timothy Taylor gallery – and now she wants to see the piece. I soothe her and say the piece is basically me saying how beautiful she is, interspersed with slack-jawed admiration of her husband's Mayfair gallery (sadly true).

Stefano came in, suited and swathed in cashmere and, having agreed on the cover-design format, we cracked on with the inside.

I worked out that endless pages are wasted on profitless and depressing special offers for pen-lights, *Lady* tea-towels (mysteriously known as 'glass cloths'), calendars, snuggly leisure socks, and so on. I need more editorial pages – at least four more, to launch our crack team of reviewers in January 2010, and to include an actual review on the spread called 'News and Reviews'. I announced to Ben that my last remaining child at home – Charlotte Millicent – is going to boarding school in September because I am so busy doing two events a night and twelve-hour days.

'Good,' he says.

Julia Budworth calls. I am worried we are going to have to row about the killer buttons on the teddy again, but she gets to the point, and announces that Debo doesn't know what an agony aunt is, and is worried. 'The Mitford family has had so much agony,' she bulldozes, while I weakly try to explain what an agony aunt means, and readers writing in with questions. Mrs B. suggests Debo files a country diary instead.

'Lovely, Julia,' I say (thinking, 'Not a bad idea'). 'Will you call her or will I?'

There is a silence. 'I'm not going to call her,' she sighed. 'I can't take it. Whenever I do, the Prince of Wales is there for tea, and Henry, the butler, says, "Her Grace is with His Royal Highness the Prince of Wales. She says could she possibly call you back in five minutes?" It's slightly lowering.'

Lesley White from *The Sunday Times* is in all day writing a magazine piece. I stay relentlessly on message and say things like, 'Being a lady is not about blood and breeding but behaviour,' and that we have to 'search for the lady inside ourselves' until I feel like getting drunk, going cougar and falling out of a taxi knickerless with a toyboy after a long night in Mahiki. At the end of the long session with Lesley, I crack.

'Do you think you're going to make it work?' she asks, smiling as her pen hovers over her notebook.

'Listen, Lesley,' I reply. 'We are in a perfect shitstorm of economic crapness.' I presumed that Lesley wouldn't quote me exactly, but would come up with some elegant formulation instead. 'The women's weekly market is down 14 per cent year on year. I really don't know.'

3 *December* 2009

Stefano back in after lunch. We carry on working on the redesign of the columns, features and regulars – such as food, house and home, beauty, health. We go through images that Wendy – the archive editor – has scanned in from the archive to doll up the inside pages (all the mags dating back to 1885 reside in cellophane in the Fred West basement – the staff are frightened to go down there alone and always tell someone they're going, in case they never come back).

We pick a *soigné* line drawing of a man twirling a ballgowned lady on the dancefloor for 'The Gents', and wonder whether a picture of a terrier stealing a roast chicken from a table would do for Mary Killen's column about the grottage, called 'Week In'. We find line drawings of a woman doing callisthenics for our medical page, and a glamorous nightclubby scene for the Penny Smith column underneath Mary Killen, called 'Week Out'. Then we get the two Helen Taylor covers up side by side, as an experiment. On one side we have Helen in the old-*Lady* format with the white rectangle at the top and 'The Lady' in its clunky navy script. On the other is Helen in the new format, all glowing, three-dimensional vibrancy with 'The Lady' given proper spacing, rather than as now with 'The' crouching above the 'L', with everything framed in a two-tone border so all the colours pop.

It is thrilling. I do hope that Ben is behind the redesign. To get him behind it, I said, 'This is the sort of magazine that chicks will read – this'll totally bring in the chicks,' I repeated.

'I was hoping that you were going to bring in the chicks anyway,' he said. Which gave me pause. I always knew that his mission was not merely to find an editor for *The Lady*. It was to find himself a wife, too. That's why he treated a succession of twenty-one women journalists to a fish lunch in the Forge restaurant in what is now known as the 'I have a bream' series of dates.

Any time I bring a girlfriend in, he insists on having her brought through to the boardroom so he can inspect her, and Googles her quickly when she's gone. When I brought (Lady) Liza Campbell, who is a sultry blonde daughter of Cawdor Castle, for example, he was very excited, until he discovered she had two teenage children, one called Storm and the other Atticus.

4 December 2009

Today is the office Christmas lunch in Browns on St Martin's Lane. Everyone is quite dolled up. Merry atmosphere. I regret having had hissy fit about it. It was, I see now, very ungenerous of me. I showed a telling lack of seasonal good cheer to all men.

We mill about with champagne while a band plays, then we all sit down. I am next to Ben, and opposite Mrs Budworth. At one point, as the starters are being cleared away, Mrs Budworth seemed to launch herself for no reason at James Le Fanu, and suddenly snapped across our round table for ten in his direction, 'Were you laughing at me? I'm sorry you find me funny,' and he looked beatific (he is used to it, luckily, as is South London GP). Ben went into rapid-reaction-force mode and doused the flames expertly. Ben made a nice speech from a podium to which I could not reply, as I had completely lost my voice by this stage and was anyway on the verge of total breakdown.

There were lots of contributors from the *ancien régime*, including a man who wrote a 16,000-word piece on garden mazes. At the adjoining table, I noticed that Lindsay was placed next to Janina. On another table (we must have been around a hundred in all), Mary Killen was between our fashion writer Vanessa de Lisle and the bearded man called Keith who supplies the Ladygram. The Ladygram is a word puzzle at the back of the mag beloved by all our readers. I get tons of letters saying things like, 'Whatever you do, please keep the Lady-gram.' So I went over and told him with honesty, 'You are the only thing in the magazine that remains popular with the readers.'

The lunch was very good, and it was held in a vast banqueting hall upstairs. There were not one but two camera crews on hand to capture every festive moment. I drove home with two of my top columnists, Clemmie Fraser and Sof McVeigh, who had appeared on the seating plan, thanks to Ben's bellydancing PA Maureen, as 'Clemmie Fisher' and 'Soy McVeigh', to their unconfined delight.

As I left with Clemmie, and Sof, the band – comprising lawyer friends of Adam's in reduced circumstances – played on. As we baled out it felt a tiny bit like disembarking from the *Titanic*.

7 December 2009

Had to go to a Bentley lunch thing, so nipped in for a blow-dry at Mirror Mirror, the hairdresser on Chandos Place (slogan: 'A better-looking you or your money back') before heading off to West Halkin Street.

The lunch was at the Mosimann club, with Julia Marozzi, the über-skinny, glam PR who used to work with me on the *FT* (and more recently introduced me to the miracle of J Brand jeans), Prof. Wendy Dagworthy the fashion designer, ex-*Daily Mail* deputy Christina Appleyard, etc. We stood around in the Bentley room – all curved twenties gleaming sheening luxury – with champagne. Christina Appleyard revealed that she had been to lunch with Ben in the Forge, i.e., had participated in the long 'I have a bream' series of lunches and had been scoped out as a possible editor. 'But you're a former deputy editor of the *Mail*,' I pointed out. 'Why would you . . .' And trailed off in case I put my foot in it.

There followed a long presentation of Bentley products, i.e.,

cufflinks, skis, Dinky toys. Tried to look keen. Thank God delicious bangbang chicken appeared in crispy baskets, followed soon
after by sea bass, followed by crumble, followed by *le chef* himself,
who had forgotten he gave me lunch back in June and when I
reminded him did manage to remember who I was and said, with
pride, 'We had your brother in the other day.'

I rushed back to the office for a features conference. I have sent
an email round in which I asked Carolyn, Lindsay, Janina, Jess,
etc., to come 'armed with suggestions' for our Christmas cover –
which hangs around for two weeks, i.e., it is a double issue. Janina's
picks were Madonna and Heidi Klum. Ben exploded. 'How could
you have an old tart like Madge on the cover over Christmas? Our
observant readers would be outraged,' he ranted. 'You can't have
Madge when our readers want the Blessed Madonna and Holy
Infant! I still have nightmares about that ghastly coffee-table book
she did' – Ben was clearly too traumatized to mention the title,
SEX, published in 1992 – 'with the aluminium cover.'

I suggest Judi Dench and the Queen, with sense of *déjà vu*. We
would indeed look like *Majesty* magazine. Not the forward-thinking
vibrant image we are trying so hard to project. Then I suggest a
series of women all called Kirstie/y, i.e., Kirsty Young, Kirstie Allsopp, Kirstie Alley, Kirsty Wark. When I run out of Kirsties I put up
Judy Finnigan. Then we workshopped ideas for cover girls upcom-
ing – Jane Asher, Darcey Bussell. Then Jess piped up, 'Don't forget
we have a bid in for Julie Andrews.' So in the unlikely event we get
a cover interview with Mary Poppins in time, we have pencilled in
Darcey Bussell with her daughters in sparkly fairy costumes with
wings for the Christmas cover. Which left us with finding a fall-
back cover image of Jane Asher. Even pouring from a coffee pot in
a fifties-kitsch kitchen, she looked just a little bit pale and thin and
bloodless, as redheads sometimes do. She didn't convey lush car-
nality and caramel like Nigella.

I felt the feats meeting had a poisonous atmosphere. No one made an effort. I was mean to Lindsay. I was horrid to Janina. Even the C4 crew seemed dejected by the prospect of casting the Christmas cover.

Everyone slunk out of the boardroom, but Ben and I stayed, because the cover meeting bled into the next meeting, which was with, I know now, the Chief Exec. of Aga and the Aga 'brand ambassador' writer Laura James. However, I'd forgotten all about it – who, where, why? So when they appeared – Ros bearing trays of cake and teapots – I hadn't a clue. Nor did Laura give us the Chief Exec.'s. name, which was William McGrath (as I discovered far too late). I couldn't introduce him as CEO of Aga, because I didn't know his name or job title. So Ben was unsighted and the whole meeting was total shambles. Ben didn't know who they were, and started talking, for some reason, about internet porn. Eventually, the penny dropped my end, and I managed to steer the conversation towards an Aga cookery course for *Lady* readers. It was all my fault. As Ben pointed out later, if only he'd known, he could have had us 'lining up a nationwide programme of mutually lucrative events'. I went in to see him after they'd gone and grovelled.

8 December 2009

This morning I swung into damage-limitation mode. To William McGrath, CEO of Aga, I wrote:

Dear William (if I may)

It was lovely to have you and Laura, Brand Ambassador, into tea yesterday afternoon. Thank you very much for the magnificent Aga-themed gifts.

I do think that we could both do well out of a reader event – maybe we should consider doing something nationwide?

Thank you for being so sporting about the general level of chaos and ignorance – we were so honoured to have the Chief Executive in our midst, and I failed to give Ben Budworth (my publisher and CEO, whom you met) a proper brief, as our features meeting ran into tea – we are having problems trying to find a fitting subject for our Christmas cover.

Best
Rachel

To Laura, I wrote:

Am so sorry abt fucking shambolic visit yesterday our end. A features meeting ran into tea which meant I couldn't brief Ben Budworth properly and I panicked and forgot McGrath's name – and then Ben clearly panicked and started ranting about internet porn. You must have thought we were deeply unprofessional. It's not usually like that.

Will you apologize? Have sent McGrath, who was so nice and came laden with gifts, an email, but he hasn't replied.

God I'm sorry
Rxx

Got this back from Laura:

Hi Rachel,

I'm laughing so hard I can barely type! I was on the phone to William a few minutes ago, and all he could talk about was *The Lady*. He read me your email and was positively delighted with it.

I promise tea with you both was the highlight of our day yesterday and we had a lovely time. I smiled all the way home on the train and

I'm sure people thought me quite mad. William is very keen to be
involved with the magazine as much as possible next year and I
promise it was all down to our visit. I thought the best bit was when
Ben – who I thought was divine – started talking about chamber
pots.

As for me, I've almost got over being filmed with wet hair, no
make-up and an ancient jersey!

Lots of love
Laura

I sent it all to Ben with a covering note saying, 'Just ignore bit
abt internet porn.' Then when I was packing to go tonight, I asked
him if he had a big sack to put all my stuff into, and he said, 'Yes, I
do have a big sack,' much in the same way as he enjoys talk of
'squeezing in a small one from behind', and so on.

Following lunch with Mrs Appleyard, I have asked Ben if I can
see an unpurged list of the twenty or so other women he interviewed for the job of Ladyship in the 'I have a bream' series. 'Did
you just scope them out to be the next Mrs Budworth, or were you
really looking for an editor?'

'I'm not a dog on heat the whole time,' he remonstrated mildly.

We had a good meeting this morning with someone called Corky,
yet another of Ben's hires on the PR and marketing side. Corky has
roadtested the new Stefano arty covers at WHSmith in Gatwick.
Of the twenty-five people tested ('We couldn't get airside,' she said.
'Problem with the passes') more than 50 per cent of people ques-
tioned preferred the new covers. Total result! We all celebrated with
a chocolate biscuit in the boardroom. Only thing is, now Ben has
given the thumbs-up to the cover redesign we just have to get on
with the inside even faster. We can't raise expectations of a, er, visual
feast that we can't deliver. And we have to have a cracking cover

every time. 'If you haven't got your new dress, full make-up on and fuck-me shoes, there's no point in going out,' said Stefano. 'As no one will pick you up.'

Just before I left, Jess rang up. We've got the only print interview with Dame Julie Andrews, anywhere. She's not doing any other newspapers: no *Daily Mail*, no *Hello!*, no *Telegraph* – only *The Lady*! I squealed with joy and, it has to be admitted, disbelief.

We only have to give her picture approval, copy approval and agree not to syndicate it, which is absolutely fine. For a cover story and exclusive with Dame Julie for our relaunch issue, I would be more than happy if she wanted to write the interview and edit and distribute the whole magazine herself.

I went off to *Today* presenter Justin Webb's diabetes party at the House of St Barnabas, lugging Ivo's birthday pressies, blocks of A4 paper, a small teapot and a traditional fruitcake I'd been sent from the Fabulous Fruitcake Company from a nice lady who signs her-self 'Samantha Wickham aka Mrs Fruitcake'. Every day, as well as several mainly green-inked letters, I get care packages and strange parcels. From now on, I will itemize each freebie, letter, book, etc., as it arrives in a proper log.

9 *December* 2009

Ben v. perked up by our Dame Julie triumph. Claire the Olive Oyl designer is singing, 'The hills are alive,' every time I pass. I don't want to risk it, so am keeping at bay John Dower and Wesley the cameraman (who now wears plunging V-neck sweaters without a shirt and is so boyband pretty that the subs have rechristened him Weslife) at bay. They are already churning with fury that they can't film us interviewing Tracey Emin about needlecraft.

Janina entered my office in Battersea Dogs Home mode, i.e., with pleading, red-rimmed eyes. She's found out I have appointed a new opera reviewer as I go about dismantling her mother's empire brick by brick. So while Arline Usden remains for the time being on the masthead as 'editor-at-large' I have appointed Kate Shapland beauty editor and now Penny Smith of the *GMTV* sofa as opera critic, while Lindsay has taken on travel.

'Is it true someone else will be writing opera?' she asked with admirable directness.

'Yes it is,' I said, gently.

'Can I ask when?'

'Next year.' Then she asked me to let her mother (she refers to her as Arline, as if she was no relation to her at all) know in writing, which of course I did.

10 December 2009

Got in late. Dower the director was waiting for a cab en route to see Arline Usden, who lives in East Sheen. He has snagged an interview with the previous editor for the doc! 'She's been gagged from saying anything negative about the magazine,' he said dolefully.

'Bad luck,' I said. I have a joke with Dower that whenever anyone says anything positive, i.e., Debo saying she likes *The Lady* or whatever, or someone saying they enjoy reading it – any compliment really – I turn to the camera and say, 'You won't be using that then.' All they want is friction, drama, confrontation, or in the dread TV word, 'jeopardy'. So they went off to East Sheen.

I had lunch with Carolyn in one of those unchanged, Formica-tabled, Italian cafés serving chicken escalopes and omelette and chips. Polished off the remains of today's freebie – Whoopie Pies from Harrods in strange flavours, i.e., pistachio and peanut – for pud. The C4 crew came in with their tails down. They'd heard that Percy Gibson, the fifth Mr Joan Collins, is refusing to sign the release form, and that Joan Collins's agent is asking for a £20,000 fee for Miss Collins to appear in the documentary, and meanwhile, Arline's interview was disappointingly unexplosive (the main scoop was that she said that Gillian, my PA and her former PA, and her daughter Janina were 'brilliant writers'). Oh yes, and apparently, A. Usden said I only got the job because I was, and I quote, 'connected to someone famous', and moaned that I had contacts and a budget to pay for writers and images, and that she never did. Which is not entirely untrue.

So Dower and Weslife were glum, and am not so chirpy myself. Though the mag is no longer sensationally bland, and has some articles that even men might read on the loo, advertising is dire. There is none for our showcase Christmas redesigned edition on 22 December apart from a few pages of prepared meals-on-wheels, walk-in baths, stairlifts, incontinence pads and special offers for slipper socks and pen-lights.

So I rang my chum Julia Marozzi at Bentley, who'd just had me to the Mosimann lunch. I offered her a free page so she could show off the new Bentley Mulsanne (retailing at £200,000) to our readers. I also contacted Justin Cooke Burberry but he, inexplicably, didn't leap at my offer of a free spread in the new super-soar-away *Lady*.

It's a bit worrying when you can't even *give* away ads in a national magazine. And you can't put women on the cover without getting some earache. Apparently Rosamund Pike was spitting about the fact that she was on the cover last month (we used a library image that had been cleared for release). And when Lady Helen Taylor was on the cover, she said that friends called her to titter, 'I'm standing in the middle of Waitrose laughing at the fact that you're on the cover of – hee hee – *The LADY*!' One day, I told Helen, you'll be showing off about that shoot. One day *soon*. I am *very* proud of the magazine and hate it when people slag it off.

In the middle of this, Daisy Prince, who writes for *Vanity Fair*, came in for tea looking blonde and lush, and I appointed her my

New York correspondent on the spot. Now I have a Paris correspondent, a New York correspondent, a Royal correspondent, a top team of book reviewers, a spiffy new design, and writers queuing up to contribute.

All that's missing is readers and advertisers.

11 December 2009

Tore around buying flowers and shortbread (from Poundland in Portobello – awfully good) and tidying up in readiness for the arrival of a dozen French journalists (my novel *Notting Hell* is being published in Paris under the title *Le Diable Vit à Notting Hill*). Then I get a text. They are held up by an illegal immigrant on the Eurostar. When they finally arrive, I have eaten all the shortbread and drunk six cups of coffee. In a frenzy I march them around the communal garden pointing out various offending £8 million mansions while they smoke furiously. Then I bootmarch them down Elgin Crescent, pointing out the old family flat at number 61, where me and my brothers lived with my mother. 'This is where I lived since 1978,' I said. 'This is old Notting Hill, when poor people actually lived here. Now it's a ghetto – *comme Srebrenica* – for the super-rich, super-models and international celebrities.' I waited for the woman from *L'Express*, who had a naughty face, to take note. I showed them the Grocer on Elgin ('Eet is like Dean & Deluca,' one said), and Couverture and Garbstore, owned by James Dyson's daughter, and we pressed our noses against the window of new bookshop, Lutyens & Rubinstein. Robina Rose, a neighbour in her fifties who's been here even longer than me, sailed by on a sit-up-and-beg bike, and I made her give a short speech about old Notting Hill and new Notting Hill, old money, new money, or in my case, no money. Then we walked to Jade Jagger's new shop on All Saints Road. Mick's daughter was sitting at a round desk at the back, not front of house, tapping into a laptop, looking haughty. I approached and told her who I was and asked if I could bring in the hackettes. 'I'm off then,' she said, gathering her things, and tossing her head, snootily taking herself downstairs as if to avoid contamination.

Late Friday night, younger brother Jo was selected as a parliamentary prospective candidate for Orpington (Con, of course). I am thrilled for him. It went to five ballots. As I've always said, he's the one to watch. Called the mayor, and before I could say anything, he said, 'Have you heard the bad news about Jo?'

13 December 2009

Weekend in Wiltshire. Today, Sunday, my eye fell on my own name as I was reading the News Review section of *The Sunday Times*. Had been laughing heartily at Roger Lewis's (author of *Seasonal Suicide Notes*) diary extracts about living in poverty, his disappointing children and being Welsh.

Things You See When You Haven't Got a Gun (2): Boris's sister, Rachel Johnson, came running out of the hairdressers and chased me along Holland Park Avenue. 'Get back, lady, unless you like the taste of mace,' I was ready to say.

'Are you mad Roger from Hertfordshire?' she asked in a non-hostile way. Indeed, she was almost hearty.

'There's more than one category mistake in that sentence,' I ventured, ripe for a philosophy debate. But I don't think Rachel wanted to go into that side of it.

I think what Roger is saying oh so subtly is that I am a person that he would like to cleanse from the streets, like in *Taxi Driver*.

It's slightly startling to discover that one has a strong negative impression on people one meets. I had stupidly assumed he had fallen prey to my charms.

14 *December* 2009

Today is my interview with Dame Julie Andrews. At the Langham Hotel. Her suite. All morning, am very nervous. I keep leaving my desk to see if anyone has sent any food to Carolyn. As she is our food writer, she gets tons of goodies – there was a red-letter day last week when Bighams (posh foodies) sent us a box of canapés, including pigs in blankets and devils on horseback. I get odder offerings. I open a box that has arrived for me from a lady (all our readers are, by definition, ladies) called Clarissa. In it are the following: two teabags of Twining herbal tea, 'blended to recover'; a blow-up globe; bookmarks of famous explorers; some wrapping paper; a face-pack; DVDs; and a bar of Lindt 70 per cent chocolate. I eat the chocolate as I read the letter. 'I made these short fun films about famous people for my own children,' she wrote, and suggested that I wrap presents, put on a face-pack and eat chocolate while the children watched the improving DVDs about explorers. It's sweet, but I don't think so. It upsets me that people have to try so hard to sell anything to anyone or to get a mention.

The taxi arrives. I get in with Weslife and the Nagra – a broadcast-quality recorder I have borrowed from the BBC. I am wearing a fur Russian hat, which has a dribble of candlewax on it from having been left on the table of Mary Killen's grottage during supper at the weekend in Wiltshire. Also in black coat and a black dress. Earlier in the day, lots of people have pointed out the candlewax (it does admittedly look disgusting): 'You've spilt yoghurt on your hat.' Weslife films as I sit there chewing my nails, and he asks

me, as is his wont, the same question over and over again in different locations.

In the taxi: 'So, is this a big deal for *Lady* readers?' In the hotel:
'So, is this a big deal for *Lady* readers?' I keep repeating that Julie
is one heck of a cover story and that our readers love her, etc. I am
shown up to her suite, and Weslife is sent packing. I get hotter
and hotter. Am bright red in the face and glugging water when
DJA arrives. I have been sitting in a large hotel room for hours, it
seems. When she floats in, long legs scissoring in black slacks, loose
shirt, white scarf – my mouth goes dry. I cannot speak I am so
excited. This has never happened before in my whole life. She is
adorable, and spending an hour with her is like sixty minutes of
heaven. I think it goes brilliantly.

When I listen back to the interview on the tape, I am appalled
by how unprofessional, wet and thick I sound. Also, Julie Andrews
has given stock answers to most of my questions, although she
does reveal to me that she is thinking of taking out US citizen-
ship.

I think maybe we won't podcast it after all. Afterwards I meet
with her manager, Steve Sauer (by name), in another part of the
suite – I think she has whole floor reserved – to talk about cover
images. He has sent us some, three in all; the problem is – we don't
like them. He is tall and wisecracking and very Hollywood. In his
turn, he doesn't like the vintage cover Stefano has picked out for
him to approve either. So, we wrangle. He wants to see the copy I
write. 'Well, I'll send it over, but there won't be time for argument,
we go to bed tomorrow,' I tell him importantly.

'Do we?' he asks, in a rather nice, twinkling way.

I find Weslife outside the hotel. He wasn't allowed to wait in the
lobby, and has been standing on the pavement in the rain for ninety
minutes. As I climb into the Addison Lee mini-van, he points the
camera at me and asks, 'So, was that a big deal for *Lady* readers?'

I groan out loud. He says, 'Did you know you've got some yoghurt on your hat?'

15 December 2009

Stay home till 11 a.m. to write up the interview; appalling luvvie gush. Then race into office with Coco. Get call from Stefano. We have a big problem. The picture of Andrews makes her look as if she's dead, he says. I know, I say. As if she'd been made up for an open-casket viewing. I call her Hollywood agent, my new best friend Steve Sauer, in a panic, to see if we can run with any other images. Before I get to plead, he opens with, 'Hey there. Good morning. Have you called to ask me out on a date?' In order to avoid running the Mexican Day of the Dead style portrait, I on the spur of the moment invite him to come to the film producer Gerry Fox's Christmas party. After all, the tills will definitely not be alive if we run it.

As soon as I put the phone down, Stefano comes over, v. excited. He *has* used the open-casket image supplied by Dame Julie A.'s people to promote the O2 show, after all. It works because he has run the chinoiserie wallpaper from the Belvoir Castle spread on Emma, Duchess of Rutland, behind it, and it looks fabulous. I laugh. We have Christmas cover, and I have a date with agent-to-the-stars Steve Sauer.

Just before I leave, I nip into the boardroom, where Ben is sitting with little blonde Becky from Optomen, John Dower and his brother Adam. They are talking about filming in the Budworth house, Deerbolts Hall, in Suffolk. The Budworths seem unkeen. Either for the crew to go to their house, or to talk to their mother. Mrs Budworth, the matriarch, is also a director of *The Lady*.

'So you want to snoop around the stately,' I say unhelpfully. Turns out Deerbolts hasn't been in the family very long. Lord knows what Mrs Budworth would have to say. We talk about the title of the doc and how it started off being 'The Devil Wears Barbour'. I suggest we call it 'Coming Inside *The Lady*' instead.

16 *December* 2009

Rattling through the massive festive double issue plus the relaunch is testing us all. Claire is keeping calm. Stefano has pretty much moved in – we have only a few days to go before the new design goes live. He's been working round the clock, has even redesigned the classified pages at the back, and it's looking good. Nic Boize/B-Cal the pipe-smoking in-house PR chap wants to run a flap of the old masthead over the new cover so people recognize the magazine in the newsagents, so there is much flapping about flaps as well as Ben's *double entendres*. But there's so much to do – not just the Christmas double relaunch edition, there are also the issues for 5 and 12 January to do, and everyone's ill.

In the in tray: an outfit called 'Cami Confidential' has sent me a hot-pink-lace post-mastectomy collection vest top.

17 *December* 2009

We pass the Christmas double issue (i.e., send it all off to be printed, one page at a time) as if we are passing a grapefruit-sized gallstone. Then we feel hugely relieved. The new design looks wonderful, old but up-to-date at same time, elegant but accessible. Stefano has wrought wonders, and the design and subs team have been quite magnificent. Chrissie and the subs team start work on the 5 January issue immediately.

18 December 2009

Did some Christmas shopping in the morning and then continued work on the issue for 5 January, which we have to 'pass' – still can't get over that word – before the office closes for Christmas on 23 December.

It's unreal! We all need a holiday.

21 December 2009

Walked in wearing black tracksuit bottoms that had trailed through the mud of three London parks – Kensington Gardens, Hyde Park and Green Park, and then through the slush in Trafalgar Square. The climate-change camp has gone. But there's always something new in its place. Last week the square became a huge canteen with farmers giving away produce such as wonky carrots or outsized sprouts that they can't sell to the supermarkets. So there is such a thing as a free lunch. It was organized by a freegan called Tristram to call attention to food waste. You couldn't make it up.

I love what the cops call 'T. Square'; there's something going on every day: Stephen Fry reading the lesson in between tweets; the bloody Gormley daily exhibitionist on the plinth; the Christmas carols; the bring-our-boys-home services; the skateboarders and rollerbladers; the ever-changing *va-et-vient* out of the National Portrait Gallery; this week, the Norway spruce tree with grid lines of white lights ... the square has become the stage-set for the whole of London, providing free entertainment on a daily basis (must stop that – sound like stooge of City Hall).

As I enter the Irish funeral parlour lobby in Bedford Street, I notice someone has draped tinsel around every computer, and that little robins squat on desks, and signs saying 'Happy Christmas' in slopey writing that look as if they date from before the First World War hang over the flimsy wooden partitions. Kath and Joan in Classifieds are virtually wearing reindeer antlers, and carolling. There is also tinsel twined around the banisters. Upstairs, there are lots of cards from staff on my desk. Sweet.

I walked in covered in mud and muck, and Gillian said, 'You're doing ITN at lunchtime, do you want one of your cars?' Aaargh! ITN! I'd thought I was having a down day. But no. I had to go and have my hair done in Mirror, Mirror and buy yet another whole new outfit in Topshop on the Strand.

22 December 2009

Went Christmas shopping again. Trying to pass the 5 January issue, which is going to have Bahamas-based island beauty (have lapsed into fluent glossy-speak) India Hicks on cover, barefoot, looking bronzed and inviting. Ben spends most of his time nipping off to Sloane Square on his motorbike to buy toys for his nephews and nieces. 'Just off to load the sleigh,' he says.

A festive mood is definitely abroad in the office. Gillian has bagged up all the swag we've been sent during the year – Jo Malone bath oils, Martin Miller Gin, etc. – and doled it out. There is a Christmas cake slowly eroding by the kettle – people keep digging in with teaspoons, as if it's a Stilton.

As I'd rather had the pick of the beauty stuff already, I made a great show of declining my own unearned portion of the goodies. I spent most of the afternoon trying to buy a particular sort of very thick-rimmed brown porcelain espresso cup from Italy online and ended up finding them on a US website and clicking to buy, a split second after seeing that the P&P alone was $50.

The in tray (and logged in the 'gifts' file): Christmas-pudding-flavoured biscuits; travel guide to Angola (as *Lady* readers would really want to go to a war zone). Michael Winner has also sent Janina a Christmas card with quotes of how wonderful he is from Sir Roger Moore, Sir Michael Caine and John Cleese.

23 December 2009

Last day of *The Lady* year. Office closes later, reopens 4 January.

In the morning I had to do a dreaded *Sunday Times* photoshoot for the pictures to accompany the Lesley White magazine piece about me taking over *The Lady*. Zipped into Bedford Street to send some emails, cleared my desk for 'festive period', saw Carolyn, said 'Happy Christmas' to Lindsay, and Janina, went upstairs, and Adam was uncorking bottle of white with a broad grin. 'We've just had our Chambers lunch,' he slurred. 'Drink?'

'Where's Ben?' I said, declining. It's not the same when Ben isn't here. There's no one to scrap with.

'He said he might come in if the drizzle stopped,' said Adam. Then I pushed off to J Sheekey before *La Bohème*, at the Royal Opera House. It all felt very decadent. I gurgled oysters soaked in lemon and shallots and smiled at Ivo. Then I said, 'I'm so lucky, this is the absolutely perfect job for me. I don't want to do another one now.'

Then I had a terrible flashback of something that Carolyn had said after the Christmas lunch, during which I couldn't speak, because of laryngitis. Mrs Budworth the Matriarch had said something ominous. I'd asked Carolyn to try to remember exactly what Mrs B. had said. 'I think she said there was money until September,' she said. 'But that she could pull the plug at pretty much any time.'

So as it's end of December, that gives me nine months to turn her Ladyship around. Three months to get circulation staying above 30,000 (if it hits 35,000 and stays there – ha ha – I get a bonus). As I write, the *Guardian* is laying off dozens of journalists, the *Observer* has only narrowly escaped closure, there is blood all over the carpets at Condé Nast. So what chance do I have?

When I got home, I spotted that a flier from the cake woman had been sticking out from the pen-tidy on my desk during the shoot. So I'd been posing for the *Sunday Times* mag the whole time in front of a postcard saying 'Real Fruitcake'. A perfect end to my first four months at the helm.

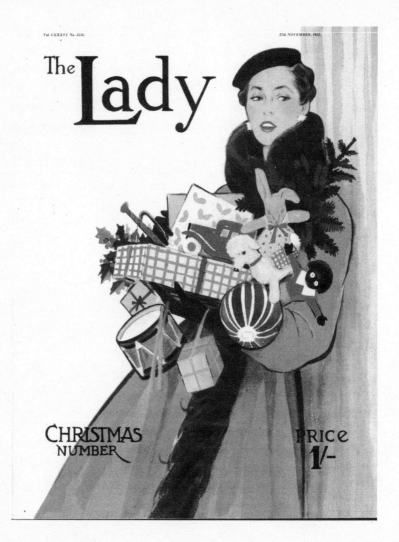

Vol. CXXXVI No 3536.   27th NOVEMBER, 1952.

The Lady

CHRISTMAS
NUMBER

PRICE
1/-

January

5 January 2010

Twelve days out of the office, and now back to a flapdown. No one knew I wasn't in on 4 January. Some of the wrong pieces are being laid out, with the wrong pictures, in the wrong places, i.e., instead of ex-BBC 4 radio producer Olivia Seligman's treatise on *The Archers*, complete with Vanessa Whitburn quotes (Whitburn is the editor of *The Archers*), the subs were laying out an extract from Charles Collingwood's autobiography about playing smoothie Ambridge rotter Brian Aldridge and Aldridge's long affair with Siobhan and their lovechild Ruairi.

So I tried to remain calm. The truth is, they do the lion's share of the work, not me. And they never complain. However, people are still ill, or cut off in snow, so God knows how we are going to put out and distribute the mag. According to the *Evening Standard*, an 'extreme weather event' is on its way. Our friend, Milly's godfather, novelist Henry Porter, has just rung to say that the M4 is shut, so I'm unlikely to get Ludo back to school at Marlborough tomorrow. Just now, someone on *The World Tonight* said that Gatwick, Luton and Liverpool airports are all closed, and has just interviewed someone who is cut off somewhere in Lincolnshire. The presenter asked, 'Have you had a problem with grit theft before in Market Rasen?' Honestly, it's all about the weather at the moment. When I worked on *The World Tonight* it was all about the rise of China and 'Who cares for the carers?' and was so intergalactically worthy that Ivo rechristened the programme 'The World Tosleep'.

Over the Christmas holiday, between cooking and washing up and shopping and wrapping, I'd tried desperately to clear mental space to think about the direction of the magazine. I'd been too busy before, cranking it out week after week.

Who is it for? Would I buy it? Who is it aimed at? What is its audience? But these are questions to which I still cannot give very clear answers, which is a problem. It's a magazine that – were I not editing it – I would definitely flick through, and so would most of my friends, if it was lying around. But we wouldn't, necessarily, *buy* it. I think the mag's miles better than it was. For a start, it looks like a magazine, which helps, and it's well written. My columnists are among the best around. Above all, *The Lady* is unlike anything else in lots of ways: it's simply not trashy, and follows a different agenda. We do masses on the secret life of the lady's maid, and we are planning a five-parter on old-school nannies that will be endlessly reassuring. My reckoning is, if I can come up with features that will make it a must-read for people who have *staff*, just as *Country Life* is a must-read for people who have country piles, or wish they did, we'd be on to something. Am worrying about this pretty much all the time. And I'm not sure I'm on the right track; I'm losing old readers (I should add that Ben keeps insisting I call them 'established' rather than 'old' readers) faster than bringing new ones on board.

Over New Year on Exmoor, a friend of Ivo's called Lady Henrietta Rous told him the magazine was too *Spectator*-ish and upmarket. 'The only people who read *The Lady* are the lower orders,' she told him earnestly. Aaaggh! What if she's right? Then the twinkling charm of Clemmie Hambro and Mary Killen will be falling on stony ground.

On the plus side . . . Coco's column, launched in the Christmas issue, is a surprise success. Joan from Classifieds now sends Coco emails in the voice of her dog, Meesha, which I have to answer. Coco is also getting lots of letters and emails starting with the salutation, 'Woof woof' and ending, 'Tailwags'. Have had a slightly less pliable response from within the office: an anonymous email from someone who called himself (or herself) Office Plank saying that I am a flea-bitten old bitch. This forcefully reminds me that I have only been in the saddle for a few months, my champagne got nicked and not everyone necessarily likes me.

It is very cold in Bedford Street. There is no central heating, only radiators, so rooms are either hammam-temperature or freezing. Uncle Tom Bowles is haunting the central staircase in his pyjamas, over which he has layered his outdoor clothes.

Edwina, the beauty in the marketing department, is cross – she wanted to pen the Coco column, and is pitching to interview Joanna Lumley. Am all in favour of youthful ambition; I want her to write; but I know just the chap I want to interview Joanna Lumley.

Roger Lewis – the writer who wants to shoot me – is clearly the right man for the job.

6 January 2010

Text from Dada. 'See Rowan Pelling in the Tel!!' it says. I am en route to the boardroom to see Ben and have a fight about the Penny Smith cover (he wants an image of presenter Penny Smith wearing a depressing blue dress with a ruffle front that looks funereal; I want her in a sparkly sequinned jacket). So I surged into boardroom and, as I got the row underway, I plucked the *Telegraph* from his table, opened it to the comment pages and speed-read Rowan's piece as we ding-donged.

Then I almost threw up.

It was entitled – 'So the G-spot doesn't exist after all? Thank God for that!' I searched for my name, and quickly came to it, in the first and longest gobbet of Rowan's notebook. She says she has always thought that the G-spot was invented solely to terrorize women, and admitted in the public prints that she didn't have one. 'The next day I ran into Rachel Johnson, now the exuberant editor of *The Lady*, whose opinion had also been sought and who admitted to no such deficiency. Johnson was aghast at my lack of G-ness, a particularly poor show in the then editor of an erotic mag.'

I didn't have the heart to fight Ben after my internal genitalia had been publicly discussed in a national newspaper.

I wrote a letter to Roger Lewis. In it I said I was sorry that my brief meeting with him had sent his trigger finger into spasm, but did he want to interview Joanna Lumley for us? I told him we paid terribly badly and had only a very few readers left, mainly in care homes. I thought that would appeal to him.

Rosie Boycott – Boris's food czar is one of her many hats – came to supper. She looks incredible. I won't even say 'for her age', because I have decided to try to ban any reference to female age in *The Lady*, unless it is the hook, i.e., 'Dame Jennifer Jenkins at ninety'. I told her about my daily walks through Trafalgar Square, and warbled about the fourth plinth being, in a sense, redundant – the whole square serves as a plinth anyway, with a different protest or installation, or service or whatnot, or climate-change protesters or hardwood trees there daily. I said that a year in the life of Trafalgar Square could be a good book and graciously allowed her to steal my idea and offer it up to Boris as a tidbit.

7 January 2010

Roger Lewis called twice in ten minutes. He has received my card and said he loved it and has agreed to interview Joanna Lumley, so long as I pay his return train fare to Wales, or wherever it is he lurks. I told him there was a catch. 'You have to go with an astonishingly beautiful twenty-four-year-old called Edwina,' I teased, expecting him to start panting like a hound.

'No, all that's over,' he said. 'Not for years now.'

So then I said that she was like something out of the Mick Jagger song: 'She'd make a dead man . . .' I started.

'No,' he cut me off. 'Not a sausage.'

We had a long talk which I concluded with, 'Well, I'm glad we're such good friends now.'

Kate Shapland, who writes our beauty page, came in to discuss selling beauty advertising and noticed that her beauty notebook, with luscious references to luxury products from Guerlain and Dr Hauschka, and so on, was placed adjacent to a quarter-page ad from Tena with the words 'TENA *Pants* Discreet in NEW cotton-like material', and a photograph of a woman pulling up her trousers over her bottom. She screamed and covered her face.

The in tray:

- free sample of Replens MD, the leading vaginal moisturizing gel. 'Clinical studies have shown that best results are achieved from regular use, three applications a week, preferably in the morning. It means you can be flirty and fabulous for ever!' the accompanying leaflet puffed. Have left it prominently on my desk to frighten Ben.
- an assortment of Sarah Smith vibrant floral 'flower-power scourers, cleaning cloths to add a splash of colour and make my household cleaning fun and easy to help remove stubborn stains'. Like the Tena pants, the cloths claim to be 'ultra absorbent'.

11 *January 2010*

Discover there is a kindly message from Jeremy on the answering machine that I haven't listened to. 'Hello. It's Jeremy (modest, dactylic pause) Paxman here. Just to say that I think *The Lady*'s looking really rather good. Much better. There are articles that I could theoretically imagine reading. Maybe. Anyway. Well done.'

Also one from writer David Jenkins, Alex Shulman's inamorato, saying, 'Just thought I'd pass on that everyone keeps saying what a good job you're doing. Gratters, old bean.'

Now I'm getting plaudits, I fear I should be even more worried. It must mean the mag is destined for the plughole even sooner than Mrs Budworth intimated. And tomorrow we get the figures for how the Christmas-relaunch Julie Andrews cover has done, so fear really grips.

Had a session of acupuncture with a lovely creature called Annee de Mamiel at Home House. She asked me lots of questions, i.e., how often I opened my bowels and whether I had well-formed stools. I answered positively. Then she stuck needles into my legs and arms and said that my right side was blocked. And that my skin was dry because there was no 'energetic activity in my womb'.

I felt very spaced out afterwards and had to eat the entire presentation box of Betty's of Harrogate's box of white champagne truffles which were sitting on my desk when I arrived.

12 *January 2010*

The circulation numbers for the 22 December issue have come in. We sold 32,000 copies. That's a 20 per cent increase week on week and year on year. 'But I thought we were looking for something nearer 40,000,' I said, when Ben unveiled the numbers. This is what I had been told a double Christmas issue cover would sell in the good old days.

Ben bridled. He went on about how we are a publication bucking the trend in a recession that has hit print media hardest of all. So I am to think that 32,000 is good news. We're up a bit, and everyone else is down. Have asked Ben to send over the figures so I can see the trend. Adam emailed, saying that Graydon and Anna Carter (editor of *Vanity Fair* and wife) just luuurve *The Lady* and read it every week and want to come in and have tea.

So we will roll out the Joan Collins memorial walnut cake again.

Hugh St Clair is slowly transforming my office. The wallpaper looks delicious and uplifting. He has covered two *bergère* chairs with his own fabric, and hung twelve or so *Lady* covers in identical silver frames (chosen by me). And now my *chaise longue* has arrived. Joan (fluffy slippers) and Kath (longest-serving member of staff, at thirty-four years) – both marvellous – stood around and laughed at it. It is upholstered in orange velveteen (it seemed a good idea at the time) and is not a *chaise longue* but a doll-sized *chaise courte*. Even my abbreviated limbs dangle off the end. Ben came in – after all, he has paid for the new wallpaper, the framing of *Lady* covers, the furniture. 'Those are the worst-framed and hung pictures I've ever seen,' he said, then shuddered at the bottle of Replens on my desk. 'And what the hell is that?' pointing at the fun-sized Tango-hued piece.

'It's the *chaise courte*,' I said, sitting on the doll-like item and hoping it wouldn't break.

'The *chaise* shit more like,' he said, before disappearing for his forty-fifth Silk Cut of the day.

Went into the boardroom to find Ben, Edwina and Nic Boize (B-Cal) working up ten key points I have to make in the BBC *Brekker* interview tomorrow morning.

'Which celebrities would we never have in *The Lady*?' Ben asked. Before I could answer, he spun into an anecdote about being a witness to the crash that left Heather Mills legless. 'I was proceeding down Kensington Gore on the A track and saw a DPG Hunter pack of two diplomatic policemen on separate bikes,' he explained. He always talks like this, because he flies helicopters and has been in the army. 'And Mills stepped out into the street. The claret was running down the pavement,' he said. 'It was all her fault! The sirens were blaring and everything. I felt sorry for the police bikers. I mean, it was all right for *her* – she went on to marry Paul McCartney, but the one who hit her was in bits and was probably invalided out of the service.' I think at one point Ben even said he was one of the 'lucky few' who've ever seen 'Heather Mills's other leg'.

13 *January 2010*

Car arrived at 7.55 a.m., to convey me to TV Centre and on to the BBC *Breakfast* set, where I am booked to appear on the sofa at ten to nine. I arrived at the same time as Kevin McCloud, who is immediately ushered to a swanky dressing room with his name on the door. I am shooed into Make-Up, don't get my own dressing room. 'This has got to last till a party tonight, so lay it on thick,' I urged. Did my spot, which came on after what seemed like interminable package followed by live interview with a man who had had hiccups for two years and was on to tell the nation all about it. My first question from Sian and Bill of the Sofa was – Was I taking *The Lady* upmarket and/or in search of younger readers?

'No,' I gushed, mindful of what Lady Henrietta Rous had said over the festive period, i.e., our readers were all from the *lower orders*. 'It's all about age, not attitude.' What I meant was, of course, attitude not age, as Ben reminded me the second I came off air. The only time the interview came alive was when they asked if it was true that there was a dog on the staff. 'Yes,' I pealed. 'She writes her own column!'

Next, a car arrived to take me to the Cath Kidston shoot and interview at a riverside 'dream house' in Chiswick in lee of Fuller's Brewery. The air by the Thames was a heady mix of hops, mash and riparian vapours.

I apologized for my heavy pancake as soon as I'd got through the security gates and into the dream-home interior, filled with light and colour and art. Cath looked at me carefully. 'I want even more make-up, and for you to Photoshop me too,' she said. 'Just Photoshop away, won't you?'

She was heavenly, the house was heavenly, it was all heavenly. Stepdaughter Jess's bedroom was a poem of white bunks and pretty colour, as was the study, bedroom, sitting room, hall. Modern art mingled with film posters, i.e., still from original of *St Trinian's* with gymslipped schoolgirls brandishing hockey sticks from the windows of the school train. Whenever I asked who did anything, she airily replied, 'All on the cheap,' or 'It's white lino,' or 'Shepherd's Bush market stall'. I can spend thousands on something and it still looks cheap and nasty. Kidston spends a few pee, and makes it look like *World of Interiors*.

I rushed back before the crew from *Madame Figaro* arrived, which they did promptly at 2.30 p.m. Did interview and photoshoot in the snow in the communal garden while little children called things like Romilly and Lilac romped around with puppies and mummies. It was like something out of the Boden catalogue, with a slight Ingmar Bergman feeling, with the light very grey and the ground very white and the stucco looking almost dirty against it all, and the bare branches etched against the snow and the stucco like filigree. The round topiary bushes by the playground had bonnets of snow and looked just like Christmas puddings in *Beano*.

Later, I went to the opening of the Ruddock Medieval Europe and Medieval/Renaissance galleries at the V&A. Jill Shaw Ruddock made an adorable speech which mentioned the Middle Ages but, thankfully, not the menopause. I was chatted up by David Willetts. He wanted to talk to me because I sit on this quango, called 'The Family Commission', I think.

'It's not merely that the old are getting younger, but the young are getting older,' I pronounced, as if addressing a studio audience on *Question Time*. I saw his eyes gleam behind his specs. 'That's mine. I've copyrighted it,' I said. It was cold in the galleries, but the mojitos were good and I recognized the chilli-caramel roasted nuts – they were Ottolenghi and about £25 a kilo.

14 January 2010

Want *The Lady* to profit from the blanket publicity surrounding
Lady Antonia's book, *Must You Go?*, about her affair and marriage
to Harold Pinter. I have rejigged things so our reviewer Susan Hill
interviews our reviewer Antonia for what I hope will be a cover
story with welly. After all, it's not often that a *Lady* columnist is
headline news.

Then I have to go to a meeting upstairs about our coverage for
the mag's anniversary, which falls on 16 February, by which time
The Lady will have been in continuous publication for 125 years.
I have the idea that we will come up with a list of 125 Ladies of Today
to mark the occasion, plus lots of other stuff. I can't believe the
pressure never lets up. Stop the train – I want to get off. The sales
of the 22 December Julie Andrews issue have collapsed to 31,700
after Sainsbury's sent back 700 unsold copies.

15 January 2010

Susan Hill called to say that whenever she asked Antonia any questions about Daniel (Harold's son), Vivien (his first wife), or the
children's reactions to the loss of family life, she merely replied, 'Pass.'

'You're both my writers, and you're friends,' I told her. 'You're not
Lynn Barber, and *The Lady*'s not the *Mail*. Just have fun with it.'

16 January 2010

Car arrived (I seem to be writing those words too frequently) to take
me to Broadcasting House to record *Loose Ends* 'as live' at 11 a.m.
Clive Anderson was hosting, Emma Freud guest interviewing.

There were three luvvies and a hack on. The actress Emilia Fox talked about *Silent Witness* and pathology and dead bodies, interrupted by Paul Whitehouse, who has a sort of comedic Tourette's. John Hurt talked in a husky voice, interrupted by Paul Whitehouse and his own hacking cough about his hoodlum picture, called '44-inch Chest', I think.

Emma Freud – astonishing huge violet eyes, skinny legs, glossy hair – and I had already compared breast cup sizes in the Green Room over filthy BBC coffee. She says she is DD, sometimes E. 'Same,' I said. 'Snap!' I was pathetically trying to get her to like me. Then, when we were recording, she went for me rather, as I would, to be fair, if I had the grim task of interviewing me.

She opened the interview about me trying to put the ooh la la into *The Lady* by mentioning the full-page Stannah Stairlifts ad, her eyes goggling at the very idea. 'I'm grateful for all our advertisers,' I responded stoutly. Next up came the Charles Glass piece. 'I think you're referring to the fiasco known as humping the help,' I confirmed. Then she had a go about me writing endless columns about myself and Notting Hill neighbours and said I was an outcast in our hood. At this point I sort of collapsed like a pricked inflatable and just rambled on about *The Lady* and broadcast an apology to all those I have serially offended. I should have snapped back, 'You clearly regard both me and my readers as equally incontinent,' and pointed out that she and our Notting Hill neighbours are not exactly huddled masses in need of urgent international aid – the news from Haiti gets more awful by the minute – but live in vast mansions staffed by tiny Filipinos. But, as ever, it didn't occur to me at the time.

Repaired to the pub, where beige platters of re-formed meats and pastry in the shape of sausage rolls, mini-pasties and spring rolls awaited us. I sat in between Whitehouse and Freud in the pub and had a lovely time, as Whitehouse did impressions and made up a special face for me (eyebrows raised in mock surprise combined with cheeky grin). He asked me what I was doing later. 'I'm playing tennis in a tournament,' I (rep)lied. 'In the rain, wearing a shortie skimpy white tennis dress and no bra.'

He nodded approvingly. 'Thong?'

'I haven't decided,' etc., etc. We went on like this. Jumped into taxi.

'Don't forget to text me a picture when you're on court,' said Whitehouse.

On the way home, I became New Best Friends with Freud and talked about fathers, cancer, blended families, schools, children, men. 'No man has fancied me for years,' she said sympathetically.

'Me neither,' I said. Whether true or not, I wouldn't have dreamt of replying otherwise, as we were now in the throes of bonding over both loving the same Topshop blue velvet jacket. We parted on the best of terms. I made her pay for the taxi. When I got home, I felt incredibly depressed by the experience. Emma Freud had actually used the phrase 'social pariah' of me on BBC Radio Four and it would be broadcast to the nation at 6.15 p.m. How did I get here?

18 January 2010

Monday's always good for post. Today's in tray:

- Rescue® Remedy chewing gum: 'Feeling a little frantic at work or worried about something in your personal life?' Cue Rescue® Chewing Gum.
- a batch of aromatherapy oils from Annee, my facial acupuncturist.
- copy of 'Veteran's World' January newsletter.
- a leaflet from Phoenix-Diamonds. Real memorial diamonds created from the ashes or hair of your partner, loved one or

pet: 'They possess the exact same characteristics as mined gems without the social stigma of blood, sweat and tears of conflict diamonds.'

- a CD of Barry Manilow's *Greatest Love Songs of All Time* with quote from Manilow saying, 'I think this is the most beautiful album I've made.'

Have approached Nigella again and Kirsty Young to do covers. Both turned me down like a bedspread. But later saw freshly single Trinny Woodall at dinner looking skinny and utterly ravishing at financier Peter Soros's Notting Hill mansion ('house' simply doesn't do it justice). She told me she has been busy 'archiving' her wardrobe and had spent three days on coats. This week was dresses. And that she had taken a decision not to buy any more clothes for a year. I asked her to be a cover girl. I can already see the long piece all about the skinny clotheshorse and the joys of not shopping in the mag! I dropped the names of my cover girls Lady Helen, India Hicks, et al. She seemed keen, and pretended to send me an email on her Black-Berry so I would have hers – but it never arrived so, presumably, she'd rather kill herself than be on the cover of *The Lady*.

19 January 2010

Family Commission meeting all morning then lunch at Ivy with Sarah Baxter – editor of the *Sunday Times* magazine – whom I adore. Extraordinary Nordic catlike blue eyes. George Weidenfeld – Antonia's long-standing publisher – tottered past. I detained him. 'I'm Rachel Johnson, you published my first book,' I said. He was with George Walden, the former MP. He looked totally blank. I forgot – I should have said something about him, not me, i.e., 'I'm editor of *The Lady*, and we just ran a big interview with you by Candida Crewe to celebrate all your achievements.' No one wants to hear about you – they only want to hear you talking about them. I must remember that. Email from reader to the editor has come in:

Dear Madam

The Lady has always seemed to me unselfconscious and polite, with a lucid prose style which I hope will not become elliptic, hurried and gossipy, like most other magazines.

The best thing about *The Lady*, apart from its useful update, was the concise biographical gems on historical figures . I remember particularly ones on Handel, William of Orange and the astronomer Herschel and his sister. Yes, I know one can get it all on Google, but that is not the same as sitting down in comfort with *The Lady*. I have not missed the 'Handy Hints' page with its wartime requests as to what to do with scraps of left-over soap or how to remove quite simple stains, nor do I miss the fashion, which seemed a little matronly to me, although it was infinitely preferable to the ugly shooting gear which appeared in an October issue. I had always thought *The Lady* was concerned about the preservation of birds rather than with the glorification of killing them. I have always imagined *The Lady* to be as much a town magazine as a country one, and although I have always lived in or near the country, I rather dislike the somewhat sentimental ersatz paeans of praise to Agas, etc.

However, the real reason that I will not be renewing my subscription is the fact that you have chosen that simpering adultress [sic] Lady Antonia Fraser as your book reviewer. She has never shown any remorse for the misery she caused Vivien Merchant and her son, and I can't help thinking that she and the social-climbing, 'poor man's Samuel Beckett' writer Harold Pinter rather deserved each other. I have not been influenced by the Robert Harris article in Culture in this. It is what I have always felt.

Ouch!

I wrote back saying that we are none of us without sin and that I had no doubt that Antonia was aware of hers. I thought 'simpering adultress' was rather good. Bad news.

The India Hicks cover tanked – we're down to 27,000. I don't know what to do. Hix Nix Hicks Pix! Maybe it's a lesson that our USP is that we're old and unsexy, and we should just hang in there. Next two covers are women around eighty – Honor Blackman and Antonia Fraser – so maybe they will do better. On the other hand, it could have been the snow. As Ben pointed out, there was an 'extreme weather event nationwide', so little old ladies in rural areas were probably struggling to make it into their post offices. Probably.

20 January 2010

To Annabel's for a small party for Graydon Carter. I went with Adam Budworth, a friend of the Carters, in a cab. Coco was banned from entry. It was my first time in Annabel's. The champagne wasn't quite chilled enough. Someone present who must remain nameless revealed that at dinner with Sam and Dave Cameron on Monday (this was of course private, but I can't resist wanting to spread it abroad), Graydon had struck the table senatorially and announced, 'You know what my favourite magazine is in the whole world?' 'Tell us, Graydon,' they all begged. After all, he is the most powerful man in the glossies. '*The Lady!*' I imagined Graydon and Anna lying in bed chuckling over our ads for walk-in baths and sheltered accommodation and couldn't help wondering – *why?* I think I know. It's our way with classified ads, those genteel feelers for little couples who can cook and drive and polish antique furniture and prestige cars that reassuringly speak of a more elegant age, where people can be cared for and looked after.

21 January 2010

Graydon and Anna flaked and cancelled coming in for tea. So Ben's plan to fill an envelope with £20,000 – the sum his great-grandfather sold *VF* for in the 1900s – and slide it across the blue baize table-cloth and offer to buy back *Vanity Fair* cannot, now, be executed. Relief in the boudoir. Weslife is going to doorstep Graydon at the Dorchester and try to get him to repeat his line about his favourite magazine being *The Lady* to camera. This ploy was unveiled in the boardroom, where we all sat in a PR meeting. When I heard this with the PR company Taylor Herring, Edwina, B-Cal and Co. I have to say it made me wince. A very uncool idea.

22 January 2010

Total disaster. Nic Boize was instructed to brief the *Press Gazette* about our soar-away circulation and bumper Christmas edition. The result that appeared online was this:

> *The Lady*, one of the country's oldest magazines, is looking to triple is weekly sales from the 15,000 it sold before Christmas to in excess of 45,000 by the end of the year.
>
> The 124-year-old title, which was originally launched as a 'jour-nal for gentlewomen' and famed for its classified ads for domestic staff, underwent a full-colour relaunch in March last year.
>
> It then appointed Rachel Johnson, sister of London mayor and *Telegraph* columnist Boris Johnson, as its new editor. She joined the magazine in September.
>
> However, the new direction of the magazine, which first launched

in 1885, may have alienated some established readers, as sales fell to an unaccredited 15,937 by mid-December.

The last Audit Bureau of Circulations figure for *The Lady* shows that in the first six months of last year the £1.50 magazine was selling 28,721 copies on average each week.

(In September 2009, to herald my arrival, Ben introduced a price rise of 30p from £1.50 to £1.80, just to make my job even easier . . .)

I called Ben en route to Berkshire for a meeting and tried to explain the significance of this. I said the *Press Gazette* was a primary source that all media hacks would read, and it was a story of career-ending import unless it was corrected, and fast. 'No one reads *PR Week*,' Ben retorted. I said it didn't matter whose fault it was – what had happened was same as if the *Grocer* had reported that sales over Christmas at Tesco had halved when in fact they had gone up. And the magazine in question was called *Press Gazette*, not *PR Week*. So B-Cal got on the blower and it was all sorted – turns out that somehow, the figures for our newsstand sales had been mistaken as our total sales . . .

So then I called the *Press Gazette* from the car, gave a cheery quote about how I was thrilled about the circulation increase (I begin every press statement I make with the words 'I was/am thrilled'), and the story was corrected. But still. Ben has brought in high-profile (sic) editor, relaunched twice in a year, and the net result is a story in the trade press to the effect that I have finished off *The Lady* and the readers hate me. Result!

24 January 2010

Sunday Times magazine do a six-page spread, '*The Lady* and the Revamp'. Ben is unimpressed and gives it a 75 per cent rating. I am amazed it is so nice, and say so, explaining that even if the journalist had been vicious, the piece would still be bloody great. 'In fact, I'm about to write to Lesley White thanking her,' I say. 'She could have gone on about stairlifts, and incontinence pads, and she didn't. She made us look like a player.' Pictures are hideous, as usual.

Roy Greenslade has put something up on his *Guardian* blog saying I am a risky choice and asking readers to comment. I feel horribly over-exposed. I am fed up with reading about me. What on earth do other people think? My mother does not mention it when I go to her flat for tea and I see a copy of the *Sunday Times* mag on a side table. I really mind what she thinks but don't say anything. Her silence makes me wonder whether the Budworths were right and I am wrong after all. But then I reminded myself – it's still 5,000 words of free publicity, and not even the Budworths can argue with that.

Later she calls and tells me she enjoyed the piece and hadn't mentioned it because she hadn't had time to read it before.

25 January 2010

A genial PR man called Julian comes in and takes me on a personal tour of historic Rules restaurant, which is next door. If I play my cards right, I will be given a swipe-card for the tradesmen's entrance and can go straight up to the panelled bar with murals taken from the Savoy Hotel, antlers' heads from estates in Scotland, framed letters from Graham Greene (who set a scene from *The End of the Affair* here) and extracts describing Princess Margaret from James Lees-Milne's diary in the Betjeman room upstairs.

One drawback – no teas or coffees are served at Rules, just good, plain-cooked game and fish and scotch, i.e., manfayre.

Back in the office, Gillian told me that Emma Tennant kept ringing and had made Gillian send a copy of *The Lady* by bike to her in Notting Hill, even though she hasn't written anything but simply wants to see Stephanie Cross's review of her book about

Princess Margaret. She will be punished. I screech, 'By bike! By bike,' in fury at the cheek of it. We don't have money to waste on biking free copies of the magazine to readers simply because they call up and try it on!

This just in from Emma Tennant:

Dear Rachel

Just to say I'm most impressed by the new *Lady* – it reminds me of my life at *Queen* magazine when it had just got started by Jocelyn Stevens and Mark Boxer. It's quirky, clever and goes into any topic it feels like – I think it's going to do very well, and congratulations again.

All best
Emma

So all is forgiven.
In the in tray:

- a Simnel cake.
- a National Trust Plant and Garden Notebook.
- a letter from the people who run Safe Haven for Donkeys in the Holy Land (Julie Burchill had asked that her fee go to them – she is turning into living saint).
- a letter on Basildon Bond from a woman who said she's advertised herself as a carer in Kent in the Sits. Wanted columns of *The Lady*. 'Before I did so I rang the classified dept for a chat; would it be worth advertising, etc., and what would be my chances of successfully gaining employment.' I wondered where this was going. 'I had nothing but perverts ringing me up. I can tell you it was *extremely* [her itals] disturbing and upsetting. I did not expect this at all because of the prestigious nature of

your publication.' Then she went on about our care of duty and how we'd failed her. I am most surprised. So, perverts read the mag, so Lady Henrietta Rous – who told me only the lower orders did – has been proved deliciously wrong.

Tomorrow I have to go through the slush pile of unsolicited submissions to *The Lady*. The fun literally never stops.

26 January 2010

Figures came in. The Penny Smith 12 January cover of the *GMTV* presenter in sequins has ... worked! We are up to 32,000 plus. I am worried that the uplift is down to my bottom on the BBC *Breakfast* sofa, plus outings on *Loose Ends* and *Steve Wright in the Afternoon* on Radio 2.

In the in tray:

* a book called *Have a Nicer Day* by a man called Rickard Fuchs: 'The best-selling guide to achieving a better life from the multimillion-selling doctor-stand-up-comedian-author'. Inside the book he's written 'Have a Nicer Day' and signed his name. Felt better immediately.

I started going through the slush pile, pieces still being considered for publication. The first one I came to in the folder was 'Solving Stonehenge's Secrets' by a man called Ron Toft (I'm sure he's one of the many freelancers who came to our Christmas lunch).

The next was a 1,163-word piece with photographs on 'Cobnuts and Filberts – fresh green hazelnuts', entitled 'Nuts, Whole Hazelnuts', which I opened eagerly and was thrilled to see that the author's intro began, 'In his famous poem "To Autumn" John Keats noted it was the season for nature to "plump the hazel shells with a sweet kernel". Then I saw that they were in a special folder called 'Accepted for Publication by Lindsay A. Fulcher'. Now, can't wait to see the ones that have been *turned down*.

In the features meeting I announced that we are henceforth to call random, old-*Lady*-type articles about nature subjects 'cobnuts' in honour of this last submission.

27 January 2010

The newest Big Idea for the 125th anniversary edition on 16 February from the marketing team upstairs is a specially designed rose. I got this from the head of press and promotions:

Introducing the new Lady *rose created by David Austin (the top rose producer in the UK).*

The Lady's *Blush*

Ausoscar
Alba Hybrid

A particularly beautiful semi-double variety whose flowers start as elegant pointed buds and develop into open rounded cups. The colour is a pure soft pink, the inner petals often having quite a prominent creamy white strip up the middle and a creamy white eye in the centre. Perfect for all types of borders.

The Lady's Blush is a new rose that has been created by David Austin to celebrate the 125th anniversary of **The Lady** – England's longest-running weekly magazine for women.

Is it just me or is that description of *The Lady*'s Blush not pure filth?

29 *January* 2010

The Lady literary lunch. Guest speakers – Ben Fogle, Gyles Brandreth, Juliet Nicolson (sister of Adam, daughter of Nigel, granddaughter of Vita and Harold). All spoke brilliantly – Gyles terribly mad and funny, full of quotes and pep, with mad swivelling eyebrows and curious dead-straight lashes such as you sometimes see on pigs. Talked about Oscar Wilde and how he was reburied in Père Lachaise cemetery. 'How do you get to be buried there?' I mused. 'You buy a flat right next door like me,' he bragged in a nice way. Am so old now that all I talk to people about is their funeral and burial arrangements. Ben Fogle was ridiculously handsome and had the most beautiful hands I have ever seen on a man. Juliet spoke very well and illuminated to all how important *The Lady* was as a historical resource, with its ads for Victory Toupées ('impossible to detect') and Epilastic corsets. Sat between Ben and Gyles and talked about diaries. Gyles has published his – *Something Sensational to Read on the Train* (a quote from *The Imp. of being Earn.*) – and then he smirked, 'Only good girls keep diaries, bad girls don't have time.'

John Dower asked for a show of hands from the room – a sea of sparkly suits and white hair, one pretty black woman, about five men, including a diarist – of how many approved of my changes. It was like *Any Questions*. About half the hands went up. My favourite part of the whole day was being handbagged by a reader who was quivering with rage and said, 'You've changed everything!' and complained about everything, even how easy the crossword was, as Dower filmed every foam-flecked word.

My second favourite part of the day was when the events manager, Andrew Kaye (this was after Brandreth had made a break for
the border after his speech, saying he had to hotfoot it to Lough-
borough to address some double-glazing salesmen), came over to
Ben Fogle like a puppy and said, 'Well, I hope *you're* stopping for
sweet,' with a pleading look.

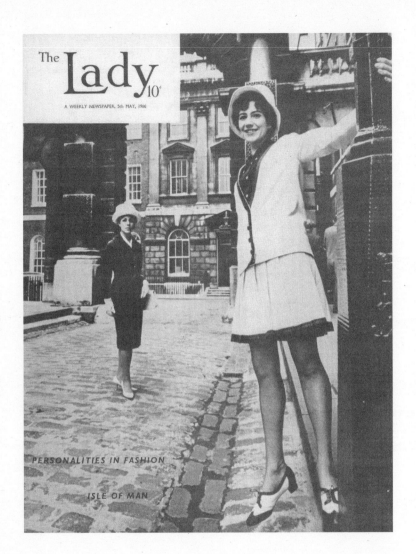

The Lady 10ᵈ

A WEEKLY NEWSPAPER, 5th MAY, 1966

PERSONALITIES IN FASHION

ISLE OF MAN

FEBRUARY

1 February 2010

Was reading the *Mail* idly over breakfast and my eye fell on my own name.

> Since no one in public life ever seems able to say sorry for anything these days, Rachel Johnson, editor of *The Lady*, has stepped into the breach and refreshingly apologized to readers for changing the 124-year-old magazine. At *The Lady*'s literary lunch at the Institute of Directors, Rachel, 45, announced: 'Tony Blair might be answering to God, country and Sir John Chilcot. But I have a harder task in that I have to address you, our loyal *Lady* fans. I put my hand up and admit that mistakes were made. To my great regret, readers were lost and I'm sincerely sorry for this.'
>
> Let's hope her elder brother, London mayor Boris, is big enough to say the same if the need arises . . .'

It went on. Annoyingly, they have added a whole year to my age!

At 6 p.m. I cabbed to the premiere of *A Single Man*, where there was a parade of slebs on a black carpet at the Curzon cinema. Hurley twirling in front of paps and massed flashbulbs in sleeveless dress. In February! Sat glumly through the film, wincing at the endless scenes of men snogging and choosing impeccably laundered shirts and performing elaborate toilettes. Tom Ford made a little speech introducing Colin Firth and Nicholas Hoult, and so on, to the stage, and revealed he had shot the whole movie in just twenty-one days.

Meanwhile John Dower and the crew from Optomen have been in the building for five months in order to make a 48-minute doc. I must remember to tease them. Over dinner, I told Colin Firth that he would defo be nominated for an Oscar, because the entire movie was about displacement activity (he prepares meticulously for a suicide he never carries out) and delayed gratification and as such was in the same mould as *Brief Encounter* and *Lost in Translation*, two of my top movies of all time. Firth looked very unimpressed with these aperçus.

I sat between A. A. Gill at Harry's Bar (for the dinner for Tom Ford, given by Graydon Carter) and Graydon. Made the mistake of telling A. A. Gill that I was being filmed for a docusoap. Then I made the mistake of telling Gill that the same guy who did *When Boris Met Dave* was directing. 'That was awful, awful,' he grinned happily. 'But the documentary about you and *The Lady* –' he stabbed at his endive and artichoke starter '– that will be *suicidally shit.*'

2 February 2010

The figures came in, and we're still keeping our heads above water, at around 31,000. Which is like the weather – not bad for the time of year.

After Harry's Bar, a blank. At 10 a.m., I went into Ben's office to hear the progress sales (i.e., the estimated rather than the net figure, which we calculate after returns) of how the cover after Penny Smith – Honor Blackman – had done. Still above 30,000. But not, I think it can be agreed, close to the crazed, skyrocketing figures the Budworth boys have in mind.

4 February 2010

Today's in tray:

* brownies baked by Helene, who plays Despina in *Cosi Fan Tutte*, courtesy of the PR at the Royal Opera House.
* a whole box of Lovedean Granola from Lucy O'Donnell, which I have also already eaten.
* a letter from John Springs offering himself as cartoonist.
* one horrid, unsigned four-page letter written entirely IN CAPITALS from a woman who attended the Fogle/Brandreth/Nicolson lit. lunch headed, 'Points of Dissappointment [sic] shared by many': 'Why not ask for a show of hands of who doesn't like the new *Lady*?' it asked. It said that those who were interviewed and said nice things had been bribed with a free lunch, that she and others – readers of forty years' standing – would be cancelling their SOs (standing orders), and ended after complaining about the Bucks Fizz, the Antonia Fraser cover and the lack of flunkies to meet and greet at the Institute of Directors. 'Such a great shame for *The Lady* magazine to have changed so much and in many eyes not for the better.'
* also a short letter marked 'Personal'. 'A little note to say how much I enjoyed your literary lunch. Your hard work organizing it was very much appreciated. [I should admit all I did was turn up, make eyes at Ben Fogle and eat a delicious lunch.] I am a lady GP from the Cheshunt area.'

8 February 2010

Went to work this morning and, when I let myself into the building, I felt gloom settle on me for the first time since I started.

There doesn't seem to be much uplift in advertising. Circulation is where it was when I arrived (the 1 September issue sold 31,164). This morning I received a letter that said, 'It is so refreshing to pick up a magazine that isn't littered with ads,' as if this were an aesthetic decision on our part – no nasty advertising for the new-look *Lady*!

Janina is lobbying me every time one of her interviews with ageing hoofers and Hollywood has-beens is held out or cut; she has just spent an age poring over the flatplan for the 23 March issue and sent me an email complaining that the William Blacker interview about Romania – for which I have commissioned portraits from Laura Carew, and copy from Stephanie Cross, late of the *Guardian*, is over three pages. 'Linda Hamilton has been reduced to two pages, and she's beautiful and all the quotes are new. Could she be back to three please?'

Meanwhile, the subs have discovered that Lindsay has put a piece of mind-blowing dullness called 'Arbours' into our Spring Gardening issue, a piece that was considered too tedious to have run even last year, when the mag was full of long pieces about small furry creatures, as I can prove. Have just received this from a long-standing contributor:

Dear Ms Johnson

I am a freelance journalist and former regular contributor to *The Lady*. You have three commissioned articles of mine (dormice, endangered mammals and Stonehenge) which, it would seem, are now unlikely to be used. I am advised that if this IS the case, I should ask for a 50 per cent kill fee. I look forward to hearing from you.

Of course *The Lady* is a work in progress: I have to bring Debo on board, probably get rid of 'The Gents' (our readers will never accept the name), reintroduce the short story and banish our rather fizzy serial written by Susan Hill's daughter Jessica Ruston to the website, as it leaves our readers cold. For my part, I've relaunched and overseen the redesign, I've sat on daytime sofas and exposed myself to radioactive amounts of self-publicity.

And now I think, 'Mmm, what next?' I sort of know what will make a good feature – Paul Johnson on the passing of the lady's maid – and what won't, as some strange alteration in my news sense has occurred. If someone offers me an interview with a Holly-wood actress in panto with a memoir to promote, I groan out loud. But if someone tells me about a woman called Patsy who is a textile designer in her eighties who lives in a cottage in the New Forest and who has designed tea-towels for the National Trust that have become collectors' items, I feel a warm glow inside.

But still – the future is incredibly opaque. When I write a book, I know what the last line is going to be, and I sort of push the boulder uphill towards it. I have no idea what the last line of this diary is going to be. There are three in-house PRs and two PR companies working on *The Lady*. But I still can't help wondering, 'What's the plan?' So I said to John Dower, every time I see Ben or Adam, I can't help thinking, 'What's the plan?'

'*You* are the plan,' he answered.

Me? ME? If he's right, then we're well and truly fucked.

9 *February* 2010

Today's in tray:

- two more Simnel cakes.
- one handmade gemstone necklace with river pearls and intri-cately faceted amethyst drops and crocheted with purple thread made by destitute Jaipuri women for a jeweller in Killin, Scotland, and a nice letter saying, 'We know that if you were

to feature our website in *The Lady* it would really help our business, which in turn would help needy people, particularly women and children in India. A stamped addressed envelope is enclosed to return the necklace.' The envelope isn't stamped.

- a letter from a reader in Cambridgeshire – v. shaky handwriting – saying, 'Dear Editor, I really love the new *Lady* (altho' I rather liked the stuffy old one as well) ... The lovely Dr Le Fanu has cured my mystery bladder problem – Halleluja! God Protect Him! My GP most interested in the relevant literature he sent me.'

- three cellophane-wrapped packages of Fiona Sciolti 'botanical chocolates' and a letter explaining how, for Fiona, handcrafting each chocolate is a labour of love, and commanding me, 'Prepare to Indulge.'

The 125th-anniversary issue is being subbed and laid out, and Lindsay and Mrs Budworth are gently steaming to each other telephonically about the fact that I am holding out the 2,000-word piece about Lewis Carroll's tenuous links with *The Lady* magazine from our gala collectors' issue.

On which subject – Stefano Arata's cover design for the anniversary special has come in this morning, and while it's pretty, it's very ungrabby. Just a profile of the woman from a vintage *Lady* cover, like a black medallion, and some trellis-like flowers in the background. Have set Claire on to making it look as if it is 2010 as well as 1885.

10 February 2010

Massive kerfuffle between our design team, and lots of tears before bedtime as we try to pass the anniversary edition for 16 February.

Claire, Stefano, Tammy at each other's throats. Too many cooks, I think. Not sure the plan to have Stefano overseeing the cover is going to work, as he calls Claire's designs 'disgusting' to her face, tells Tammy that her choice of pictures is naff, and has on occasion reduced them both to silent sobs. As they are both very calm and level-headed, I can see I am going to have to step in with the water-cannon.

Today's in tray:

- a very nice letter from someone in East Langdon, Kent, saying that she has advertised her apartment on the Italian-French Riviera in the magazine for years and that she is always inundated with enquiries – 'All our guests, without exception, have been delightful and many return as regular guests' – and calling the magazine 'a treat and a tonic'. When nice letters come in I hardly know where to look.
- a letter from Dartford, Kent, from someone who wants Gillian to spend an entire day looking for a back issue from 1937 and enclosing an air-freshener in the shape of a cat and ending, 'All the best for 2010. Another air-freshener enclosed, I guess you can use it.' *Another* air-freshener?

The cover has ended up with the black profile and, inside the profile, the cover line, 'Who is today's lady?', in the hope that the readers will open the magazine to discover in a frenzy of excitement just who is on our list of 125 Ladies of Today.

11 February 2010

On editorial front: have asked Alexander Chancellor to do telly for us, and Dafydd Jones wants to provide a photo essay showcasing the country's *vieillesse dorée*. Ben wants us to run a slot for widows/dowagers/divorcees called 'Back on the Market'.

On doc front: the film crew is finally going to interview Julia Budworth. At Deerbolts Hall. I tell them not to mention Buttons the Killer Teddy. Then Mrs Budworth actually manifested in Bedford Street. I was in the boudoir and got a call from Ben. 'Can you shoot your chuff in here for a sec to meet Mum,' he said, very formally. I walked in.

'You're a very rude girl,' she said in a wig-lifting voice, holding out a hand for me to shake.

'Am I, Julia?' I said weakly.

'I wrote to you last week. Did you reply? No. So rude!' I told her I hadn't got her letter. 'I posted it on Thursday,' she insisted. 'First class!' I told her I hadn't received it.

'Ask Gillian,' I said to Ben. 'She opens all my letters.'

'It had "Personal" on the envelope!' said Mrs Budworth.

'Even the personal ones,' I said.

'Gillian, has any mail arrived for Rach from Mrs B.?' Ben enquired. She denied it had; good girl. Then he shook his head, to convey Gillian's message to the boardroom.

'Well, I definitely sent it,' said Mrs B. with finality, as if between us we had conspired to be rude. We have arranged to have lunch, in Terroirs.

When I got back to my office, Debo telephoned, just as I was on the other line to ebookers, i.e., a call centre in India, trying to change a return flight to New York (Ivo had complained about me going for six nights and had told me I would 'feel guilty' if I went for that long). So I had Delhi on one line, a duchess on the other. I told her that Julia B. had made one of her papal visits. 'And how was she?' Debo asked, mischief in voice. I told her that it would have been possible to distinguish Mrs B. with a grievance quite easily from a ray of sunshine. Then I talked about Debo doing a cover, and she said she had a new photo of herself in a long Hartnell taffeta skirt that we could use. She said everyone there was at sixes and sevens because of the exhibition at Chatsworth. 'It's not about

Chatsworth, it's about me and my life,' she said. 'It's been absolute *purdah.*' Then she explained that 'purdah' was a pet phrase and hybrid malapropism for 'murder' and 'purgatory'. Then she talked about her first cousin, Ben's ma, Julia Budworth. 'She's rather sharply right wing,' she said fondly. 'It makes one rather good value, don't you think?'

Stefano came in, and we spent hours trying to come up with a cover for the 125th gala special, an afternoon which left Claire shaking and in tears and Tammy quivering with rage. He has been a brilliant designer, but all good things have to come to an end. More to the point: Claire came into my office and announced that if Stefano remained to oversee covers, she would go. He did the redesign but wants to stay on and make sure the covers remain true to his vision. But this isn't working. The atmosphere is terrible.

Claire has told me she can't take it any more. So I will have to tell Stefano, regretfully, his services are no longer required.

12 February 2010

The 125th issue has – unbelievably – struck a chord. Our list of 125 Ladies of Today is running on PA and the *Telegraph*, and passim. So, am pleased. I had an idea; it carried the issue; and people seem to have noticed. It's not like this every week, that's for sure. Received a corrective letter from Callander, Perthshire (on A4), in case I was beginning to rest on my laurels.

Dear Madam,

Many years ago, I first started taking *The Lady* for the Ladygram but found many of the articles interesting. Since the relaunch, however, the Ladygram and puzzles are the only intelligent offering. Can I, I ask myself, afford to pay £1.80 just for the Ladygram? I am very saddened that a good magazine has been reduced to pathetic offerings designed for the flighty unthinking in our midst. Tackling up-to-date topics seriously rather than insulting the readership with such rubbish would have been far more acceptable – etc.

Never mind. There is a whole page of coverage in the *Indy* on p. 3. Pictures of three ladies – the Queen, Tracey Emin, Jacqueline Gold – and a piece which starts, 'When Boris Johnson's sister Rachel assumed the editorship of *The Lady* promising to double the tiny circulation of the venerable publication, she knew that the shock waves from her cultural revolution would get the teacups rattling in the parlours of the nation's gentlefolk . . .' It goes on to reference my own 'quinoa-eating, Range Rover-driving Notting Hill set'. Tsk! How dare the *Indy* mention our tiny circulation? Talk about pot and kettle!

Meanwhile, Kelvin MacKenzie (old mate of Ben's from his radio days) is in. He's taking tea in the boardroom as I write. We have two – actually three – possible covers this week: Joanna Trollope, Alan Titchmarsh, or a still life of some secateurs and cut hyacinths on a trug (very old *Lady*), as it is the hardy annual Spring Gardening issue. We are going to ask him to pick it, then tell him how it does.

Kelvin has just left. He marched into my office shouting, 'Luv a duck, you don't need to publish a magazine, this place is old fashion, innit! What year is it! You should close *The Lady* down and open a museum, charge everyone to come and look at this. You could all sit here doing nuffink and folks would pay good money just to look at yer.'

I agreed that entering the Bedford Street premises is like slipping through a tear in the space-time continuum and is stuck in the fifties (i.e., 1850s) and we are all indeed preserved in aspic. Then I took him through to Claire and she got up the three covers on the Mac. He picked the Titchmarsh cover and told us we had to have more pieces about women in their fifties whose Viagra-fuelled husbands had left them. 'It's the marital equivalent of the government boiler-scrappage scheme,' I said. 'Let's call it "Goat Alert".' He liked 'Goat Alert', then said that just because our readers were old ladies, we didn't have to have an old-lady mentality but, like *The Spectator*, had to grab readers with our attitude instead. Ben plugged his 'Back on the Market' idea.

MacKenzie had lots of other ideas, but he spoke so loudly and fast and mugged for the camera so much that I just allowed his genius and expertise gathered from years of editing the *Sun* to wash feebly over me like a neap tide, in the hope that, eventually, like a migraine, he'd go away, which eventually he did.

15 February 2010

Tammy, the picture editor, has resigned. 'It was nothing to do with Stefano,' she said (citing a better offer at picture agency Corbis).

I whinged all day to Ben about the weekend. He'd twisted my arm to go to review a place called Barnsdale Lodge, a hotel on a reservoir and an A road in Rutland, a low-lying, benighted county with howling Siberian winds. The Edward Faulks family came too. I took the children on Friday night and Ivo met us there on Saturday morning. We had a perfectly nice time biking and lounging around watching the Six Nations Rugby and eating cream teas, but at the end of the weekend I was appalled. After listening to all that PR guff from the Rutland Tourist Board, buying lunch in the 'Rutland Pub of the Year' for everyone, including the manager of Barnsdale, I had to *pay the hotel bill*! That wasn't the deal AT ALL. They'd only knocked off a hundred quid as a press discount.

So I laid the hotel bill (a not unreasonable £451, not including lunch at the Horse & Jockey, Rutland Water) on Ben's desk to await arrival. When I saw him I whined, 'I gave up a weekend to go to stay in a hotel by the A606 in the freezing cold, listen to the hotel manager talk about his eco-development holiday-cottages scheme for the whole weekend, then I had to pay the bill,' I bleated. 'And write the piece.' Ben crumbled. I do love him sometimes. He had just told me that his family name 'many moons ago' was Dutton de Budworth and as a result that his army nickname was Mutton Spudworth, and I had screamed with laughter.

Ben carried the bill himself into Geoffrey, who sits in a cubby hole beyond the boardroom, and asked him to deal with it. Geoffrey does the traumatic *Lady* accounts.

16 February 2010

Was reading the *Guardian* and, as one does, had moved swiftly on to jolly features section G2 and found this on page 3:

Passnotes 2,729: *The Lady*

Age: Is that a question you'd ask a lady? I'll whisper it . . . 125 this year.

Speak up, I'm 93, and a little deaf. Exactly the sort of reader *The Lady* no longer wants, I'm afraid.

Don't be so insulting, young man. I've been reading *The Lady* since I was knee-high to an Irish wolfhound. My mother read it, too. Used it to recruit my nanny, governess, all our domestic staff. I remember Mr McCrindle, the butler, saying . . . Madam, we haven't got time for this. *The Lady* is now a whizzy, happening publication edited by Rachel Johnson, printed in full colour, and seeking to double its circulation by connecting the venerable magazine to the modern world.

Was thrilled! *The Lady* has been Passnoted! And the *Guardian* Passnotes column is totally cookin'! Yesterday, Passnotes was on the Brits. And the day after, Greggs. Yes. Greggs! That's how hot we are.

Greggs is also rebranding. Just like us. Greggs hopes to become 'the Skoda of pies', and kit out its stores in southern England with soft lighting, dark-wood fittings and decorously displayed baked goods. As today's haul included a large – and when I say large, I mean the size of my head large – handmade, hot-cross bun from Betty's (with label 'a spiced Easter speciality'), we very much do seem to have much in common with Greggs, with our dark-wood fittings and endless cakes. At least Betty's of Harrogate didn't send another Simnel cake garnished with marzipan balls to represent the Apostles or whatever.

I don't think even Coco can manage any more marzipan balls.

18 *February* 2010

Lunch at Hix, swish new Mark Hix vehicle for purveying seasonal English fayre, like elvers, sea kale and pennywort, at New York prices. Little blonde Becky Clarke and Pat Llewellyn from Optomen were taking me. When I nipped down to loo I found Blur bassist, the lush-locked Alex James, sheltering from the rain with his four tiny children in the basement. I do like a posh lunch. We ate green salads (£8 – oof, not that I was paying) and I have to say they were absolutely wonderful – green chlorophylly crunch, dressed with an oil none of us could identify. As we tanked up on white wine, Becky and Pat revealed they've seen rushes (translation: literally hundreds of unedited hours of footage) and are concerned the documentary was too 'soft'. Translation: this means John has gone native and has produced a film in which we come across as *identifiably human*.

'You're OK,' John told me on the telephone, before lunch. 'We only go for you in a couple of places.' Translation: you don't screw up too badly. I know, because I've been told, that people who make documentaries do endless 'decoy' filming, for hours and hours, just waiting till you come a cropper, say something awful, shout, cry, break down in tears, swear, wet your pants, i.e., they wait for some kind of gotcha moment, when they can exhale with relief, because they've got a result. The thing will be aired, and viewers will sit on their sofas agog at how awful you are, which seems to be the underlying principle of most TV programming.

We carried on drinking a lot of white wine. Then John Dower called before pudding. He was on his way back into London from Deerbolts Hall, the Budworth pile in Suffolk. He said the interview with Mrs B. 'had gone very well' and that the matriarch was 'sharp as a tack'. I could have told him that. Saved him the trip to Suffolk.

He also said that when he'd brought up the subject of Buttons, the Killer Teddy, Ben had panicked and made a guillotine motion with his hand. He'd ordered, 'Don't answer any questions about the blue teddy, Mum, they're only trying to make you look stupid!' So, sadly, Buttons has hit the cutting-room floor.

I felt woozy all afternoon and was unable to finish the second book I have to read before doing *Late Review* on BBC2, for which I have to fly to Glasgow tomorrow – Natasha Walter's *Living Dolls*, in which she deplores the Return of Sexism, porn, Asda bras for eight-year-olds, and so on. Also have to read 500 pages of Late Period Amis in the shape of *The Pregnant Widow* and watch a three-part documentary on feminism by Vanessa Engle, by Friday.

Meanwhile, just to make life even easier, Ivo is in hospital having a knee operation. He will not be able to walk – or even hobble like Hopalong – when he exits, and all the children are lying around at home calling me on my mobile when I'm at work, to ask me things like 'Have you moved my iPod/mobile charger?' and 'Why aren't there any Coco Pops?' in aggrieved tones.

I feel very stressed suddenly. It could be reading all these books which explain how little I earn and how much housework I do compared with men, and those surveys reported in the *Mail* that say that marriages wouldn't crumble to dust so fast if men did their share of sock-picking-up and dishwasher-loading.

Also, this week's crash course in whither feminism – in which it has become painfully clear that women are still expected to supply geisha services to men, women have failed to capitalize on the She-decade of the seventies, and women have only succeeded in lumbering themselves with another job on top of the one they've already got – didn't help much either.

23 *February 2010*

Reader's Digest has gone down with the loss of over half a million souls. I mean, *sheesh*. If a world-famous mass-market monthly with a loyal circulation of 500,000 plus who want to Increase their Word Power, chortle over Humour in Uniform and discover all there is to know about John's Thalamus (three historic *Reader's Digest* columns) can't survive in today's market, *there is precious little hope for us*.

A bearded C4 photographer came in to take stills for the doc. They kept making Ben and me pose like man and wife in front of the portrait of the founder, Thomas Gibson Bowles (a gloomy oil show-ing the moustachioed proprietor with quill in one hand, cigarette in the other), which is in the equally gloomy boardroom. I felt like the Queen, with Ben at my elbow standing in for the Duke of Edin-burgh. As a result, I am scowling and frowning in all the pictures.

The in tray:

- a proposal from a Bexley-based freelancer for an article on other things that happened on Guy Fawkes night entitled

'Remember, Remember the Fifth of November' with an out-line specifying some notable events that happened on this date in other years: the polishing of the Cullinan diamond, the appointment of the British Censor of Films (1912), the Discovery of the Body of Tutankhamun, and the Hither Green rail crash (1967). Proposed length: 1,350 words.

- a sweet letter from a reader (on pink writing paper printed with roses) in Lowestoft, which enclosed a cutting of an interview with Ben Budworth in the *Eastern Daily Press*. My correspondent revealed she had been a devoted reader of *The Lady* for forty years and explained that she had started reading the magazine after answering a catering advert. 'This opened a new life for me after my family left the nest,' she wrote. 'My husband didn't return from World War Two so I was on my own, with a living to earn.' Some of these letters are really touching. Then I read on – and it turned out my Lowestoft correspondent had been on the staff of Deerbolts Hall, Budworth Towers! And the letter was about Mrs Budworth, whose husband had been killed in a private plane crash in Suffolk when Ben was ten! 'The Lady of the house was very kind to me,' she recalls. 'She was pleased with my work.' And she even remembered cooking for the oldest son's twenty-first birthday: 'I cooked two geese and a pancake feast soaked in Grand Marnier.' The letter ends, 'I had a wonderful life, all due to *The Lady*.'

Honestly, I could cry. I picked up the telephone on my desk and called this lady – an Eva O'Reilly who turned out to be ninety-six, to thank her for her lovely letter.

I raced to the Burberry catwalk show for London Fashion Week, held in a marquee adjoining Tate Britain. As I got out of the cab I could see that a weapons-grade goatfuck was underway outside. There was a heaving melee of buyers, photographers, bloggers, models, slebs, men in high heels and yellow suits, editors, liggers, all pushing to get past the velvet rope.

'Take a STEP back,' the heavies kept shouting. Inside, I spotted Anna Wintour in cherry-tweed twinset and brown boots, her tawny bob swinging. As soon as the show started, she put on sunglasses. Why does she do this? Beautiful show, loud music, thin girls who don't look as if they've given up anything for Lent; they never took up a single thing to start with. As I now know, having studied reviews in the fashion press, it was a *military-themed* show. I had a nice chat with Sam Cam, who looked lustrously beautiful and said nice things about *The Lady*. She has a wonderful dewiness about her, long-lashed eyes and sheeny hair. When she first turned up at St Mary Abbots CofE primary with Nancy aged four in tow, some-one pointed to her – a drooling daddy, no doubt – and drawled, 'So . . . who does that gorgeous Iranian au pair belong to?'

Then on to Duff Cooper Award party (it's a literary history prize) sponsored by Pol Roger at the French Embassy. It's always very grand. The embassy – on Millionaire's Row, i.e., Kensington Palace Gardens – has been redone since I went to the same party last year, and the year before that, back till year dot. Now the resi-dence looks like a cross between an advertising-industry crashpad in Soho and the Palais de Versailles, so is eloquent of a nation in deep cultural confusion. Ancient poets sitting on sofas, drinking Pol Roger, with faces like mountain ranges seen from a plane – deep, snaking runnels and craggy outcrops. I had always believed, until this moment, anyway, the line that people never felt old, they just looked old. What is clear, however, from the line-up at the Duff Cooper (one ancient past editor of *The Times*, my old tutor from Oxford, etc.) is that this lot were clearly feeling jolly old too. Artemis Cooper, daughter of Duff, granddaughter of Diana, made a lovely speech. I was sneaking out before *l'Ambassadeur*, embla-zoned with discreet *Légion d'Honneur* rosettes, embarked on his traditional interminable speech in honour of the winner.

I was creeping past a sofa on which sat distinguished men of letters Paul Johnson and David Pryce-Jones, man-about-town Claus von Bulow, etc. Paul Johnson audibly hissed the words 'Stupid girl!' as I passed.

Dinner with Lady Helen Taylor and art dealer and gallerist hubby Tim. It was just the six of us, the Taylors plus a very *soigné* pair – one a hedge funder, the other the half-French CEO of Sisley. The Sisley CEO looked about eighteen, but was thirty-four. Her husband looked about fifteen, but was forty-three. So the pair were a walking advertisement for their product. I stared at them in wonder and when I got home ordered all her 'plant-based' miracle products on the spot, especially after she'd told me my exciting bottle of Crème de la Mer (despite all the guff about 'the broth of the sea', etc.) that had appeared by magic in my in tray was 'too rich' for my skin and how the magic Crème de la Mer formula 'was way out of date'.

25 February 2010

Went to lovely Annee in Home House for my third session of acupuncture. She took my pulse on both hands. 'Your yin pulse is very slow,' she said, with a look of concern. 'And your lung function is weak. Have you been constipated?' Basically, she explained that the yin side is your female side and mine was 'struggling' and I needed to 'release my chakras', and so on. So I told Annee, blinking away hot tears of self-pity, about managing half-term on my own in the February sleet, the fact that Ivo had had an operation (he still hasn't left the house after ten days; am beginning to doubt he ever will) and that at the end of half-term I had to fly to Glasgow to appear live on *Late Review* show with Toby Young, who was funnier than me, then fly back and have people for lunch.

As I whinged on, I felt terribly sorry for myself. She told me my skin was very dry and that I needed a facial. I need more than a facial! It's such a fallacy that me time and self-pampering solve anything. They only add to the sense of panic and urgency.

What I need is more MONEY and more HELP and more TIME.

Two small bottles have arrived in a large box. Carolyn Hart – hardened food editor of many years' standing in Fleet Street – saw them and sighed, 'In the winter it's pies with annoying names, like Higgidy Pies. But after Christmas, it's like a cuckoo, the arrival of the first bottle of garlic vinaigrette. It's the start of *the salad-dressing season.*'

The in tray:

- a letter from a reader in South View, Ilkley, cancelling her subscription and explaining – at length – her decision. After naming and shaming several columnists, she concluded, 'The decisive reminder to drop you was the current issue showing Alan Titchmarsh on the front page – I can't stand him.'
- a letter from a reader in Somerset who had sent in an article about the Forest of Dean in May 2007 which had been accepted for publication by Arline Usden, and enclosing a photocopied note from the then editor to that effect, and asking me to 'clarify the situation'.

I have finally gone through the unsolicited folder containing the most recent submissions, and was enthralled to find the following gems:

1. a piece of 1,000 words entitled 'Ottawa, Tulips and Dutch Royal Family', about the sixty-fifth anniversary of Princess Juliana's gift of 100,000 tulip bulbs to Ottawa, submitted by a freelancer who has contributed to a variety of print and online publications such as *The Stage, The Pink Paper* and *Out in the City.*

2. a proposal for a piece about Anna Korda, a film dialogue coach who worked on the Bond films and with Marlon Brando, Sean Connery, etc., submitted by someone who once published an article in *The Lady* about an 'ex-Bluebell living in Rome'.

3. a sweet letter enclosing a piece about hip-replacement surgery which starts, 'I know that since you took over as Editor you are planning on rejuvenating the image of *The Lady* – so an article on hip replacements might seem totally out of order!' The piece – titled 'Hip, Hop, Ouch' – was surprisingly readable.

4. a piece from a reader in Mottram St Andrew about the duties (empty slops, blacken grates, etc.) of servants between 1914 and 1938, written by her late husband's grandmother. In the submission, she points out that servants were not exclusive to grand establishments. The author cites as evidence her late husband's grandmother's house, which was 'a large house in Warrington owned by a solicitor'.

5. a pitch for a 900-word article called 'Turning the Tide' which tells how a reader in Huntingdon 'turned his life round after a life-shattering experience'. The reader has written for *Waterways World* and *Good Woodworking*. I read the piece – it was a cockle-warming tale about a woman whose partner had died and who, in the absence of a partner, had bought a narrowboat instead.

6. an article (SAE enclosed) about the Mayan calendar.

7. a proposal for a nature column about a different mammal, bird or insect each week with a specimen column entitled 'A glimpse of . . . the Hazel Dormouse' enclosed, length: 928 words.

8. a piece sent in from KwaZulu-Natal about a memorial to the fallen horses of the Boer War which starts, 'They died in their thousands, far from their homelands, for a war they neither understood nor cared about.'

Part of me wishes I could commission them all, because each and every one would reassure antique readers (never forget – the average age of our readers is seventy-eight, so whenever I commission anything my rule of thumb is partly 'What would Mrs Budworth think?') that nothing has changed on the Ladyship. But I can't. I have taught myself that when I read pitches, and emails, and written submissions, or take calls from freelancers, that I must imagine myself running the piece in that week's issue, and dropping something else to make way for it. Just as I have trained myself not to say yes to an event unless I'd be really looking forward to it if it was tomorrow.

As a result, I bin almost everything, and 100 per cent of the short-story submissions (which are almost always about ghosts at Windsor Castle anyway).

26 February 2010

Friday. My shirking from home day. Ivo still crippled after knee op. I finished *Must You Go?* – Antonia Fraser's memoir of her marriage to Harold Pinter, as I am interviewing her Ladyship tonight in front of a paying audience at Waterstones, Notting Hill. Over brekker my eye fell on a snippet in the *Mail*. It ran: 'Two women in Waterstones are standing in front of a poster: "Antonia Fraser in conversation with Rachel Johnson about her new book, *Must You Go?*" the poster says. "Friday 26 at 7pm. Tickets £3, redeemable against cover price of book." One woman is heard telling the other loudly, "Well, I'm certainly not going."'

I met the writer Gilbert Adair at Kitchen & Pantry on Elgin Crescent, to ask if he would be our film reviewer. He explained that going to a screening and writing up the review takes two working days and that the first thing a film critic does when he is sent details of a new film is to see how long it is, and that anything over 100 minutes was to be avoided. He didn't seem very keen.

I rushed home to put on my new silk Bree Van der Kamp-style

blouse, bought specially from West Village for tonight's event. White wine was flowing in the Green Room – i.e., a back office at Waterstones. Antonia was resplendent in a sort of black and white zebra coat with a red lining. The first thing I did was tell her she looked beautiful, which she did. Then she told me she had an idea for a column: a woman of distinction and mystery (a mysterious look crossed her distinguished face as she said this) described an item of clothing she has kept for years and why. 'Like this Jean Muir coat,' she said, gesturing to the zebra. 'I've had it half my life, and it's still going strong.' Having just had an inconclusive conversation with G. Adair about a culture column, I am struck with what I regard as inspiration. 'What a good idea,' I said. 'We should call it "This Old Thing".'

When we go on to the shop floor, the events manager tells us the mics are broken. So we sit on raised office chairs as if facing Magnus Magnusson. 'Hello to all my descendants,' smiled Antonia. The crowd included two of her six children – Natasha and Benjie – and one grandchild.

I launched my cheeky first salvo: there'd been some family reaction to the fact that Sir Hugh Fraser MP, Antonia's first husband, to whom she was married until she had her midlife *coup de foudre*, got shortish shrift in the book. 'So, Antonia,' I asked sweetly, 'what first attracted you to the rich, internationally renowned playwright Harold Pinter?' She either didn't pick up or totally ignored the implication and replied that when she first met Harold he was rude and disruptive and he'd told her that he was rude and disruptive pretty much all the time. 'So I can't say I wasn't warned,' she said, with her superb smile.

She revealed that Harold was a non-observing Jew. 'He made his Bar Mitzvah, but only to pick up the money,' she said. 'He said that he needed it to buy a copy of *Ulysses*. But I'm not sure I believed him.'

During questions, she was asked by a wild-haired man at the back if Harold had contacted her 'from the other side'. She appeared to ponder this for ages, and then said that one day she knew she had to go to his grave. So she took a cab to the cemetery, in Kensal Green, and when she got there she found a languid youth contemplating Harold's unmarked grave. She engaged him in conversation, and he told her he was an aspiring playwright who had come to pay his respects to Pinter. 'He was from Hackney,' she concluded, shortly before revealing that Harold voted Lib Dem.

PS. Harold's grave is now marked. I had this from Antonia:
'In lines from the top it reads:

HAROLD PINTER

PLAYWRIGHT

NOBEL LAUREATE

BELOVED HUSBAND

OF

ANTONIA FRASER

October 10 1930–Christmas Eve 2008

'He typed out everything himself in 1992 except, clearly, the terminal date and "Nobel Laureate", which I added on the grounds that, if you've got it, flaunt it. It was such a relief that he wrote "Playwright", which he also had on his passport, so when people made other helpful suggestions I was able to rebut them. They ranged from "Poet" to "Polemicist".'

27 February 2010

John Dower and Weslife came to do a final and rather unexpected last interview with me at home in Notting Hill, to provide a final scene for the doc. As it was Saturday, Ivo was in bed upstairs reading papers and drinking tea, a ritual he can extend to Sunday night if necessary. I was in jeans and T-shirt. They've come because, apparently, Channel 4 think the doc is still too tame. So poor John Dower is having to recut to provide a posh *EastEnders*, complete with shriekings, firings, sackings, and all into one 48-minute episode rather than muck-spread over twenty-five years.

'It's got to be all blood on the carpet,' said John, dolefully. He is a real filmmaker and doesn't like being told what to do, how to cut, etc. As a result of this ding-dong – John says he has made an intelligent, nuanced documentary, where the main characters are multi-dimensional, etc. – the viewing of the edit has been cancelled in order to give Optomen more time to make the doc embarrassing and buttock-clenchingly awful for the principals concerned, i.e., me and Ben.

The Lady 12p

A WEEKLY NEWSPAPER, 20th MARCH, 1975

6 pages about
BEAUTY
hair—
skincare—
slimming

on offer
King's Pattern silver-plated cutlery

MARCH

1 *March 2010*

Joan – the lady on Classifieds who wears the fluffy slippers, who has plastered her office walls with studio portraits of her collie called Meesha – is having a birthday celebration.

AS KATH MENTIONED AT THE END OF LAST WEEKS SUPERB
STRAT & DEV MEETING IT'S MY 50th (five hail Marys for that one)
[said Joan]

FEEL FREE TO POP DOWN TO CLASSIFIED FOR HALF A LAGER
AND A ROLLMOP ANY TIME FROM 12PM
LOOK FORWARD TO SEEING YOU LUV JOAN X.

I realized the invitation was not so much for me, but for Coco, to whom Joan is devoted and brings in doggie treats. I sent her an email saying that Coco would be sorry to miss the herring and stout but I was thinking, 'Fifty? She looks at least sixty!'

Made me feel very old as my big Five Oh is in six years and seven months.

2 *March 2010*

The sales team here is henceforth led by tall blonde glamazon Helen Robinson, Ben's newest hire. Hels – as she is known – wants us to find sponsorship for our various columns. So I have emailed all our regulars asking them to come up with ideas for corporate sponsorship.

> Dear much-appreciated columnists [I whizzed round], As a revenue-raising *Lady*-saving exercise, can you all come up with suggestions as to who if anyone might be prepared to sponsor your cols., as Martin Miller Gin does the letters page? i.e., Mary Killen, who writes about life in her Wiltshire grottage – Rescue® Remedies; Clemmie, our gardening writer – some seed company; Sarah, who writes about her allotment – sheds; James Le Fanu – indigestion; Penny, weekly diarist – Moët et Chandon/Beecham's Resolve, etc. etc.?

Mary has emailed back her list for possibles – includes Eggleston Hall, the finishing school, Sheepdrove Organics, Norland Nannies and Aga.

Sarah Langton-Lockton has come up with Wyvale (garden centres); Gabriel Ash (upmarket greenhouses); Hunter wellies.

Penny Smith, the *GMTV* presenter, opera critic and diarist, says, 'I have a feeling I might not be able to do anything which was sponsored . . . being a news bunny and everything.'

I have decided that I am going to approach Elizabeth Grant of Astroglide to see if she wants to sponsor my ed's letter and, if she doesn't, I feel confident Replens will.

I have discovered that Joan of Classifieds is not fifty but seventy. She looks marvellous for her age. Like many of the fantastic characters here, she is both past retirement age and has worked here almost all her life. You gotta hand it to the Budworths. They are old-school, paternalistic employers of the first water. Once people come into the cream-and-eau de nil HQ of Bedford Street (a sort of pauper's Fortnum & Mason), they never leave. I'll probably be wheeled out of here in my bath chair. Or so I hope, anyway.

My lunch guest today was Mrs Budworth. 'This is a terrible

restaurant,' she said to me when I arrived in Terroirs. She had suggested lunch; I had booked it. And I was paying. Not even Ben. 'It's terribly noisy!'

She clearly wasn't happy, so I beckoned to the waiter. 'Can we move downstairs?' I asked. There are leather booths and a bar on the lower-ground floor; it's not quite so rackety. An odd look crossed his face.

'You should know that the associate editor of *The Sunday Times* is downstairs,' he said. I peered and saw Eleanor Mills, the journalist who'd been given my column by John Witherow/Susannah Herbert, resplendent in a grey wraparound dress. This was rather eagle-eyed of him, I must say. It was where I'd taken Els for lunch (actually, she paid, as I'd given her instant quotes for her piece which I had suggested to Sarah Baxter on the key topic of 'Sleeping Your Way to the Top'). I greeted my old *Sunday Times* chum warmly and we were soon ensconced at Mills's table downstairs and she was happily at ours in the window.

Then Mrs Budworth dived under the table and did a cavity search of her capacious handbag. After rootling she withdrew a long, handwritten list of complaints that covered both sides of the A4. Then she swept aside cutlery, napkin, glass, etc., as I gazed on aghast.

'Let's start with My List,' Mrs Budworth said in a determined voice, as she laid it flat on the table. I went pale. I thought we were going to have a lovely ladies' lunch!

Her list ranged widely from the photograph we had chosen of Nancy Mitford ('Such unfortunate legs,' Mrs B. said. 'Why on earth didn't you cut her off at the petticoat?') to a typo on the '*Lady* and the Royals' piece in our collectors' 125th edition.

After having lumbered me with two large coffee-table books about Suffolk painters and ordered me to review them ('They only came out in early 2009'), Mrs B. asked me if she could write a column about rural life.

'I regard myself as a complete country mouse!' she said. I blenched and grabbed a waiter's sleeve. 'Get me a drink!' I ordered. I definitely needed a tissue-restorer. 'Yes, madam,' he said, handing me a wine list. 'You choose,' I said, thrusting it back.

The list was followed by complaints about Tom, chat about Arline, discussion of Ben's management style, of which I only said complimentary things – i.e., he was perfect for the job and very nice – we did have a lovely lunch. Apart from the filming at Deerbolts Hall, Earl Stonham, Stowmarket, Suffolk, for the documentary – when Ben had headed her off when asked about Buttons – she revealed she hadn't spoken to her son since Christmas, when they had a fight because he wouldn't do what she said he had to do at *The Lady* and put the magazine, and the other directors' interests first, and hers second.

I agreed it must be annoying for her that she couldn't have free rein at *The Lady* but she still had to hold out the olive branch.

'What would you feel if you heard he'd been knocked off his bike?' I said, knocking back my white Burgundy. 'He's your SON.'

'He hasn't said sorry yet,' she said, gathering her things and stuffing the list back into her handbag. 'The word is "sorry".'

I left the office early as it was the tenth birthday party for Mumsnet, hosted by Google in Victoria. The dress code was 'Boden', so I rushed home to put on a cheeky gingham blouse and skinny jeans. We arrived – as one does – shortly after the Prime Minister, as the motorcade double-parked in Victoria Street alerted us. There were two officers in yellow hazard jackets on the door. We went upstairs to the Google canteen (we were taken there by a runner who Reception referred to as 'a Googler'). A huge cake, home-made biscuits decorated with icing and hundreds and thousands, Moët champagne, lots of media, Johnnie Boden, Justin and Sarah Webb, Kathy Lette, thousands of female journalists, Labour ministers, etc.

Justine Roberts, the founder of Mumsnet, made a funny speech about how the Mumsnetters had bullied Brown over Biscuitgate (when he refused to reveal what his favourite biscuit was). Gordon Brown paid tribute to his wife Sarah and referred to himself as Mr Sarah Brown. Then Sarah Brown spoke in broad mockney paying tribute to Mumsnet and her DH (that's Mumsnet for 'Darling Husband').

3 March 2010

Went over to Claire to check a headline, and she was working away at a pattern of interlocking 'L's on her Mac screen instead of the Joan Collins cover. I recognized the pattern – it was the same pattern of 'L's that adorns the *Lady* carrier bags that we give away in Gatwick as part of the global promotional drive for the mag. She was playing with a red banner that went diagonally over one corner. 'AS SEEN ON TV,' it read. 'Why are you putting "AS SEEN ON TV" on the bags?' I asked.

I thought, not even Ben would regard the forthcoming *Cutting Edge* documentary, in the same strand as 'My Daughter Grew Two Heads' and 'Half-ton Mum' and 'The Man Who Turned into a Tree', as a *selling point* to potential readers.

'Ben said to,' she said, clicking the banner into green to see if it worked better. 'Because of *Corrie* and the documentary, he says.'

Corrie! Oh yes. What's happening here is that *The Lady* is being flashed up on a forthcoming episode of *Coronation Street*. In honour of this, we have had to mock up a cover image of *The Lady* with Joanna Lumley on it, so when this screen-flash happens the newsstand edition and the one on telly seamlessly match. We have failed to secure an interview with Joanna Lumley to accompany the cover image, but Ben is undeterred by this tiny detail. His thinking is, when viewers see the magazine on the small screen, they will all rush out and buy *The Lady*, and we must encourage them in this subliminal impulse, by sticking 'AS SEEN ON TV' on carrier bags at Gatwick Airport.

Upon further investigation, I find out that the way the magazine features in *Corrie* is that someone finds an escort by dint of putting an ad in *The Lady*. And the escort is none other than housewife's favourite – Nigel Havers.

Ben is full of expectation of soaring circulation when 1. the documentary and 2. the product placement of *The Lady* on *Corrie* explodes on to an unsuspecting and wondering world.

I began to get it. It's another of Ben's stunts, and it might just come off.

Big news! Having delayed the doc (because C4 wants John Dower to make it more moronic than it already is), *Cutting Edge* has now re-instated it for 9 p.m. on 18 March, as another doc has 'fallen through' for legal reasons and they need to fill a hole. With the '*Lady* & the Revamp' doc. That's in, like, *two weeks*. Got this from little blonde Becky.

We have just heard from Channel 4 that they are now putting the *Lady* doc back in the schedule for tx [transmission] on 18 March. We were really hoping for more time but it's a good slot and it means we'll be very current!

The cut is being worked on and we hope it will be in good shape for you to view next week. We'd like to invite you in to try and work something out.

Just so you know, C4 publicity will want to release a rough cut or some clips to print press this week. It means we'll get mentions in the listings, which we want. We will be able to get later cuts out to reviewers nearer the time.

Oh Jesus.

I have told Ben I am not doing publicity for Optomen/Channel 4. That's *their* job.

Got back from watching Oliver play football against the Oratory outside Reading. Ivo drove, so I could catnap. The publicity stills from Channel 4 arrived – but I couldn't open them until I got home. They are beyond hideous – dark, slightly out of focus, I look like I'm auditioning for a role in the Baader-Meinhof gang. And married to Ben.

So I pinged off frantic email to Becky.

> Becky! Have you seen the stills? Ben and I . . . *ugh* . . . we look like a
> pair of warring married undertakers on non-speaks in a funeral home.

The Welsh writer Roger Lewis's interview with Sharon Osbourne has landed. He has called it 'Secret Bud of Pleasure' in honour of a sticky and intimate passage in her novel about a pushy mother who wants her daughters to be 'bigger than Oprah'. He clearly had a lovely time with Sharon, whom he describes as 'bang tidy' after extensive renovations both to her exterior and interior.

I emailed congratulating him on a brill piece and for inserting an allusion to the clitoris both in the headline and in his piece.

'Oh, is that what it is? I had no idea,' he said in his email back. 'In any case, I always thought a Clitoris was something you kept in a cage and fed on Trill.'

I marched into the boardroom and found Ben listening to Dire Straits loudly on his iTunes. 'Good news,' he said. 'The 125 cover sold 33,800. A few could come back, of course. And some more good news. We made an actual profit last month. A small one, but a profit.'

4 March 2010

It was sunny for literally the first time in four months, but still freezing bloody cold. I was walking down the Portobello at 8 a.m. and I heard one trader say to another, 'Turned out nice again today,' in chirpy Cockney tones that couldn't fail to cheer. When I got to the office I swanked to Ben about the Mumsnet party. 'Why didn't we think of Mumsnet?' he said, as if he blamed me personally for this failure of spark. Then he told me about his website wheezes to rival Mumsnet's popularity and reach.

1. www.sitonmyfacebook.com for people who were fed up with Facebook and wanted casual sex.
2. www.unpcworld.com for people who used internet porn on their computers at work but don't want the guys from the IT dept to find out when they examine the hard drive. 'A number of Budworths and Blezard were among the first to sign up,' Ben said.

The Channel 4 team finally finished today. This involved me doing various so-called 'pick-up' interviews out of sequence about Arline and Lindsay. I had to pretend they were recorded not now, but months ago in November and December last year, when I was hissy-fitting about Arline still being listed as 'editor-at-large' on the masthead, and before we knew Lindsay was leaving, and also of course before the Stefano redesign.

So they filmed me in the boardroom wearing my Bree Van de Kamp silk ruffle-sleeved shirt. They handed me old copies of *The Lady*, with the old-style covers, such as one with a white-haired lady stroking a kitten on her lap, so that I could publicly mock them.

I did this for a bit, and during a change in the lighting I started reading an interesting article about bowel cancer. I was gripped. I cried, 'I take it all back.' The presentation of the piece was – like everything about the magazine then – shatteringly dowdy, but I had to admit that that actual article was useful. But of course they won't use that bit – me being nice about *The Lady* of bygone years when it was edited by Arline – because it shows me being reasonably human, and giving credit where due.

But the truth is, I could see why the readers loved it as it was at that moment. It was reassuring, and informative. It was not remotely concerned with being on trend. There was, I can see now with hindsight, something so old-fashionedly dull and kind about *The Lady* magazine from around the Coronation until about November 2009 that it was almost magnificent.

At the Strat. & Dev. meeting at 4 p.m. Lindsay read out an elegant and dignified speech about having had a marvellously rich eighteen years at *The Lady*. She named the highlights, such as going to interview Norma Major, and attending HRH The Queen Mother's funeral, not to mention endless travel.

At 6 p.m. I was filmed leaving *The Lady*, to provide an ending for the doc. As my get-up was a black anorak and horrid leggings, I didn't want to be beamed into the nation's living rooms in this chav outfit. So I borrowed freelance journalist Viv Groskop's coat. She'd come in to chat (am continually surprised by the keenness of freelancers, so I've asked her to interview Mumsnet's Justine Roberts, and Boden's founder, Johnnie Boden).

I had to repeat the 'leaving *The Lady*' money-shot of me exiting the glass, gold-embossed double doors on to Bedford Street three times with different expressions. As I did so, Ben and Viv (who was waiting for me to give her back the coat) were joined by a small crowd of onlookers who had gathered to laugh and point.

5 March 2010

Email from a freelancer:

Hello Rachel.

I've recently been to Buckingham Palace to interview HRH The Princess Royal about her interest in lighthouses, which you may

already be aware of. [ed's note: can he be serious?] I interviewed
her on behalf of a private-circulation magazine issued to a group
of UK lighthouse enthusiasts called the Association of Lighthouse
Keepers. [ed's note: no kidding!] The interview duly appeared in
their quarterly journal as an A3-sized 'Royal Supplement'. It caused
much favourable comment from everyone who read it, [ed's note:
I'm taking this on trust] and it has been suggested to me that with a
bit of a rewrite to take out all the technical 'jargon' that cropped up,
it would be of interest to a much wider audience [ed's note: again,
I am taking this on trust]. Her interest in lighthouses is fairly well
known in the media – mainly because of her alleged fondness for
'lighthouse-bagging' (a term she hates) but in our conversation she
was particularly chatty, open and honest about other aspects of her
enthusiasm that are not so well known.

I am nonplussed. On the one hand, our readers love the Royals,
as they do Labradors on sofas and home-made autumn chutney in
larders. But a whole interview about Princess Anne's interest in
lighthouses? Not so much, I suspect.

I shove the email in a folder in which I put all pitches and pro-
posals and invitations to speak I can't quite face confronting that
second and hope, in time, will go away.

The in tray:

- a proposal for a 'Diary from a Provincial Lady' from a reader
  in Hampshire called Dinny who would like me to give her –
  surprise! – a regular column. She sends some sample cols.: on
  playing the organ, and gardening, and a survey carried out by the
  UK Bee Farmers Association. The survey was on bee keepers,
  surprisingly enough, and discovered that 10 per cent of bee keepers were dead, 20 per cent were called John, 30 per cent had

beards, and 75 per cent were 'getting on a bit'. She adds, 'And 100 per cent were sartorially challenged. It seems I am married to a stereotype.' I will send Dinny a nice letter. It's really sad, but we don't have space! *The Lady* already has more columns – what with Mary Killen, Penny Smith, Clemmie, Dr James, Sarah L-L, etc. – than the Parthenon, and my dearest wish – to have Debo on board as agony aunt – remains unfulfilled!

- a letter from an Oxford reader complaining about Joan Collins's appearance on the cover: 'Are you trying to give us angina?' and the Penny Smith col. I get a lot of complaints about the Penny Smith column. Readers don't like her, because she is very pretty and frisky and funny.
- a letter from a 99-year-old reader, a Miss Fluck in Skipton, saying she is cancelling because her business partner has died. She conveyed her sadness at the end of a long tradition this represented, a tradition which started when her grandfather returned from Manchester Cotton Exchange on Friday afternoons bringing a copy which had to be kept in a 'mint state until Sunday p.m., when Mother would ask for quiet from the children and recline on the settee. This must have been ninety years ago.'

8 March 2010

First thing, went to a sort of media screening place with a cappuccino bar in reception – soooo Soho – to view the rough cut of the documentary, which is being voiced for the moment, until they find an actor, by John Dower.

Ben arrived mob-handed with a TV lawyer, James Herring from one of his PR companies and brother Adam. John Dower was there. I thought he'd be shitting himself, but he was very cool. '*The Lady* and the Revamp' had some laugh-out-loud moments but mainly I watched through my hands. To see oneself prat about and witter on is, truly, the theatre of embarrassment. I stared at myself. At the beginning I was pink and blonde and plump. By the end, raddled and sunken and grey-faced.

When the credits rolled, in order to foreclose any nitpicking from the Budworth side, John Dower strategically reminded Ben that he'd joked on film about filling a paddling pool with custard and getting me and Arline, Janina and Lindsay to strip off and wrestle in it. Also that he had suggested bricking them into the cab office where they both work, which Lindsay referred to as the 'gulag' in the film. And he also just mentioned that Ben had also said, 'Rach is my ho now.'

And, he concluded with meaning, Dower hadn't included any of those bits in the final cut!

There was a moment when I appear to say that Lindsay was on the 'deathlist' which made me wince. How could I? And a worse moment when I let rip (under duress – the Budworths were less than impressed by my *Sunday Times* magazine coup) and said that '*The Lady* is a piddling little magazine that no one cares about or buys . . . sorry . . . I didn't mean that.'

Ooh yes, and they announced they want Richard E. Grant to voice it. Withnail himself! Swoon.

The in tray:

* a letter from Mrs B., thanking me and running through a few items she hadn't had time to bend my ear about during our lunch at Terroirs. She enclosed a cutting from 1974 written about *The Lady* by Philip Howard of *The Times* on the occasion of the *Lady*'s ninetieth birthday, describing the mag as a 'rock of decorum in the shifting sands of permissiveness and unLadylike behaviour'. I feel there is an underlying message here for me somewhere . . .

- an unsolicited article called 'The Art of Being Polite' about the importance of 'Ps&Qs'.
- a letter from a linguist in Switzerland who served in the WRNS cracking the Enigma Code offering us the text of her talk, entitled 'A Very Personal Pre-dinner talk about Bletchley'. (I add these to my pile of pitches about Bletchley, amazing mazes and modern manners, which I receive on a daily basis.)
- a letter from a reader in Henley offering several ideas, including one called 'Trust me, I'm a witch' about her 'career as a suburban witch'.

Ben said he thought he'd buy *Reader's Digest*. I was appalled. What was he thinking? 'If it makes sound biz sense and you have the money, fine,' I managed to say. 'If your ambition is merely to be seen as a player in publishing, not fine.' I spoke with feeling, as last week we did not have enough money to pay the contributors. This is not the first time we have had cashflow problems, and I sense it will not be the last. Ben explained later that he would buy *RD* minus pension obligations with money raised from mortgaging property and it all made perfect sense.

John wanted A. A. Gill, the TV critic of *The Sunday Times*, to get a copy of the documentary and review it. Said the 'ritual kicking' by A. A. Gill was 'a rite of passage'. I emailed Gill asking for his address and reminding him of the last time we'd intersected.

I loved sitting next to you at dinner, especially when you told me my nose was too big and I was too hideous to appear on TV and that the *Lady* doc was going to be suicidally shit soooooo

where shd the producer send it so you can have your wild hunches confirmed?

Got this back:

Down the toilet obviously

Sent from my BlackBerry® wireless device

When I said this was chippy he flashed this:

Do stop sounding like menstral sloan [sic]

Sent from my BlackBerry® wireless device

10 March 2010

Predictably, the number-one story running on the *Guardian* Media website is that *The Lady* is considering making a bid for *Reader's Digest*. Words fail me. I don't think we have enough dosh to pay the printers this week. But Ben is all fired up, bushy-tailed, seems utterly serious.

The in tray:

- a copy of *Fashion in the Time of Jane Austen* published by the Shire Library (the bliss!) with a note saying, 'I'm confident you will find the book of interest', which indeed it would be if my world was rocked by line drawings of an early-nineteenth-century redingote of cream silk trimmed with swansdown, a development I certainly don't rule out at this stage.
- an invitation to lunch with the Prime Warden of the Goldsmiths' Company Rupert Hambro at Goldsmiths' Hall on 5 May.
- a copy of a book by Lady Ashcombe called *Behind Castle Walls – at Sudeley Past and Present* with a picture of the author standing on manicured green lawns in front of a massive honey-stoned, crenellated, herbaceous-bordered Poshtershire pile. Lady A.'s people have been in touch, i.e., like several million others,

she has demanded a column. I flipped through and read an amusing-ish anecdote about a mix-up one morning relating to a paying visitor to the castle who some peon thought was the plumber, and was called upon to attend to an unpleasant and ongoing situation in the children's bathroom.

OMG! There is stuff in the *Radio Times* on the doc. They call it outrageous, shocking, sad and brutal in turn, and the reviewer ends, 'Compulsive viewing.' Oh. My. God. I have banished the doc from my mind already – so horrified by what I saw of myself on screen, screeching, 'Deathlist!', rolling my eyes when Janina speaks, and going on about sackings as if I edited the *Sun*, not some genteel, cosy women's weekly that still has a place in the nation's heart. The doc goes out on Thursday next week, and in it I look and act as if I'm a cross between Kelvin MacKenzie and Tina Brown instead of a middle-aged mother of three trying to revitalize an old and dusty women's magazine with only plentiful tea-towels at her disposal.

I have to face up to reality – I am going to be a figure of utter ridicule and hatred in only a week's time.

Meanwhile, I have been quietly fuming about Adrian Gill calling me names. On the other hand, after the doc comes out, I might well look back on 'menstral sloan' (sic – Gill is dyslexic as well as rude) as one of the nicest things ever said about me.

11 *March 2010*

Lindsay is leaving tomorrow, so I took her out for coffee. We sat in Caffè Nero and I complimented her on her Thane of Cawdorish approach to her retirement (nothing in her life became her like the leaving, etc.).

She sipped herbal tea and, to her eternal credit, said only nice things of all her colleagues. Lindsay asked me how I got on with

Mrs B. and told me that I was lucky Mrs B. didn't try to make me run floral-tribute covers instead of my forty-something ladies. 'She always used to try to make previous editors have pictures of vases of violets,' Lindsay told me, as I goggled in disbelief. Really, every day here is Wonderlandish – three impossible things happen before teatime.

Gillian is proving worth her weight in gold and now seamlessly tells time-wasters who want to know whether I'm going to run their piece on dry-stone walling to send an email to Vicky instead. And never fails to offer me a cup of tea with a smile.

The in tray:

- two letters to Coco, whose column has already attracted two offers of sponsorship, one from Pet Protect and one from Por-kinson's Bangers. One of the letters is written as if it were by another dog and is signed 'Many tailwags from the Borders'. One is from Leyburn, North Yorkshire, enclosing a parish magazine containing the collected works of Polly, a cocker spaniel. I read it and decided it was much better than 'Coco's Corner' (the only reliably popular thing in the mag apart from the Ladygram). I must raise my game.
- an email from Becky Clarke:

  Sent: 12 March 2010 19:23
  Subject: C4 trails

  We've just seen the trails. They will start running this weekend, I think. They are v. lively! X

Oh yes, heard today from a source who has insisted on remaining nameless that Arline was putting it about that she wanted me to get a terminal illness and *The Lady* to fold.

Crikey. This is probably just malicious gossip – although I'd want me to die too, I'm sure, if I were her.

15 March 2010

'Three cancellations already this morning,' said Ben.

He puts it down to the fact that C4 has started 'trailing' the documentary on *The Lady* that's going out this Thursday, i.e., in three days. I was sitting quietly in the playroom yesterday watching *Glee*, and the trailer actually CAME ON. I had the horrible experience of seeing me on screen, telling Ben to 'grow a pair of balls' and stropping about saying that I wanted to sack people. Milly was sitting next to me. 'Lame,' she commented. Frankly, this documentary will see off the remaining readers in their seventies and may fail to bring new ones on board and could be a kamikaze mission after all . . .

The in tray:

- an invitation to the Society of Botanical Artists Silver Jubilee Exhibition.
- a huge presentation box of Tian Hu Shan Pure Tea in exotic, fragrant flavours.
- Rococo Easter mini-eggs in a box.

Lindsay has left the building. When I came in this morning, she'd left a picture of Lady Gaga on my keyboard and she'd written a speech bubble coming out of her mouth saying, 'Put me on the cover and *The Lady* will fly off the shelves.'

16 March 2010

Circulation figures are only just peeking above 30,000 again, according to Nic Boize/B-Cal. This was for the Joan Collins cover. She is a big star. And we can't get above 30,000. I am in despair.

What do our readers want? Luckily, an email from a reader arrived to tell me: a 'nice landscape scene' or 'some flowers on the cover'.

I called brand expert Peter York, co-author of *The Sloane Ranger Handbook*, for his advice. Basically, he said we had to be 'naice', with our pinkies out. We were the anti-nasty, anti-trash magazine for gentlefolk, he said, a print publication with a 'functional base' (translation: we are read only by either employers or staff).

'But we have to keep the brand going with the editorial,' I said. We agreed that *The Lady* was a micro-trend magazine which would always venerate the Royal Family and would endeavour to remain reasonably reassuring in a world full of uncertainties. I wittered on until we both had to go – me because Radio 2 had just arrived to ask me the difference between being a lady today and being a lady in the age of Vera Lynn, him to give a speech.

Our brand analysis was inconclusive. Being 'naice' is not going to butter many parsnips.

The in tray:

- a letter thanking me for speaking at the Wellbeing of Women lunch at Fortnum's last week and a voucher for a complimentary facial.
- a letter from a Wimbledon reader expressing approval at my changes, and so on, leading to a huge BUT: 'However, I do have one huge complaint. For some years now you have offered lovely nightwear during the summer and winter months. Quite frankly, a nightie length of 42 inches on me would not cover my nether regions once I was in bed . . . surely you could offer a few of the short-sleeved nightdresses in a longer length? I personally take a length of 54 inches, but would settle for 50 inches.' I carry it out to Gillian. 'This one's about a woman who wants the nightie company that advertises with us to produce a short-sleeve one in 54 inches. It's your lucky day.'

- a letter addressed to Arline Usden pitching a 700-word article about having your own supply of truffles, accompanied by a selection of photographs of the tuber.
- a copy of a new publication by a group called Christians Aware called 'Food, Festivals and Faith'.
- a press release from an outfit called ToDryFor promoting a new collection of designer tea-towels.

With perfect timing, just as I was opening this last item, Viktor (the *Lady*'s Bolivian housekeeper, who emerges from the Fred West basement every morning to rod radiators, hang pictures, sprinkle rat poison behind biscuit-harbouring safes and fridges, etc.) came into my office and handed me a freshly laundered pair of blue and white tea-towels. Everyone else gets one; only the editor gets two. If there's one thing I don't need, it's more tea-towels.

Trailers for the doc are now running on a loop on Channel 4.

Ben is in full overdrive and has put up a huge banner on the website saying, 'Channel 4 Viewers Click Here', which directs them to a special offer: five issues of *The Lady* for £5! He has also increased bandwidth or something to the *Lady* website in expectation of millions of hits following transmission on Thursday night.

17 *March* 2010

An email arrived from my pet webstalker Jimmy Burke, which I reproduce in full.

Ms Johnson,

I have just learnt that your brother has been confirmed as Conservative PPC for Orpington. I wonder whether dreams of political office have started to occupy your idle moments too?

If so, I beseech you to resist. I know the temptation must be tremendous, and I'm sure you know the perfect people to provide the parachute, but think of the country.

After all, if you can commit such egregious crimes against journalism with a few bashes of a keyboard, imagine the damage that could be done if you were entrusted with something that actually mattered!

Regards,
Jimmy

A call came in. Gillian said in a tentative voice, 'Rachel, I've got Deborah, uh, Duchess of Devonshire on the line. Shall I put her through?'

'Oh all right then,' I said. 'Put her on.'

Debo is ninety at the end of the month, and the papers are full of her. She has tentatively agreed to be a cover girl for us. First we talk about the lovely party *Tatler* and Penguin have just given her for the reissue of Nancy's novel *Wigs on the Green* at Claridge's.

Then she moved in for the kill. 'You were so very kindly talking about me doing a cover for *The Lady*,' she began, then paused. 'To bore you further . . .'

Her timing was wonderful. I shouted with laughter. '"To bore you further" is what my children say to me when we are talking about arrangements,' she said. Then she explained that she felt very over-egged at mo what with Stoker, her son and heir the current Duke, saying the aristocracy was finito in an interview with Camilla Long, an interview he gave to publicize both the reopening of Chatsworth and her ninetieth-birthday exhibition. So we agree to delay the cover till her book – *Wait For Me* – was out in October. 'There's a marvellous picture of me in a long taffeta skirt, you see,' she said. 'That can be your cover.'

We parted fondly then I remembered – she's star of the docu-
mentary on Thursday! So I called back and got her PA, Helen
Marchant. 'We've already pinned a large sign to the TV to remind
Her Grace to watch,' she said.

Ben bounced in to tell me – it's Wednesday – that he's briefed
all the diaries about the programme and leaked embarrassing
things about me before the doc is aired tomorrow. This doesn't
sound good. 'Such as?' I asked.

'Oh, that having you as editor has been like having a new puppy,'
he said, terribly pleased with this. 'Everyone loves the puppy very
much but it does leave messes about the place for others to clear
up.' Somewhere else he described me as a 'firework' that you lit
and you weren't always sure whether or where it would go off.

Janina has been asked – not by me – to compile a list of all the
writers, and so forth, who have contributed so far under my editorship. There are sixty-three names on the list. Ben was talking
about this and sounding pleased over lunch. I should have smelt
rat. When I go upstairs to the marketing nerve centre – i.e., the
room that B-Cal shares with Piers the computer guy – B-Cal was
working on a genius wheeze, which was to put something on the
website saying '63 Reasons to Read *The Lady*' followed by a list of
every Tom, Dick and Harry from Toby Young to Kimberly Quinn
who has contributed a piece over the past six months. 'I don't think
that it's right to project the magazine on the basis of one person
who has written one article for us back in 2009,' I said.

18 *March* 2010

Doomsday.

We had a 'celebration' day-of-transmission lunch with Becky
and the legal chap from Optomen in Scott's in Mount Street.

When the wine waiter came along Ben ordered a bottle of white wine and announced that he intended to spend the next forty-eight hours in the pub. Janina sent me emails every five minutes.

John Kercher (the father of Meredith, the student Foxy Knoxy was convicted of slaughtering) keeps sending in story ideas via email. It turns out he is an old-time contributor to *The Lady*. Today I felt a rush of compassion and agreed to let him file a diary. Obviously, in the hope that he will be moved to write about his daughter. One has to be ruthless. History of the Hampton Court Maze – no. How I felt when my daughter was killed in brutal sex-game by Foxy Knoxy – hold the front page!

It's low of me, I know, but I am in the business of selling magazines, despite the 'Journal for Gentlewomen' tag round *The Lady*'s neck.

I don't watch the doc going out as I am at a 'small kitchen supper for locals, very casual', i.e., a sit-down catered dinner on our communal garden for about thirty given by the divinely beautiful artist and mother of six, my neighbour Nicola Reed. When I switch on my iPhone at 10.15 there are seventy-six new emails and a bundle of texts. And twenty-seven voicemails. I haven't listened to them yet.

19 *March* 2010

Had sleepless night worrying about having been portrayed as a hatchet-wielding Rottweiler on nationwide TV. Also made fatal mistake of going online at midnight and putting the words 'Rachel Johnson' into Twitter and Google. OMG.

Apparently I am a 'talentless whore' and 'look like Boris in drag'. Some females tweet they have girlcrushes on me. There are whole threads on Mumsnet devoted to trashing me and analysing my wallpaper. Feel incredibly exposed. As for this morning's papers . . .

In the *Guardian*, Nancy Banks-Smith wrote crushingly funny piece correctly linking *The Lady* to P. G. Wodehouse's Milady's

Boudoir. Banks-Smith compared me first to Aunt Dahlia and then my management style to Boudicca (at one point I say, 'Ben's a dear boy, but he hasn't wielded the hatchet enough'). When it got to the bits with Paul Blezard – the doc made it look as though I sacked him in my first meeting, when I didn't – Banks-Smith wrote, 'The literary editor was slaughtered on the spot.'

The Times reviewer was good on the *Lady* readers. 'The old-guard readers emitted the *joie de vivre* of a funeral parlour: one was so steely as she described Rachel's "silly" changes that you suspected her extensive ornament collection might become a murder weapon.' The *Times* review ended with my Ratner moment and quoted me: '"In the real world this is a piddling magazine that no one cares about or buys," she shrieked, before ducking half an octave for, "Sorry, I didn't mean that . . ." (Come now, Rachel, stay real . . .)'

Felt very odd this morning. Have had masses of reaction, but the truth is I only really care about what the people in Bedford Street think. Last night at 2 a.m. I sent an email to Janina saying I hoped she and her mum were OK, and there were no hard feelings on my part, and let's all push forward to the sunlit uplands of 40,000 a week.

But she hasn't answered. I want her to be OK.

Gillian has lost no time in passing on the horrified reaction of appalled readers to the doc who have written in their droves to editors@lady.co.uk – our generic email address for anyone who wants to contact Editorial. We have had thousands of them. My inbox brims with both bile and a sort of stunned approval.

Interesting documentary – absolutely aghast at Rachel's comments relating to the *Sun Times* article – stairlifts & incontinence pads. Rachel might need incontinence pads herself one day.

Outraged by RJ's comments!!!! I'm over sixty, buy the magazine from time to time. Rachel's comments were ageist. Even if you use

incontinence pads, you can still think, you still have feelings, you're
not sub-human. She should be sacked on the spot. What she said is
illegal. Who does she think she is?

I love the bit about what I said being 'illegal'. People actually
want me to go to prison for saying stuff.

We've all been supportive to Boris up to now but Rachel's attitude to
people is appalling, has probably alienated viewers. I am forty-nine &
I feel alienated by her comments. I always enjoyed the magazine
hitherto. Dreadful to previous editor who has done her best over
the years, she was treated like a criminal, dreadful treatment. There
used to be an innocence to *The Lady* magazine & if I wanted to read
about Jane Fonda's great sex I'd buy *Marie Claire*. Sharon Osbourne
is not *Lady* material, nor is Joan Collins.

One man wrote in saying that my ideas for modernizing *The
Lady* were feeble and what we needed was a 'pet page that could be
about that new pet cleaner that just came on the market and the
London Zoo – a different animal each week, and have a plant and
exotic plant page'.

One of Gillian's emails that morning started thus – as if this was
her comment rather than a reader's – which rather put me off my
stroke at first:

Ben & Rachel,

absolutely disgraceful, I was cringing . . . to behave so abominably –
Rachel's attitude to mag & people who'd worked there for years. To
humiliate them like that . . . What does she think of herself? – crude,
obnoxious, ungallant. To talk about Arline & her daughter publicly is
disgraceful. Dumbfounded. Silly questions to Duchess of Devonshire –

a wasted opportunity. Arrogance of calling the shots! No humility or I'll tread softly approach . . . if it's so piffling, why does Rachel want to work here? No comfortable feeling at end. I've always liked the covers – much better than Kelly McGillis, say. It was a wonderful opportunity which has been wasted. Everything is brash & common now & Rachel Johnson has spoilt it all. All my friends found Rachel utterly obnoxious.

But it turns out she is merely conveying the comments of a 'Mrs. R., buys it from shop, been on a *Lady* holiday. Lives in Cotswold village, Burford.'

Still, I regret several things. *Je regrette beaucoup*. One, telling Ben to grow a pair of balls. As David Sexton said in the *Standard*, 'She was not in awe of her boss. It's one thing to observe "You live in a bubble," another actually to issue him the straightforward command, when he wouldn't do what she wanted: "Grow a pair of balls!" Few men hear that whispered softly in their daydreams.'

He went on.

By the end, *The Lady*'s circulation had gone up a bit. Will Johnson stay at the helm? She is now writing a diary of her time on the magazine. If it's anything like as entertaining as this larger-than-life documentary, it'll be well worth reading and a lot bloodier than anything to be found in Wodehouse.

I also regret my hobnail-booted manner with Paul Blezard and the rest of the staff, who appear to flinch whenever I enter a room.

22 *March* 2010

Spent thirty-six hours in Paris, where *Le Diable Vit à Notting Hell* (*Notting Hell*) has reached almost the top of the fiction bestseller list. It is number two. I am here to prop it up by whizzing past bookshops and doing interviews for France Info, France Inter, etc., *in French*. The weather is balmy and sunny, and after doing promo I went to the Beaubourg, where I stared intensely at Lucian Freud's paintings of walls in Holland Park, Irishmen in W11 and benefit inspectors in his studio in Notting Hill, and felt in two places at once. In the evening, I met Charlie Glass – the author of our celebrated 'humping the help' feature – for a drink before I hopped on the Eurostar. In the bar, my mobile rang. It said '*The Lady*' on the screen. Ben. His voice didn't sound quite right. 'Can you keep a secret?' he asked me.

'Of course I can,' I answered, downing my ice-cold Stella Artois in excitement and hurling a handful of peanuts down my throat.

'Well, B-Cal – you know, Nic Boize – came down a while ago. Obviously, not all the sales figures are in yet. It's still only Monday, and the week doesn't close till 10 p.m., but it looks . . . very . . . like . . .' He started speaking slowly, as if on horse tranquillizer.

'Spit it out, old boy,' I said, thinking, '35,000 if we're lucky.'

'Boize said he'd never seen anything like it, wasn't sure whether to believe it, but . . .'

'WHAT!' I screamed.

'54,000,' Ben said, sounding delighted.

I repeated the number several times, and said in a loud voice, 'Incredible, incredible,' while gesturing to Charlie Glass to pop up to the bar and order me another Stella. And – feeling like pushing the boat out – some more peanuts. This was a cause for celebration.

'It's all been worth it,' I said to Ben. I told Charlie immediately, then called Ivo from the taxi en route to the Gare du Nord, to share the good news.

It's not often – ever – that I can say I've had a top-three bestseller and almost doubled the circulation of a magazine in one week. So I am going to say it tonight (am sitting on Eurostar with laptop) because the chances are I'll never have the chance to say it again.

I am thrilled, and proud, and happy. For the first time since I can remember. And all I know is this – it'll be back to square one tomorrow, the book will be sinking down the charts and the doc will be forgotten, so I'm going to enjoy this while it lasts, and milk it for all it is worth.

23 March 2010

I don't know if I have the fortitude to record what happened today.

It started with me surging into the boardroom latte in hand, on a high after posting record figures. Ben's face fell when he saw me. 'Come in, come in,' he said, lifting his bottom off his chair as if going into a *schuss* down an easy blue run. He does that when I enter a room. Still. Even after I said he had to grow a pair of balls on national TV. He has lovely manners. Then he dished the bad news immediately.

''Fraid B-Cal got it wrong,' he said. 'It's not 54,000 after all.' I sank down into a Chippendale chair and placed my Caffè Nero paper cup carefully on the blue baize covering the boardroom heirloom table. 'Go on,' I said, cursing B-Cal privately.

I had been really, really happy last night, thinking I'd turned it around and all the flak around the doc was worth it because I had doubled the circulation, and now, of course, I find out it was a mirage. 'He misunderstood the EPOS (electronic point of sale) figures,' Ben went on. 'It's probably still north of 40,000, mind, and we sold out in Sainsbury's.'

Apparently, the best B-Cal can come up with, based on progress-of-sale gross estimates, is that we will sell, as a result of the doc, between 38,000 and 45,000. Now, between 38k and 45k is quite a wide margin – as Ben said, B-Cal would have quite a good career as an ERNIE-style random-number generator – but it's a lot better than 27,000, which is where I was when I started. Oh well. We fight on. We fight to win.

Gillian and I decided what we would do with the literally hundreds of letters and emails and telephone messages we've had in this week was this. Bundle them up into folders and get a workie to come in and answer them all.

All was going OK until Ben ordered me to join him for lunch at Leon on the Strand. I pottered into the boardroom clutching my wallet and Leon loyalty card, and he started saying something and I started saying something, then he suddenly snapped.

'This has got to stop. No interruptions! I need to have a hearing on discipline with you. No. More. *Interrupting!*' He almost roared.

I studied his face to see if he was joking. He is quite a student of management theory and sometimes talks about being a follower of the 'sandwich method' of dealing with staff, whereby you squeeze in something unpleasant between two nice things, in a sort of shit toastie. I still can't decide but, not unnaturally, he is fed up with people telling him I walked all over him in the doc.

The moment passed, and we trotted to Leon and had a nice lunch, during which he warned me that there was a rearguard action underway to make out I had completely sunk the magazine. He intimated that dark forces were plotting to have Ms Usden and Ms Fulcher reinstated in Bedford Street in a moving ceremony, while I am ushered out of the building via a back exit on to Maiden Lane. It appears to be being orchestrated by none other than Mrs B.

As a result, she has soared in my estimation. She simply can't forgive me for not loving and venerating the magazine as it was when her father ran it, and before I got my hands on it. And she is acting – as no one else will – to save it from moral ruin.

But I think Ben will stand by me. I'm his hire. He picked me out of a line-up of twenty-two others, after all (having said that, I have subsequently learnt that I was blackballed by at least one director-brother, but Ben ignored this). On the way back to the office he insisted that he walked the street side of the pavement. He always does this, as if worried that a brougham is going to career out of control at any point and come crashing into us, and if it did, the gentleman should take the impact.

After lunch I was getting back to work, thinking things were back to normal – phew – when I heard a commotion in the subs room. I heard chairs being pushed back, and nervous laughter. I heard Gillian falter, 'Yes, she is,' and then with a roaring sound Mrs Budworth entered my office, encased in a navy twinset. 'You wretched girl, I'm going to MURDER you,' she said in a loud voice. She stood four-square in the middle of my office, almost shaking.

'What were you thinking of? Why aren't you jumping out of the window at the sight of me?' she bellowed. Her gaze was trained on my Maiden Lane window. Outside, on the other side of the street, towards the modern building above the horrid pub saying that J. M. W. Turner was born there.

I sat down, having politely risen to my feet at her unannounced entrance.

'How. Could. You. Say that awful, awful thing you said, about how we were a piddling magazine no one cared about, or read? You MONSTER,' she said, settling down in one of my dainty chairs.

'I did take it back immediately,' I reminded her. In the next breath. My mouth had gone very dry. It sounded pretty feeble.

'But too LATE! TOO LATE!' she said in a raised voice. 'It is what everyone will remember. And it has been picked up. I read it in *The Times*, and the *Telegraph*.' She looked towards my window again, as if I was expected to auto-defenestrate on the spot.

She went on handbagging me. I tried to explain that the crew were here for six months, and filmed for 400 hours, and had caught me red-handed in one unguarded remark, but there was no placating her.

'You've done yourself no favours, I'm afraid. As for us . . .' She made it quite clear that if *The Lady*'s nineteenth-century pre-eminence, its circulation figures of 70,000, even 80,000, were never regained under my watch, it would be All My Fault, and that I had brought a horrible taint of modern nastiness to the magazine that was heretofore sugar and spice and all things nice.

I tried to steer her away from my Ratner remark and said I really regretted saying it, which I did, still do, and would do anything to take it back, but I can't. Then I said that I wouldn't mind in the least if the directors – i.e., her, Ben, Adam, Willy and Richard – wanted to sack me. I said it. 'Why don't you sack me if that's how you all feel,' I said, looking her straight in the eye.

She dropped her gaze. 'It's all right for you,' she said. 'You've got your career ahead of you, or you *used to!*'

At this point we both burst out laughing.

Eventually, I offered Mrs B. three pots of Lovedean cranberry and almond granola as a peace offering (have a whole crate of Lovedean and a whole crate of Dorset cereals that won't fit in my in tray) and steered her out of my office. 'Consider yourself murdered, dear,' she said as she left, tipping the mini-pots of granola into her huge black handbag.

I felt shattered after that but I knew it wasn't over yet.

Mrs B. had said – *inter alia* – that the Duchess was also 'incandescent'. So I called Edensor vicarage. Some flunkey told me Her Grace was in the garden. An hour later, she called back. 'Hello,' she said in a flat voice.

'Debo,' I began, feeling dreadful. 'I called to apologize. I'm so sorry that my remark about "piddling little magazine" caused such upset.' And then the Dowager Duchess let me have it too, along much the same lines as my previous handbagger, Mrs B. She asked me if I was considering my position.

'How could you sack that nice literary editor who'd been working for the magazine for forty years?' she asked. 'How could you say that awful lie about "piddling magazine"?'

Now, of course, the facts are these: Debo's father, David Mitford, was general manager here from 1911 to 1914 and took it so seriously that, according to legend, he spent his time ratting in the basement with his pet mongoose. And Blez had been working here for only two months, and was sacked by Ben for going AWOL and having his copy sent back nine times by Sarah Kennedy, the interim editor, but I just didn't have the heart to defend myself, or my big mouth, any more. I felt really, really sad that I had let them both down and had allowed the daylight of modern-day documentary broadcasting in on what they both clearly consider to be the magic of *The Lady*.

25 March 2010

After the ordeal of the Mrs Budworth ambush, I have been feeling unaccustomedly shaky. I went in to Ben and gave him my Diana look (from beneath lowered eyelids). 'Come and see Uncle Ben, sit on Uncle Ben's knee,' he said. Like me, you can never keep Ben down for long. He's a cork too. 'Do we have to put you on suicide watch? Take away your shoelaces?'

Then of course I protested that I was fine. He then asked me if I was going to resign. I said no. We passed the issue for 30 March, and tomorrow I go to New York with Milly, for her super-sweet sixteenth birthday, and nothing's going to ruin it. Ha ha.

Have got Gillian to photocopy a catholic selection of both horrified and approving letters to the office since the broadcast and send them to Mrs B. and the Duchess of D.

The in tray:

- a letter from a man from HMS Prison Brixton called Peter Wayne congratulating me on my 'Herculean effort revivifying *The Lady*' and offering his services as a contributor to 'The Gents' or, failing that, a true-life account of how the Duke of

Devonshire (Debo's late husband) saved him from arrest in Hatchards and came 'rising to my rescue like a superannuated Sir Lancelot'.

There are so many letters and emails after doc, of which below is a classic example.

From: Gillian Spickernell
Sent: 25 March 2010 11:38
Subject: reader call

Mrs Betty Ruggles from London SE1 rang:

Sharon Osbourne appalling, the likes of her! As for Penny Smith! I don't want to know about her silly little antics during the week! I'm not a subscriber, buy it when I want something to read. Been buying it sixty years. How on earth could you put Sharon Osbourne on the cover?! I saw the last 20 mins of documentary & can't imagine what advice the Duchess of Devonshire will give if she's to be an agony aunt.

Luckily, as I was leaving Bedford Street yesterday, staggering under weight of muesli, granola, Rachel's yoghurt, etc., that I had been sent by PRs following my appearance in the 'What I Ate Yesterday' slot in *The Times*, a girl plucked my sleeve. 'Hello,' she said. She had black hair, Alice band, white face, red crimson lipstick, and was working the shorts-over-woolly tights look. 'I loved you in the programme. If you ever want an intern, someone who would work for free . . .'

'As it happens, I do,' I said. 'What are you doing next week?' She is called Agnes Frimston.

It's as if there is an unwritten rule that dictates everyone at *The Lady* has to have a name from a Barbara Pym novel.

26 March 2010

Well, Ben had a meltdown at last. It had, in fairness, been brewing for weeks.

The trigger was the interview (over the phone) with me in *Campaign* magazine, the house journal of marketing and advertising. The piece started – and I paraphrase, as I am catching up with this diary in the business centre of the Plaza Hotel, Central Park South, New York:

> *The Lady* has had more publicity in the last six months than in its whole 125-year-long history. And it's all down to Rachel Johnson. Before the arrival of new editor Rachel Johnson, the only time one would expect to hear of *The Lady* was on *Have I Got News For You*'s niche slot sniggeringly poking fun at ultra-obscure publications like 'Ukrainian Goatkeepers Weekly' or 'Tractor Part Monthly'.

Ugh.

I didn't know the piece had come out, so it sat between us on the blue baize table as he went on. I was trying to leave the office to make my transatlantic flight, for springtime and my daughter's super-sweet sixteen in New York. Because it sure as hell wasn't springtime in Bedford Street.

Then Ben let me have it. Said I'd used the magazine and abused the magazine for my own fell, self-serving purposes. That I had trashed the magazine publicly (the 'piddling little magazine' comment will, I suspect, haunt me for a while). It was all about me, me, me, and when I gave interviews I never suggested that I was standing on the shoulders of giants, never referred adequately to the illustrious 125-year history of the organ, nor made it clear enough that there were a multitude of departments slaving away night and day to put the magazine out there. He was most outraged to read my answer to the question, 'What is the PR strategy?' – 'I am the marketing strategy.'

To sum up, it was all a bit www.racheljohnson.com and not enough www.lady.co.uk for his liking.

I didn't interrupt, because I worried that if I did, in order to say, 'But Ben, you hired me to make a splash, and to get everyone talking about the magazine. What matters in PR is not so much what people are saying but the volume of sound. We can't control and dictate exactly what other media outlets are going to choose to run with and emphasize, but the important thing is that they are paying attention. In that sense, I have executed your strategy of hiring a high-profile editor and revamping the editorial and creating buzz . . . To The Letter.'

Instead, I sat there staring at the blue baize while he told me exactly what he thought of me, wondering whether I should go back on my previous answer and chuck in the towel, i.e., resign – and at least I would make my flight. I tried not to look at my watch – I had to be at the Virgin Atlantic check-in in less than two hours, and hadn't even packed or picked up Milly, fifteen and three-quarters, yet. Finally, he looked exhausted and said, 'Sorry. I had to get that off my chest.'

While Milly and I were on the Heathrow Express he rang to see if I was all right. Which was a relief. Of course I was all right. I did think the documentary, and the reaction to it, were very hard on him. John and Becky made him out to be a flippy-floppy public-school boy, me the alpha-blonde ball-breaking new broom. It was a caricature. I haven't exactly emerged unscathed either.

But he was definitely the one who took it for the team.

27 March 2010

In New York. Got an email (one of many) from Janina. 'Mrs Budworth called for you.' I forgot to say. Janina has dyed her hair blonde. Several pitches have arrived by email:

- 'I enclose two articles on the theme of petsitting,' writes one aspirant contributor. 'I do have several more of this ilk!'
- a wonderful piece written by a lady in Earley, Reading, on an old typewriter on the end of the war in 1945, with lines such as, 'One thing we have missed lately has been the great friendly noise of our bombers going out on their heavy raids.'
- one called 'tea-time traveller' about how to find proper tea in a proper teapot in the UK (pics available on request).
- a letter on the same lines (these things always come in pairs) saying, 'I enclose a 930-word article with suggested illustrations on the subject of cricket teas.
- a letter saying, 'I enclose a 700-word articule [sic] with suggested illustrations on the subject of pillboxes.'

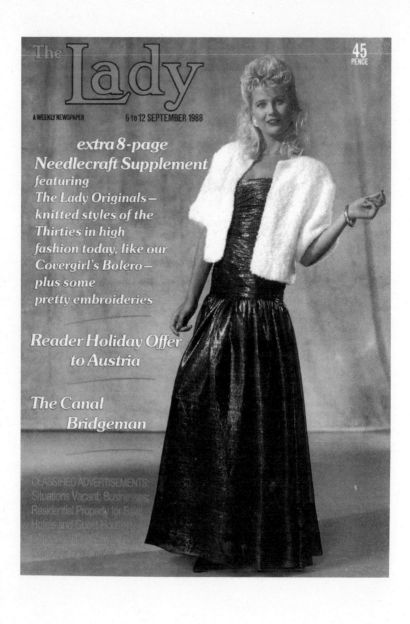

APRIL

1 April 2010

The *Mail on Sunday* has begged me to participate in a piece in which I grow potatoes for charity and see how I get on compared with other 'celebrities'.

I declined.

They emailed again saying how incredibly keen they were, and listed the other 'celebrities' who had leapt at the chance of some free self-publicity. They mentioned that they would donate £500 to charity if I just chatted about my green fingers for a few minutes over the telephone. 'You don't even have to do a photoshoot.' As I can give the money to the Parkinson's Disease Society, which is a noble and worthy cause I have a personal interest in (my mother has Parkinson's), I obliged. They agreed to send a sack of peat to the *Lady* office, and some seedlings.

The piece duly appeared in the *Mail on Sunday* with a huge picture of Anthea Turner crouching over a grow-bag, flicky hair, gardening gauntlets and huge smile all in place.

It's the great gardening trend of the year! At garden centres all over Britain, potato-growing kits are being snapped up by families eager to experience the taste of their own fresh spuds [I read in amazement].

But the big mystery is: how many potatoes can you get from one grow-sack? The *Mail on Sunday* has asked seven very different personalities – from politician Vince Cable and Radio 4 inquisitor

John Humphrys. [My name is unaccountably not listed.] We have
equipped each of them with a grow-sack, compost and five Vales Emerald seed potatoes and given them ten weeks to produce the best possible
crop. The delicious and heavy-yielding variety Vales Emerald is popular
as a salad potato. The winner, who will be chosen by BBC *Gardeners'
World* presenter Toby Buckland, will pick up £5,000 for a charity of his
or her choice. Here our contestants tell of their expectations . . .

If my as-yet-unborn potatoes win, then the *Mail* will give £5,000
to Parkinson's, so whatever it takes, my spuds have got to be bigger than Anthea Turner's, even if it means sending Gillian to the
Tesco Metro on Bedford Street for a packet of Finest.

6 April 2010

A huge grow-bag of peat has arrived. Which is lovely. There's only
one snag. The bag containing five seed potatoes and the trowel has
disappeared. I can't imagine who would bother to steal a bag containing seedlings. So I am going to lose! To Anthea Turner.

7 April 2010

It is the middle of the Easter holidays so we have lined up three
covers in advance. This should enable me to get out of Bedford
Street. They are, in this order: Liz Hurley looking toothsome in
tweed lying on a bale – cover line 'A Role in the Hay'; Tracey Emin;
and Johnnie Boden. I had just landed in Palermo airport when my
iPhone told me I had a message. It was Ben.
He has had major wobble over the Tracey Emin interview.
I was half-expecting this as, when I went to the 'beauty contest'

in Bedford Street back last summer, the one little tip Ben gave me
before I went in front of the board, i.e., Ben, Adam, Richard and
Willy Budworth and their ma, was that his mother, Mrs B., absolutely loathed Tracey Emin. So I duly announced during my
coronation that *The Lady* would have no truck with the mouthy
baggage, her rumpled and unsavoury bed, her abortions and her
Tampax. 'We would not be touching her with a mile-long bargepole!' I added for good measure.

Needless to say, months later, Tim Willis, ex-*Sunday Times* style
editor, has secured a major interview with her, written it up
superbly and I fully intend to run it in *The Lady*.

In the course of this, Emin talked about possibly voting Tory, her
childlessness and riffs – and this was the bit that gave Ben pause –
about how needlework, through the ages, since the Bayeux Tapestry
until the present day, has been a brilliant displacement activity for
women who – unless their idle fidgeting fingers were otherwise
occupied – would be masturbating instead.

So Ben now wants to circumcise this interview and remove all
allusions to needles and wanking – a private pleasure he for some
reason (he is Old Harrovian) refers to as 'bean-flicking'.

I said this would be OK had I not put out this fire once already,
to whit, I had gone into the office on Maundy Thursday, and I had
warned the reader in my editor's letter that the interview was
strong meat. Carolyn had even suggested that we run a cover line
saying 'Emin Uncensored'.

The argument is, you either move forward, or you don't. You
either run stuff that's going to move the goalposts a bit, or you just
carry on providing the same old pabulum of cobnuts and cucumbers. If you try to keep all the old readers happy while enticing new
ones in, you risk losing *all* your readers.

So as we navigated Palermo airport and tried to find the Sciacca
road, Ben said, 'Having read a lot of the letters from the old guard,
I can't stop worrying. I can't sleep at night. We've got this tricky

business going, where we don't want to alienate the old readers before we get your news on board.'

So he wants to cut the interview, remove all the nasty bits about body parts, and shove it online. Then he gave it away. 'I can't imagine what Mum would say, you see, if she read about . . .' and mentioned bean- (or was it bead?) flicking again.

I knew it! The whole cover interview will have to be pulled – all because Ben is frightened that Mrs Budworth will have the vapours. I felt my blood freeze in my veins. Then I took a deep breath. Was I being reasonable with the old family mag's doughty readers? Forget Mrs B. – would the Tracey Emin remarks about masturbation pass the what-would-Debo-think test?

No, they wouldn't.

So I told Ben to go ahead and circumcise the worst bits of the interview. After all, it's his magazine – it's their family money. Not mine.

Next up I foresee a problem with the Boden cover. I adore Johnnie more than life itself and have known him since we were both in our twenties, but Claire hadn't got a clue who he was and his PR people have so far failed to come up with a picture of him that will fly off the shelves, apart from one of him grinning as he clutches Sprout, his terrier, which has already appeared elsewhere. And I edit a magazine called *The Lady*. Not *The Bloke*.

8 April 2010

In Sicily. More emails from Janina.

Sometimes people become convinced that 'underneath', I am boiling with suppressed emotion. As Janina put it, 'You could do a Malcolm Lowry with your volcano.' It makes me want to reassure them that underneath that icy exterior, an even more glacial interior can be discovered.

Janina has found out that we are giving an email interview to the Media *Guardian* next week and has sent me an 800-word briefing note, plus points to make and topics to avoid. Meanwhile, I have whinged to Ivo in the Michelin two-starred Rocco Forte restaurant of the Verdura Hotel (we have escaped for three days with the children) about Emin, Janina, etc. He was very sound.

'Darling, it sounds as if Ben is right. Maybe sometimes you have to accept that your readers don't want to read about wanking, they'd much prefer a nice piece about embroidery. Now can we stop talking about *The Lady*? This isn't a romantic dinner at all.'

13 April 2010

Back from Sicily and in office.

Ben needed persuading, as I predicted, to run Johnnie Boden on the cover with my suggested cover lines, 'Ginger Tailor Soldier Spy' and 'Jolly Boden Weather'. My keenness to run with the Boden cover is given fair wind by the fact that the other cover possibility is Jenny Agutter and the pictures make my heart sink very slightly. They look somewhat *sludgy*. They make you realize why editors put photos of fifteen-year-old, six-foot Ukrainian honey-limbed models with eyes like infinity pools on their covers, not sixty-something actresses. It's not fair, it's not right, but it's how it is.

And as I said to Ben over lunch (in which we mainly talked about problems to do with staff), if we were going to survive having people on the front of the magazine every week, i.e., fifty-one contenders for the cover each year (Christmas is a double issue), we would need to diversify. We would have to have the occasional man. I explained that Johnnie was a seriously good egg, best of British, etc., poster boy to launch our England Special on 20 April. Then I added my clincher. 'And Johnnie's holding a terrier,' I said as I crammed my face full of fried eggs on toast with chorizo in Terroirs.

'Last time we had a terrier on the cover – it was a cover with a

terrier sitting in front of an Aga with the cover line "Aga Louts" –
it sold really well.'

The in tray:

- baby brioches with delicious crisp sugary topping from an
  outfit called Napket Snob Food.
- tons of letters and pitches and bags of cancellations from readers
  who say I have despoiled their homes by putting Tracey Emin on
  the cover. I have had to draft a statement for the PR people:

  > I stand foursquare behind my decision to put Emin on the cover.
  > She may not be a dab hand at hospital corners as far as bed-
  > making goes, but Tracey Emin, RA, has reminded a male-centric
  > world that so-called traditional housewifely skills such as needle-
  > work and quilting are in fact an art form, and always have been.

- one upset reader called Patricia writes, 'If I wanted trash there
  is plenty of choice ... words fail me. What is wrong with a
  beautiful picture of the countryside or animals or buildings?'
- one from a reader saying she liked the documentary and has
  taken out a sub which ends, 'Oh, by the way, I'm pleased you've
  kept the office dog, Coco, on staff!'
- a pitch for a piece about Harris Tweed: 'No longer scratchy
  boys' jackets that never wear out'.

But my favourite was from a lady who has been invited to a
Garden Party at Buckingham Palace in July. She pointed out that
as a forty-year-old mother of two boys, getting shipshape for Her
Majesty will cost upwards of £600, and that to add to her woes, she
is not a svelte size 16 but a size 28, and wonders (I don't see the link
but there we go) whether I will do an issue on Social Etiquette to
help her out? 'For me this is a once-in-a-lifetime event and I
wouldn't want anything to go wrong.'

14 April 2010

As predicted, the Tracey Emin cover has exploded in our faces –
like her cleavage erupting from her Vivienne Westwood dress. The
lead story in 'Londoner's Diary' is titled 'It's all getting a bit racy
now at *The Lady*'. There are pictures of me grinning and tossing
blonde hair smugly. Picture of Tracey Emin doing her sideways
gurn. 'When RJ took over as editor of *The Lady* she promised to
drag it kicking and screaming into the twenty-first century, but it
seems that some subjects are still off-limits . . .' etc. Long exegesis
explaining the difference between our two versions of the Emin
interview, one in the mag minus bean-flicking, one online complete with bean-flicking, and how lily-livered I am.

I went into the subs first thing Wednesday morning and they
were poring over it. 'It's back to the bad old days,' said Lindsay
Pine, who is second-in-command to Chrissie, 'When no unpleasant subjects could ever appear in the magazine.'

'Not that masturbation is unpleasant,' I added.

Am waiting for Ben to come in to post-mortem the *Standard*
and talk about the lines to take tomorrow, when the Media *Guardian* come in at 10 a.m. to interview us both.

I am also waiting for him to decide whether to remove his
mother's executive powers and kick her off the board. Blimey, it's
like a daily soap opera. Where are the cameras now?

It's like Wisteria Lane, only with less Botox.

15 April 2010

Media *Guardian* in all morning to interview me – i.e., persuade me
to put foot in mouth.

'Are you serious about this job? How long are you going to stay?

What's it like editing a magazine when the family is breathing down your neck all the time? How do you get on with Mrs Budworth?', etc.

I parried and puffed. I said I loved the job, which was true. I said that I understood the family's sensitivities and desire to see *The Lady* remain the repository of all things nice and remain sensationally bland. I did admit that it was hard not to run a taste test on articles like the T. Emin masturbation piece without worrying, 'What will Mrs Budworth think?' I liked the girl who came, Emine Saner, *very* much. She was a beautiful Turk (almost but not quite an oxymoron, American cheese, and am allowed to say this as am proud of my own Turkish blood). Afterwards, I warned Ben she'd talked a lot about the Emin interview. Whenever Ben mentioned bean-flicking, he made a circular movement with his right hand, like a chauffeur rubbing a speck of guano off the bonnet of a car with a moistened forefinger. This was very very disconcerting.

Later Joan shuffled in to pet Coco wearing a new pair of the fluffiest, whitest slippers I've ever seen, as if she had attached a pair of newborn spring lambs to her tootsies, and handed me today's post.

The in tray:

- a registered delivery of two new short stories, one called 'Waiting' and one called 'A Twist in the Tale'.
- an A5 postcard from Harold Pinter's only son, Daniel. In this lengthy postcard he accuses his stepmother, Lady Antonia Fraser, of a number of things and says she is aptly named the Lady Killer (as she reviews crime for us) because she is the Lady Who Kills. The postcard is big and crammed like an artwork with the tiniest writing imaginable and is still legible. 'If Lady A. is the Lady who kills, then who(m), I wonder, is the Lady who gets killed?' etc., etc.
- a letter from a lady called Rae Muddle (am not making it up) who writes from Bognor Regis saying, 'You poor girl! What a

lot you have had to put up with! I think you deserve a medal tolerating an editor-at-large and everyone hovering over you!'

Feel like having it copied round all the Budworths.

16 April 2010

Janina has finally agreed to take some holiday. I forgot to say that, yesterday, a chap came into my office to see me about something. Ben came in after he'd been in the office for under an hour.

After he'd gone Ben lunged towards my AC unit and switched it on. 'It's much too hot in here,' he complained. 'That poor bloke from the *Mail* was sweating like a rapist.'

I have decided to soothe ruffled Debo feathers by organizing a *Festschrift* for her birthday with everyone from Prince Charles downwards.

The in tray:

- a beachbag from Cabbages and Roses.
- glorious Michael Van Clarke conditioner, shampoo, and comb called '3 More Inches'.
- a tray of rocky-road brownies – YES! Big, big TICK!
- an invitation to Hogarthian Rout at Sir John Soane Museum from Rufus and Sally Albemarle saying dress code was periwigs and that sedan chairs would be at 11 p.m.

An excited email from Clemmie Hambro:

Hiya . . .

Sat next to Tim Bell at lunch today and so decided to ask him what *The Lady's* new marketing strategy was . . . he could only come up with an aged naked calendar, and getting people to write about shagging the nanny. I said you'd already tried that and everyone got a bit upset!!

21 April 2010

Everyone keeps asking me how *The Lady* is doing. Wellll . . . Since they ask.

After the doc, we topped 40k (the Sharon Osbourne cover, thanks to C4), and then the next week we were down to 36,000 (cover girl Joanna Lumley, after a few onscreen flashes in *Corrie*). But now we are back down to 31k, 32k, and yesterday Ben was in despair.

I think the problem is as follows:

1. Even if they want to, no one can find us in the newsstands. Newsagents buy two copies, and they get lost amid *Bella* and *Chat* and *Women's Weekly.* People will go into one newsagents and look, and they might even ask, but after that they will give up. As this email suggests:

    > It is little wonder your circulation is down. I can't find a copy anywhere! My local shop always had one and now it doesn't get that from the wholesaler and my local supermarket never has any copies. How can you boost your circulation if the magazine can't be bought?

2. If they do by some miracle find a copy of the mag (Ben will hate me saying this – he hisses, 'We're in most supermarkets, including Sainsbury's and Tesco, every Waitrose, and in 11,000 newsagents') and read it, the ads tell them they are in the wrong place. Even in the Johnnie Boden, bloke-on-cover, fresh-as-a-daisy issue we've just published on 20 April, there is a walk-in shower ad opposite my ed's letter, and then nothing till Tena Pants and Age Concern

on page 40 except for a few ads for comfy shoes and nighties (sorry, 'Night-Time Luxury'). We don't have many ads, and the ads we do have remind the reader that we are a rapidly ageing population and that we are all going to die, very soon.

3. People still don't want to shell out for the editorial. They are prepared to spend £1.80 to see if their ad looks nice, or to look for a job, but the engine of *The Lady* is still in the back, like a Citroën Deux Chevaux.

4. People are incredibly vain and age-conscious and still associate *The Lady* with their grandma. Or their nan. They feel it's not for them. No one wants their advanced age reflected back at them.

So Ben gave me a short but heartfelt lecture as I stood in the boardroom staring at the graph which showed our circulation falling off a cliff. 'I just feel very conscious about not losing any more of our old readers at a point when we don't have enough new readers to guarantee our survival,' he explained. This was the lecture no new editor wants to hear. Don't lose any of our old readers while you bring new ones on board – *or else*. 'That's why I wanted to tread carefully re: Tracey Emin' – Carolyn told me that when he used the word 'masturbation' he couldn't look her in the eye and blushed deeply – 'and your little forays into matters political. The three pillars of *The Lady* over the last fifty years have been: No Sex. No Celebrity. No Politics.'

'Have they?' I snapped. 'Well, in that case, why did you want a new editor, why did you want to update the editorial, and if that really is our mission statement in 2010, that doesn't leave us an awful lot to write about, especially in the run-up to a general election.'

He told me that I clearly hadn't read 'past interviews' with him in which he'd spelt out the magazine's 'mission statement', and explained the three pillars, etc., in words of one syllable. 'Where?' I asked. 'I haven't seen any of these supposed interviews.'

'Well, the interview in *Suffolk Life*, for a start,' he replied.

I said that, strangely enough, I didn't read *Suffolk Life*. 'Well, you don't know what you've missed then. It is a mass-market circulation magazine . . . in Suffolk, anyway.'

We are getting on very badly at mo. One of the reasons is – the numbers haven't *stayed up*. His strategy of getting a high-profile *editrice* on board, getting masses of publicity, getting us on telly, was all very successful. But it hasn't turned the magazine around. It has not been the Viagra he expected, the circulation-boosting little blue pill. And we are miles from selling the magic 45,000 copies a week, the critical threshold for advertisers. Below 45,000 we have no chance of snagging decent ads that don't just remind readers of their own mortality. So the magazine continues to lose money. Meanwhile, Uncle Tom – upstairs in abject luxury in his huge apartments in the Anne Frank annexe – won't allow him to sell the magazine. Even though – before, that is, Ben arrived hotfoot from the crocodile-infested Everglades – he'd been planning to 'slit the old girl's throat'. ('Slit the old girl's throat' is Uncle Tom's phrase, delivered with lip-smacking relish.)

If Ben sells up, his chances of inheriting the family silver in the shape of the Covent Garden property portfolio would go down Swanee. So he's stuck. It's a pig in a poke. Poor Ben. When he could be training pilots for Bristow Helicopters in Titusville, Florida. Or as he calls it, 'Hepatitusville', or 'Shitesville'.

I could see the despair in his eyes as he talked. As he went on, I took the *Daily Telegraph* off the table underneath the gloomy portrait of the founder and leant over the blue baize to read it. As he passed me to get something from the table, he smacked me on the bottom, with a rolled-up copy of a 2008 *Lady* which had an oil painting of a bunch of lilacs on the cover.

After this I returned to the boudoir, pausing only to ask Ros the receptionist how my potatoes are doing (I had to get the *Mail on Sunday* to deliver a replacement bag of seedlings). I haven't been to see them once, but Viktor has chitted them in and is under strict instructions to water them every day. They have sprouted lustily.

I know this because the *Lady* potatoes are his pride and joy, Viktor's screensaver on his mobile phone.

22 April 2010

Mrs Budworth has sent me a photocopied letter from a cancer patient in a hospice that she has received about me and the Channel 4 doc.

A hateful performance by a not-nice person who degraded long and faithful staff who kept the magazine going for years – was this so she could storm in and wreck it? [the reader/viewer wrote]

Until you stamp out her penchant for pushing herself into every issue [ed's note: that's weird, have ditched my own byline pic] most people will continue to detest the present magazine – not the changes *per se* but this brash, common tendency to stamp on everyone because she has a vulgarly-monied background [ed's note: I wish – the Johnsons have never had a bean].

Mrs B. has slipped in a note ordering me to 'Reply personally.' Sir Tim Bell, marketing guru, has had further thoughts. This from Clemmie:

Hi Rachey. Another thing SIR TIM asked was, are you interviewing all three leaders??

Also a special subscrip. offer for grandmothers to give *The Lady* to granddaughters or daughters . . .

Just passing on the PEARLS!!!

C xxxx

Just made a pilgrimage up to Mumsnet Towers to interview Justine Roberts. Or should I say, I sat there eating a delicious beetroot and ginger cupcake with lemon icing while Viv Groskop interviewed her. As I left I signed the visitor's book. There were only two names, feminist writer Natasha Walter, whose new tome I have just read, and PM's wife Sarah Brown. There was a space to leave comments, and I noted Mrs Brown had said, 'Thanks for the lovely biscuits!' and drawn some kisses. So I signed my name and left a crawly comment about cupcakes, suck-up that I am.

The travel-copy nightmare will never end. Before I got here Arline sent tons of freelancers and office pets on little trips as rewards, and the copy is still sitting on the system at *The Lady*. This is a typical email from a PR:

> I am contacting you from Axis Travel Marketing, we represent Cancun CVB in the UK.
>
> We did a press trip last year in July and had the participation of Lindsay Fulcher. I wanted to get in touch, to introduce our selves [sic] and also too [sic] see if you could give me an idea as to when the article is being published. I am preparing a report for my client so any news will be much appreciated.

The truth is, I could publish travel articles that are sitting in the 'Travel' folder from now for a whole year and still not run out.

24 April 2010

Have to go on *Newsnight* election 2010 special. Well, I don't have to, but I've been asked, and Jeremy Paxman is presenting, and the others are going to the musical *Hair!*, so I thought, 'Why not?', and said yes.

In Make-Up, Theresa May sat having pancake applied and, in

reply to a question about lipstick (Did she want some? If so in which colour?) replied, 'Pinky-browns.'

I made small talk about having been in Orpington to canvass for brother Jo earlier in the day. As a result, I know absolutely nothing about the Conservative manifesto, entitled 'An Invitation to Join the Government', a navy hardback, but all there is to know about free swimming for the over-60s in Biggin Hill. Theresa May clearly didn't want to be my new best friend (I am regarded as off-message by high-horsed Tories) so I shut up and closed my eyes while they made me camera-ready.

Then Harriet Harman came in, so I was sandwiched between Theresa May and Harriet Harperson, who – like Cherie Blair – is very pretty 'in real life'. Both MPs were wearing black slacks, little jackets and chunky jewellery and have had blow-dries. I haven't washed my hair for ten days. I looked at my neck anxiously in the mirror as the make-up professional eradicated the shadows under my eyes and my sun blemishes with Laura Mercier concealer. I felt a terrible pounding headache start. I asked the make-up woman for aspirin, but as a techie with an earpiece confirmed, the BBC is not allowed to give it out to guests. When I ask, Harriet Harman piped up, 'I've got a headache too.' Which made me like her. At least someone was talking to me.

Then it all started going pear-shaped.

I was brought on to the set with two comedians off the TV (Rufus Hound, Ed Byrne). I was placed to the left of them but – ho ho! – *to the right* of no less a personage than Nick Griffin, of the BNP. The symbolism of the placement did not elude me. When it was our turn we chattered on to Paxo about the election campaign and the debates. I said that up until the telly debates, the election campaign was like the Oxford *v*. Cambridge boat race, i.e., Labour and Conservatives battling it out to be head of the river every year. 'Then the Cleggasm happened,' I repeated (it was an inspirational coinage that came to me in Make-Up).

The studio went into shock. One of the comedians asked if I wanted a multiple Cleggasm. Paxo's eyebrows hit the ceiling. I pressed on. 'So it started like the boat race and then turned into the Henley Regatta, only it's still a festival event dominated by white, public-school middle-class males,' I concluded.

'Well, I don't think that Gordon Brown would agree with that,' said Paxo, who pointed out later that my analogy was not apposite as the Henley Regatta always pitted two boats against each other in a two-horse race. And Gordon Brown was not privately educated.

Still. Simon Hughes for the Lib Dems laughed heartily. Harman and May sat stony-faced.

When I got home from doing *Newsnight* with two comedians, and Nick Griffin, someone had already tweeted it and the Cleggasm was on YouTube. I know this because I was idiotic enough to check (the first rule of life – never self-Google).

'You were shite,' texted a friend who used to produce *Question Time* and who prepped Cameron for his second and third telly debates.

26 April 2010

Felt shattered.

Media *Guardian* interview out today, replete with pic of self lounging on orange *chaise longue* in boudoir. I was wearing a careful outfit of Hennes matelot top, Topshop blue-velvet smoking jacket, J Brand jeans and hemp trainers, to convey the message that *The Lady* editor is moving with the times.

I gave it the once-over. Immediately detected that Emine Saner, the creamy Turkish blonde interviewer, has been judicious and fair. Her piece was a jolly romp with the headline 'They may want someone lower key'. I paused over the pull-quote from me, 'I can't speculate as to whether *Lady* readers have masturbated but my wild guess is they might have done.' The *Guardian* cites our new soar-away figures (40,000 post doc, settled back to 35,000 and heading south) and quotes the publisher saying that *The Lady* is past the worrying point, i.e., we are not, in Lesley White's peerless phrase, merely wasting our time putting dancing shoes on a corpse. The piece was much nicer than I would have been about me.

I sent Ben a text saying I was having brekker in the Wolseley with adman Robin Wight, but added jokingly that I would be 'in for my spanking later'. At the Wolseley, I devoured eggs Benedict and a whole pot of coffee, and an order of crispy bacon on the side, while adman Wight told me it was all hopeless until we completely refreshed our advertising, and we should get in Kimberly Quinn, who is feted and famed for her ability to get luxury ads in *The Spec*.

'I'd love to get in Kimberly, she is advertising gold,' I replied. 'She's already come in, in fact. But if we got in Kimberly, 1. Ben would be out of a job and 2. we'd have to pay her salary.'

'Put her on commission then,' said Robin. To sum up, he said that until we get some high-end advertisers in, we were dead in the water. Given how many ads we do continue to have for walk-in baths, he's not far wrong there.

Then I went into Covent Garden.

Ben was furious about the Media *Guardian* interview. Just as he was furious about the *Sunday Times* interview, the *Campaign* interview and the Channel 4 documentary, and all the free publicity we've got – brackets, thanks to me, close brackets.

'We've got to get away from the jolly-japes, bedroom-farce type of article that keeps being written,' he raged. I couldn't think what he meant, then remembered there is a bit in the piece where I show Viktor the Bolivian housekeeper's cupboard full of loo rolls and Vim, etc., and tell Emine Saner that I like to push Ben inside it, that runs:

Pointing to an understairs cupboard in the corridor, she says: 'Sometimes I ask Ben to get something from the back, he goes in and then I shut him in!' What japes! I'd like to see John Witherow do that to Rupert Murdoch.

'This piece is nonsense,' he fumed, as he reread it in front of me, 'right up until the bit about the history of the cherry tomato.' He did some counting under his breath, like a pre-schooler in literacy hour. 'There are at least *six lies* in the piece,' he ranted. Leaving aside Ben's decision to call inaccuracies 'lies', I could only spot one. (Uncle Tom's flat is not sixteen-bedroom, it's sixteen-room . . . for now. He is gradually annexing more rooms, in a sort of Anschluss of our office space. He's taken the Thora Hird room upstairs, where I used to disappear for power-naps, and now he has his sights on several more rooms on the marketing/advertising floor. When asked why, he explained that his friends didn't like tramping all the way up to the top floor. So we are all being squeezed into the editorial and ground floors as a result, like rabbits in hutches.)

At all this, I felt a twinge of despair.

Then Ben told me that Mrs Budworth has called a board meeting in May to demand my resignation.

He also showed me a letter that Mrs B. had written in reply to a reader who complained about the documentary. Mrs B. had copied her reply to Ben. Her letter said, 'If I had my way, I'd have shown Rachel Johnson the door straight away!'

'Nice,' I said, and handed the letter back. She has always given me the impression that she regarded my entrance into Bedford Street as about as innocent as a fox prowling around a hen coop.

When I trotted back to the boudoir, Gillian forwarded me an email from a happy reader/viewer.

Dear *Lady* Magazine

On Thursday March 18th I watched a television documentary about the new magazine. I approached this with a completely open mind since my mother has been a loyal fan for many years and I have enjoyed her passing me her older copies. For her birthday one year I sent for *Lady* binders and receiving the magazine was a special moment in her week, especially since my father died in 2003. The *Lady* she loved was uplifting, interesting and interestingly quirky in a positive way.

At 49, I suspected that I was probably part of the new audience you might be targeting. I didn't tell Mum about it since she was already disappointed with the cynical tone of the new magazine and its attempts to be fashionable by upturning traditional values. My sister also watched. It soon became clear that the older ladies who spoke on the programme were the object of ridicule so my decision stood not to phone Mum, and I didn't. My sister did try and found an engaged tone so went back to the programme.

If only we had kept phoning her that evening. For she was lying alone on her kitchen floor having had an ischaemic stroke that lunchtime. She lay there all that night, unable to move or contact anyone. Her oven was on with her lunch in it. The following lunchtime her friend found her. Mum had been there for 24 hours and was in a very serious condition so I travelled in the ambulance with her to hospital in Bournemouth and phoned the family.

The irony for me is that, for part of that time, her loyalty to your magazine was being ridiculed on that programme with bickering, silly arguments and brazen rudeness. There was no acknowledgement to all the loyal readers who have kept the magazine going. They are not eccentric old ladies but decent people who have worked hard, treated others with respect and know far more about life than we do. They also know how to treat others with dignity and respect.

Mum is still in hospital with dysphasia and dyspraxia so she finds it very difficult to speak or express herself. She is learning to write with her left hand, having had beautiful handwriting and taught many children to read and write herself. She nursed my dad through cancer for three year without complaining until he died and still didn't complain. I am upset that, with the power you have, you feel it necessary to force radical change that verges on bullying. I am studying writing and I am interested in many kinds of magazines but I shall probably not be buying this one. Mum had just cancelled her subscription when she was taken ill. It just seemed very ironic that she was lying so ill and so alone whilst this programme was aired with all its bickering and docu-drama overtone.

Jane Dey

You couldn't Make It Up.

I have pushed it on to Becky and Pat at Optomen, so they feel guilty too.

27 April 2010

When I went into Ben's office the next day, there was a note on his desk. I read it upside-down. There were about ten points scrawled in felt tip on the back of an envelope.

'Sack the editor' was number four.

When he saw me reading it, Ben explained that, last week, he was summoned to the Royal Overseas League to have dinner in an empty dining room with his trustee, Jonathan Lawley. This was on the fiat of Mrs B. The trustee went through Mrs Budworth's agenda item by item.

'I see,' I said.

Nice email has arrived from Gillian.

Miss Lynn Barry from Northampton called. Been buying *The Lady*
from her post office for 40 years, now 61 years old. Thinks the way
Rachel has turned it around is nothing short of fantastic. Absolutely
brilliant! Miss Barry did Barbara Cartland's hair for years & years. She
loves the way Rachel is highlighting charities as well, such as the
Dogs' Trust.

According to Ben, Mrs B. is planning a boardroom putsch to
oust me *and* Ben, and install Adam as publisher and presumably
editor in May.

Meanwhile, the fact that Jo (standing as PCC in Orpington)
has been using the office to telecanvass has leaked.

This is lead story in the 'Londoner's Diary' tonight.

Tories find *The Lady* is for turning

How will the Tories beat the forces of Cleggmania? Simple – engage
the services of *The Lady*. The mayor's younger brother, Jo Johnson,
a prospective Tory candidate in Orpington (Tory majority: 4,947),
is using the offices of *The Lady* magazine, edited by his sister, Rachel
Johnson, to telephone-canvass for votes in order to see off the Lib-
Dem threat.

'As you may know, a few of you attended a telephone canvassing
held at *The Lady* on behalf of Jo Johnson,' says an email from Einy
Shah, a member of Johnson's campaign team, sent to party workers.
'On Tuesday May 4 and Wednesday May 5 we will be giving one last
plea to call the Cs (definite Conservatives) and Ps (Probable Conservatives) to get out to vote. Cleggmania briefly hit Orpington
but we need to call our voters and tell them to stick to the blue

corner ... we'll be relentlessly campaigning ... we need as many boots on the ground as possible. We need all the help we can get and would really appreciate one last push to get Jo elected in Orpington.'

It is certainly another sign of Rachel Johnson's pioneering approach to editorial duties. In a recent Channel 4 documentary she described her new offices as 'a cross between an undertaker's and a lunatic asylum' and said there were far too many fusty old members of staff there by dint of the hereditary principle. 'Ben's a dear boy, but he hasn't wielded the hatchet enough,' she said of her publisher boss, Ben Budworth.

Some of *The Lady*'s more traditional staff might be shocked to learn their organ has now been hijacked by 'dark forces' to serve the Conservative Party cause. The magazine has never been overtly political in its 125-year history. Staff were so confused as to how to operate a newly installed hand dryer they had to have their freshly laundered towels restored while they were given tuition on how to use the baffling contraption.

I slunk in to see Ben to receive another spanking for this. But for some reason he had taken this one on the chin, despite reminders that, when I got here, *The Lady* was a Jacques Tati version of goings-on in the Tudor court, with mothers passing on titles to daughters, falling down staircases, resident ghosts, and so on.

I asked Ben whether he wanted, following the *Standard* story, Jo to cancel his planned telecanvassing session. To his credit he said no and insisted that bro Jo should come in as planned. 'The crusade for common sense and the return of the Conservative regime must continue unheeded,' he said, rubbing his hands. I'd forgotten how 'sharply right wing', as Debo puts it, the Budworths were/are.

It also crossed my mind that the reason he wasn't furious was because he'd leaked it himself ... like he did the Dyson driers and the Emin masturbation.

Frankly, Ben leaks so much he should really be wearing a pair of Tena pants at all times.

28 April 2010

The Channel 4 'Lady and the Revamp' doc was repeated on Monday, so there's another spate of online comment, emails, and so on.

> I've only just caught up with this programme, and was mesmerized by Ms Johnson's mercurial tits. She came out of Rigby & Peller with both of them pointing in the same direction (natch – you get what you pay for at the great R&P), and then we saw her chairing an editorial meeting with the two of them slumped under her sweater like two tired puppies that were no longer talking to each other. Most distressing.

. . . blogs someone called Waldo.

The in tray:

- a letter asking me to consider a 'Poetry Page' enclosing a Kiplingesque cutting from the *Sunday Post* of 1970 which begins, 'If you would like to see a better Britain, a country worthy of its daily bread . . .'
- a letter from a reader called Cyril Bracegirdle who wants to write a column about antiques. He is kosher: he's written a book called *A First Book of Antiques* and *Collecting Railway Antiques*.
- Madame Arcati, a media blogger whose name for *The Lady* is the 'old cunties' weekly', has also blogged again:

> Astrologer Eric Francis foretold on Madame Arcati that masturbation holds the liberating key to better relationships in the

future. A sign that he must be on the right lines comes from Rachel Johnson in the *Guardian* today, invited for the umpteenth time to talk about her once-genteel magazine *The Lady*: 'I can't speculate as to whether *Lady* readers have masturbated,' she says, 'but my wild guess is they might have done.' I wonder if the magazine's stately owner Mrs Budworth has given the matter any thought.

There are small mercies. Thank God Mrs B. is offline at Deerbolts Hall, Suffolk, and only communicates by letter first, and telephone, second, and by loud hunting cries, third.

Someone has hacked into the website and replaced the biographies of our fragrant *Lady* bloggers – Meredith Ogilvie-Thompson, Tania Kindersley, Jane Alexander, Lucy Denyer – with spammed ads for female Viagra and date-rape drugs.

John Kercher's diary has come in. It's all about his holiday, and each paragraph begins with the word 'Then'. I stare at it glumly.

I can't make Janina deal with it, or even Lindsay, because they're not here.

29 April 2010

Emma Freud has refused to be our cover girl to accompany her eulogy piece on Clement. Quite correctly. You can't be on the cover of *The Lady* because your dad has died. So we are stuck. Until, that is, Judy hacked into Janina's computer and found all manner of goodies, among which was an email from *goddess* Olivia Williams, the slight and wounded star of Robert Harris's movie *Ghost*, in her inbox. Hurray! Hallelujah! Janina saves the day.

30 April 2010

Mrs Budworth rang to complain about the Camilla cover, which has HRH The Duchess of Cornwall in a pink hat adorned with pink roses. She asked to speak to Judy (Ros our receptionist is like GCHQ when it comes to telephone traffic, as all calls to *The Lady* come through her). 'She has a moustache like a sergeant major!' she told Judy, and then added a complaint about a wrinkle on HRH's upper lip. 'What on earth was Rachel thinking?'

When I got in, I stared at the cover and could see no trace of upper-lip down or what the French call 'a duvet' at all, not even the wispiest of summer-weight togs.

It is *Marie Celeste* on Fridays, which is why I try to work from home Fridays. Today when I went in there was no Janina, as she is still on holiday. No Claire the designer. No Carolyn (on some foodie jaunt to Helsinki). No Jess, as she only comes in on Mondays, and is having a baby in September.

Meanwhile, Chrissie chief sub is screaming for more help and earlier layouts from the design team. Tammy the picture editor has left for her new job at Corbis, and her replacement, Tamasan, also known as Tammy, has arrived and she doesn't work Fridays. So Tammy is the new Tammy. This from Chrissie:

Judy has just emailed me the bones of her chat with you re: getting Tammy Myers (i.e., old Tammy) back in as picture editor on Fridays when Tamasan (new Tammy) is off (forwarded here to you). I want to concur with what she says and add my view.

We really need to be able to send the magazine to press on Wednesdays in future. This means keeping up the momentum that we have attained this last week. The only way to achieve this is for Subs to get layouts by Thursday and Friday. The only way they can do this is if copy and PICTURES are in. Copy is now usually here in good time, but PICTURES are a hold-up. We very much need to have a Picture Editor in on Fridays not only to get pics but to chase up caption and credits information so it is ready for Subs.

The person who needs no training to do this properly is Tammy Myers, so it would seem like very good sense to get her in on Friday in place of the extra person coming in during the week.

I went in to Ben and said that it was no good, I couldn't do editorial single-handed as I did this week, and also the design team needed an extra pair of hands at the Mac on Fridays. I mentioned the chap from the *Mail* again.

He repeated what he said before, which was that there 'was no budget'.

I understand Ben's reluctance to spend money on a picture editor and the new chap from the *Mail*, but still. I can't help fizzing with fury. After all, unless there's actually a good product, there won't be anything worth PRing, period.

The Lady

THE VERY SPECIAL
WEEKLY MAGAZINE

60p

25 to 31
MAY 1993

ROYAL CHELSEA
Preview of the Chelsea Flower Show

HOLIDAY OFFER:
Gertrude Jekyll's gardens

TEA FOR TWO
Talking to Thora Hird

CHESHIRE GARDENS
A paradise for plants

JOBS AND HOLIDAYS
*CLASSIFIED ADVERTISEMENTS:
Job vacancies at home and abroad, holiday cottages, hotels and guest houses, bungalows to let and for sale*

9 770023 716035

21

MAY

3 May 2010

Roger Lewis has asked me to canvass for him so he can become Oxford Professor of Poetry despite the fact that he hates the stuff. So he copies me in whenever there is a little snippet/interview. Someone called Duncan Fallowell has asked me to set up a Facebook group to help promote Lewis's campaign. This is beyond my level of social-networking competence. Today, this from the Welsh troll:

> Dear Rachel,
>
> I was watching a DVD of an old black & white John Betjeman documentary – and in the voiceover he said something you might like to put on the masthead:
>
> 'I shan't get up yet. Not now I've got this new number of *The Lady*.'
>
> Amicalement,
>
> Roger

5 May 2010

Up at 6 a.m. to go to the Strathmore Hotel in Queen's Gate Gardens to do a live '*emission*' (do love that word) for Radio France. As *Le Diable Vit à Notting Hill* is still miraculously on the bestseller list in Paris; and as the publishers are flogging it on basis that it's a richly comic satire on the Notting Hill Tories and bankers, etc., I feel duty-bound to turn up. But it's in French. Have sort of mugged up on basic words – like *banquiers gras* (fat cats) and *chefs de fil* (party leaders) but still, it's a car crash. We all sit around a table in front of mics, in the middle of a large function room in the hotel. With the overexcited presenter are me, Jon Henley from the *Guardian* and a lot of gabbling Frenchmen. To one side of the room, there's a sort of mixing desk, and lots of people on computers, and producers, plus people standing around openly talking throughout the broadcast. It couldn't be worse. It's 7 a.m., noisy, I have an audience of attractive dark Europeans. I have to fill the airwaves for forty-five minutes and I don't really speak more than restaurant French.

I whisper this to John. He says, 'Don't worry,' and claps me on the arm: 'You'll be *fiiiiine!*'

I feel better for a second, until he tells me he lived in Paris for ten years and is married to a Frog. Whenever I open my mouth to utter in the tongue the people in the hotel seem to be laughing, silently. It is very distracting. I was so drained and depleted afterwards that I had to stop at a café on Pall Mall at 8.30 a.m. to eat a full English breakfast to recover.

Lunch with Rupert Hambro at Goldsmiths' Hall in the City. Once you accept something, you sort of have to go. Lots of very old men in very elegant suits approached me holding drinks and said, 'Ha ha ha – so you want to know all about us, do you?' I didn't. But they then proceeded to tell me all about silversmithing and palladium. I sat next to a retired man called David Peake, a former head of Kleinwort's, who told me he was ashamed to say he was a banker and that when he was head man at Kleinwort's, he was paid (or he paid himself) about the same as a junior trader at Goldman Sachs. The lunch was enlivened by a delicious 2006 Meursault, but otherwise unproductive, even though I got a guided tour of the assay office, and was frisked upon leaving.

6 May 2010

Election Day. Brother Jo is standing for election in Orpington. The subs have put up a gallery of pix of Boris culled from newspapers – Al with Indian dancers, Al on bike, Al rumpling hair at City Hall – and now they've pinned a little Photo-Me-sized pic of Jo to the wall too. Which is tactful.

The prospective parliamentary candidate came in last night for his final telecanvassing session. His 'Get the Vote Out Script' is on my desk when I arrive. It includes the line 'Every vote is crucial and we really need your vote.'

The in tray:

- a letter about God from mad reader.
- a furious letter from a reader in Blackpool saying she'd written in a couple of weeks ago enclosing an SAE asking for the address of someone who dispatched olive oil by mail order and that she has been 'disappointed not to have heard back' from me about it. 'I sent letter to Office Dog Coco,' the letter ended.

Ben came in. I am trying to get him to spend some money on editorial rather than expensive PR accounts, so I showed him some snippet in the *Standard* 'Diary' about me (an item that Taylor Herring copied round as if they'd placed it) and said, 'And for this you are paying a PR company five grand a month?'

Then he told me I was a slut and to fuck off.

Newsweek has gone down. Sheesh. First *Reader's Digest*. Next *Newsweek*. Titans of the newsstand! If they can't make it, what hope for us?

Carers Week is now following me on Twitter. And ooh – so is *Dementia* UK. I now have 500 followers (to India Knight's 15,000 – go figure).

Had an email from a contributor:

> I was wondering if you've been able to find a slot for the piece I sent
> you on Helen Bertram, the new chairman of the Beatrix Potter
> Society. Could you let me know when you've got a mo, please?

Judy, having hacked into Janina's email, has found that she has
set up a Google alert so that whenever my name comes up on the
web, she gets the link. What a brill idea! I immediately set up a
Google alert for myself. However, I find out very quickly that there
is a champion hurdler of the same name in the US, so I am getting
real-time updates of her achievements in track and field – and
ominously little about anything here at *The Lady*.

7 May 2010

Up all night as Jo elected in Orpington with historic victory,
trebling Tory majority, and delivering modest speech as he was
declared MP. We all went down to sit in Bromley Civic Centre as
the long hours passed. The first thing the returning officer did was
hand him a brown manila envelope saying 'Rules and Regulations
for MPs, Important and Confidential'.

I am so proud of him.

Following the crash course in assay and silversmithing, this
gold-plated invite has arrived from a PR:

> I am hosting a small media dinner with Carol Marlow, MD of P&O
> Cruises, and Peter Shanks, MD of Princess Cruises and president of
> Cunard Line, on Tuesday 15 June at 6.30 p.m. at the Groucho Club.
> Whilst it will be very informal [the email went on] topics will
> include cruise marketing, the changing face of cruising, attracting

new-to-cruise customers, Azura launch, looking ahead to Cunard's
Queen Elizabeth, launch of Adonia and fly/cruises for P&O Cruises,
business projections, cruising and the environment, 2011 launch
and world cruises.

The fun literally never stops!

Google has alerted me to the fact that Edwina, our twenty-
something beauty in marketing, has given a long and considered
press interview to a journalism website about the future of *The
Lady*. Well. I've always thought that she would make a cheaper,
younger, and much slimmer and more sensible replacement for
me in the boudoir, and now I have proof.

Meanwhile, good news. Apparently Debo has finished her book.
If she wasn't furious with me, I'd call her up and try to bend her to
my will again and ask her to be my agony aunt, but I don't dare.
I think that she has been turned against me by Mrs B. They are
cousins, after all. I have proof. The Dowager Duchess has declined
my unbeatable offer to address readers at our next literary lunch at
the Institute of Directors in October, on the grounds that she is
'ridiculously booked up'.

This makes me want to sob uncontrollably. I mean, apart from
Jilly Cooper and the Queen, Debo is one of the few women that I
utterly and completely revere, and her rejection cuts me to the
quick.

8 May 2010

Drove to Pershore to stay with Nick Coleridge, the MD of Condé
Nast, and Georgia, his wife, who is a friend from school and university. Absolute heaven, very relaxed. I don't have house envy (though
the place is late-Georgian perfection, light, and airy, and even better, he has a splendid young Russian 'cook-general' couple to make

beds, delicious meals, drive, etc.). No, I have organizational envy. Let me count the ways, as Nick is very methodical and would doubtless approve of this.

1.   He has copies of every single one of his stable of magazines leatherbound in zinging boiled-sweet colours, i.e., *Vogue, Tatler, Interiors, House & Garden*, ranked together in tall white fitted bookcases.

2.   He has twenty-seven bespoke vellum Florentine photograph albums filled with amusing pictures of clever friends that he is still friends with many decades down the line, complete with hand-inked names and captions.

3.   He has an entire breakfront bookcase filled with his own works in their various foreign and domestic, hardback and paperback editions.

4.   He took photographs during lunch and swimming and walks that Georgia revealed would be stuck in and annotated within a few days, if not hours.

I know people bang on about how wonderful and marvellous, etc., women are when they manage to get children to school *and* go to work, but really.

I DON'T KNOW HOW HE DOES IT.

9 May 2010

Gaaahd! Must learn to control myself. I will go down in history – if at all – not merely as Boris's sister, but also as mistress of the unhelpful remark after my performance at Bromley Civic Centre. Jo wisely ran his whole campaign under the radar, declined press interviews, refused to have *Times* sketchwriters follow him round, and confined media to the *Bromley Advertiser*, etc. At the count, we'd been sitting for hours with not so much as a beaker of tea, and the exit polls were predicting a hung parliament and the Tory total was inching up, but not nearly high enough to claim victory, and I tweeted, 'It's all gone tits up. Call for Boris.' At around 4.27 a.m. I was bored. And had got rather merry at the Café Anglais earlier – much earlier – in the evening.

Then I went back to watching Dimbles TV. When I looked at my iPhone twenty minutes later I had about a hundred new messages, as for some reason scores upon scores of people had decided to follow me on Twitter, which prompted Twitter to tell my iPhone this via messages. Then I got a text from Jenni Russell, the *Guardian* and *Sunday Times* columnist: 'Is your tweet giving you problems?'

Eh?

Help. I looked at my Twitter account (only a few hundred measly followers) and saw that India (who has billions) had retweeted it, i.e., sent it to all her followers, and then *Guardian* editor Alan Rusbridger retweeted it, and it went into the *Guardian* website's live election blog and then . . .

That morning, it was a headline in the *Sunday Mirror*. Page lead. 'IT'S ALL GONE T*TS UP. CALL FOR BORIS,' it screamed in twenty-point headline. 'Johnson sister in Twitter swipe.'

In the piece – tagged 'Exclusive' – Vincent Moss, the political editor, wrote, 'The despairing sister of the Mayor Boris Johnson, Rachel, took a swipe at the Tory leader to Twitter saying . . . etc.'

Oh Jesus. What a galumphing fool I am, verily the Fergie of the Johnson family. Luckily, we are in hung parliament, so people so enraptured by wall-to-wall constitutional coverage from Westminster and Downing Street and Lib-Dem HQ as Clegg flip-flops between Brown and Cameron that very few have pointed out that I have been 1. disloyal (I am always presumed to be good Tory gel, simply because I have two openly Tory siblings, an assumption that always makes me want to join the Socialist Workers' Party) and 2. inappropriate (the editor of *The Lady* should not have strong opinions, let alone voice them). Apart from Sarah Sands, the minxy deputy on the *Standard*, who invites me to expand my 140 characters into 1,200 words for tomorrow's paper. I decline. She is very artful about persuading writers to write the one piece that will do them most damage, and I have to side-step my natural urge to jump in with hobnailed boots when she comes calling.

The second rule of life is clearly: Don't tweet.

On the plus side, Dave Shelton, who is in charge of distribution, has done a micro-survey in his West Sussex rural locale. We are now selling six out of eight copies in Sweets 'n' Things in Lancing, and two out of three in Wick News, Littlehampton, which is, respectively, two copies and one copy more than the same week last year.

Wahay!

10 May 2010

Gordon Brown has resigned. Or announced he will by the time of conference in the autumn. William Hill has posted odds on Jo Johnson being PM by 2010 as 13–1, so maybe I am overestimating the impact of my tweet (which is still being repeated *passim*, with result that now have 1,000 followers on Twitter).

Meanwhile, as the Tories and Lib Dems and defeated Labour parties try to form a government, I have important pitches to consider:

- would you be interested in a 1,000-word feature entitled 'Founding Mothers' asking two female vicars about the realities of life working in the Church of England and their hopes and aspirations for the future of the institution?
- a letter from a lady in Blackburn, Lancashire, which begins, 'Dear Rachel Johnson, I wonder if you would consider a series of articles on Margate? I enclose three, and have a further five in the pipeline.'

- another letter: 'I am a staff nurse and started to write poems to cheer people up at work; they seem to like them and I would enjoy seeing them in print. I also write short stories, but have not had anything published yet.'

BLESS!

I have also received six typed letters, obviously all from the same nutbag, about the Camilla cover, all equally poisonous. Goodness, some people do use bad words!

Janina came in today, but is off again now for a week.

11 *May* 2010

As I write, there is no new PM, Jo is an MP, the country is glued to the TV, and here at *The Lady*, I have been invited to various important events. An email just in:

> I have just spoken with your PA and sorry to hear you have yet to receive your invitation to our very special Designer Hat-Making Tea Party at The Gore Hotel, hosted by celebrity milliner Katherine Elizabeth and presenter and interior designer Linda Barker, in aid of The Eve Appeal's Make Time For Tea campaign.

Party Pieces (the Middleton family firm) is now following me on Twitter and oh, yes! Paul Blezard is, according to the *Indy*, writing a *roman à clef* called 'Saving Grace' about 'a balls-to-the-wall lady editor' who comes in to try to relaunch ailing, old cunties' weekly and sacks all and sundry.

As it's Tuesday, the figures came in. We're up to well over 32,000 again, so Ben is being v. nice to me, so it's all good. Or at least, better.

A woman called Denise came in to interview me for a newspaper with a readership of 800,000 that prints out of Dubai. It's called the *Khaleej Times*. I've never heard of it. How does everyone do it? Why are we only bobbing above 30k? She was a clever woman in her fifties. She queried my cover choices, such as Camilla PB and Tracey Emin, and then admitted she hadn't read *The Lady* since she was in her twenties and her chums were training to be nannies. 'What did you think of it?' I asked. 'Then?'

'Dunno,' she said. 'Never read it. It was just something benign in the ether.' A rather good description of its nebulous charms.

What I ended up saying to the lady from the *Khaleej Times* was this – what I love about working here is, almost above all, the classified ads. I could burble on for hours about how proud I am that we are a trusted global *entrepôt* for domestic staff, and in our glossy pages (and online) we provide a forum where those who employ and those who seek employment in a domestic setting can profitably meet.

In our 'Situations & Appointments' column this week, for example, there was a long, long ad – must have cost hundreds to place – in search of a live-in couple for a 'busy Grade 1 listed residence of national importance' where hospitality and good service were required to be of the highest standard. It was clearly a grace-and-favour residence, and the gig came complete with a three-bed house attached. As ever, I was very tempted to apply myself. I told Ben that I've always thought that the real juice in the mag was in the back, and all the best stories, which is why I've launched a column in the mag called 'Small Ad, Big Story', which Vicky Murden, our letters and website coordinator, researches and writes.

'You're not wrong there,' he said. 'There's a whole bunch of them down in *GMTV* who when asked what their guilty pleasure was said it was reading *Lady* classifieds in the bath.'

12 May 2010

Have had two meetings with telly peeps following the doc. The first was with Simon Shaw, the editor of *Antiques Roadshow* (10 million viewers can't be wrong ...) He came up from BBC Bristol to see me in the boudoir. Gillian made him a cup of tea.

His idea was – me going round advising regional papers how to survive the savage recession in publishing. I didn't think this inspiring. The last thing I want to be seen to be is some blonde bitch Trinnyishly telling people what to do. Then I went to see Optomen in their groovy, open-plan HQ in Camden complete with Gaggia machines for in-house macchiatos. I told them that BBC Bristol (i.e., Simon Shaw) had had one idea and that it hadn't grabbed me and I started to tell them what it was and I saw them look down, and then one of them – little blonde Becky – said, 'That was the first idea on our list too!' and merrily scored a line through it. They clearly want me to come up with something glittery ... so sent them this.

From: Rachel Johnson
Sent: 12 May 2010 13:04
To: Becky Clarke
Cc: Pat Llewellyn
Subject: 3 and a half thoughts

Off top of head before I go to have lunch with Ben and discuss our collaboration with Mills & Boon and National Trust called The National Tryst (am not making this up):

1. a tongue-in-cheek series on couples who have second homes and who decamp between two places:
    'Two for the Price of ... Sanity/Our Marriage'.

2. a weirdly compelling Exmoor piece springs to mind (if I can't buy the *Exmoor* mag) – have you heard of LIZ JONES of the *Daily Mail*??? If you have, call me, if you haven't, ask someone else to explain. And read this. She moved near me on Exmoor. She is sort of publicly committing hara-kiri in her *Mail on Sunday* column. She comes to me for a week. Then I go to her. You film us until . . . one of us dies.

3. also like the thought of me finding my old schoolmates (all nine of them) from Winsford First School in 1972 – that could be fascinating and tell the story of rural decline in nine vignettes.

13 May 2010

Have had an email from a couple who used to be pastry cooks for the Beckhams and the Queen Mother. Of course, everyone knows that the Mitfords' nickname for the late HRH Her Majesty The Queen Mother was 'Cake', so that bit made sense, but I couldn't imagine a crumb of scone or a spoonful of Sussex Pond Pudding ever crossing Posh's lips.

> We have in the past been offered to do various things for publications but with our Royal Household past, we believed we would be more suited to *The Lady*!

Well, the line 'with our Royal Household past' was the clincher. This was more like it. Posh and Becks, and the Queen Mum, encased in one package – like a sort of Royal Beef Wellington.

Have had to pull a massive spread on weddings by a writer who has been pitching a piece called 'Weddings: Then & Now' since I got here. The piece arrived, with three interviews with couples who got spliced in wartime. I thought this article about weddings of yore would go very well with a feature on the Lucy Mangan book about her own London wedding called *The Reluctant Bride*, in a something old, something new, sort of way.

Plus it's May – i.e., wedding season. Then the subs started subbing it and discovered that one of the main interviewees in the main part of the piece – a general – was dead. Not just a little bit dead, but very dead indeed. 1995 dead. Yet the author of the piece had conducted a long interview with the general about his wedding reception in Fleet, where he wore his khaki Marine uniform and bride Dorothy wore white. It's one for Derren Brown. We kept ringing the journalist, but she never rang back.

There are two possible solutions. 1. She did the interview more than fifteen years ago and has been sitting on the piece for that long. 2. She conducted the interview with the general from *beyond the grave*.

14 *May 2010*

Last night at dinner Peter Soros looked at me and said, 'You've had work. I can tell.' I couldn't have been more delighted. Have written crawly cards to the Osbornes and the Camerons and parcelled them up with commemorative *Lady* tea-towels and got Gillian to send them to atone for my Tits-Up tweet. I sent Clegg an email on his BlackBerry asking for his address so could do same for him and Miriam, but he never answered. How quickly doth power go to the head!

17 *May 2010*

I bumped into James Pembroke, the publisher of *The Oldie*, at cricket tea at Dragon School, Oxford, while Oliver was playing in the Third Eleven against Papplewick. I shoved scones laden with jam and cream into my mouth as Pembroke told me that Ben was very resistant to hearing pearls of wisdom from the old hands of magazine publishing, such as James Pembroke.

According to Pembroke, trying to sell copies at the newsstand is expensive and hit-and-miss, and what we should be focusing on is subs.

'Ben said on your Channel 4 documentary that he's been running media companies since he was a nipper,' said Pembroke. By this stage we were back on the green Dragon playing fields watching our sons play cricket in their whites, on a golden May Saturday, as students passed by languidly in punts on the Cherwell. 'But that's only if you count dealing in pornos from his dorm at Harrow as running a media business.'

In my view, we should give away copies of *The Lady* like the *Evening Standard* does, then advertisers might pay attention.

When I sent Ben a text challenging him to confirm that 'running media companies' since he was 'a nipper' meant renting out wankmags at Harrow, he responded immediately.

There have been many media ventures since Harrow, but whilst at Harrow at the tender age of fourteen I had a booze bootlegging business, a 'magazine', ahem, rental business and an illegal radio station pumping out vile sketches suggesting what we thought a lot of masters (beaks) did in their spare time. Of course since then a number of them have 'done bird' for just such 'indiscretions'.

18 May 2010

Matt Warren from the *Daily Mail* came in to have lunch with me and Ben at the Forge restaurant. Matt, should he come to work here, is nigh on perfect. He raises the testosterone level in Bedford

Street by about 100 per cent, he's an Old Shirburnian, he got a First from Edinburgh, he's an experienced motoring, travel and features hack . . . and he wants to work at *The Lady*!

Over lunch Ben admitted he feels outnumbered by the number of women in the building. 'One week in four I definitely feel tense and tearful,' he said. Then he and Matt snorted and gasped into their napkins.

The in tray:

- three more bottles of vinaigrette.
- a presentation box of teas in round tins rather like snuff/ rubbed tobacco, in strange flavours such as Pomme Prestige, Singapore Breakfast, Darjeeling Okayth.
- an anti-UVA product for Face and Neck called Symmetria.
- Her Ladyship's guide to the Queen's English, which helpfully tells me whether to say napkin or serviette, by the author of a book called *An Apple a Day*.

I do wish PRs would stop sending anti-ageing creams, endless speciality teas in pompous packaging, and salad dressing. What we want is CAKE.

Have had testy email from the journalist David Jenkins.

Dear Rachel,

I'm pretty appalled by this – see below. You've had my invoice for more than two months and I was always told that you had a twenty days after acceptance payment policy. I assume the Budworths are not cutting back on their lifestyles: it's just not on not to pay your writers. You've been a freelance, and you should know that it's an editor's prime duty to pay her/his contributors. I'd like to know what you're going to

do about it: in fact, I'd like to be paid tomorrow. Meantime I shall
phone other contributors and find out what's happening to them.

David

> Forwarded message
> **Date:** 17 May 2010 15:59
> **From:** Tracey Allsopp
> **To:** David Jenkins
> **Subject:** Payments
>
> Hi David
>
> Thank you for your email regarding payment of the invoice for
> the 30th March. At the moment we are doing our very best to pay
> what we can, when we can, from our outstanding invoices, and as
> the cash situation will allow us.
>
> I can only but apologize for any inconvenience that this is causing
> you.
>
> Tracey

This was bit of a shocker. Not only are we not paying contributors *again* but one of them is David Jenkins who *knows everyone*
and is Alexandra Shulman editor of *Vogue*'s boyfriend. I called him
and told him I was very sorry and would sort it out.

Oh God, we've just had another testy email from a contributor,
Drusilla Beyfus (Shulman's mother-in-law, aaagggh, so the word
is out). And Ben said that Hugh St Clair rings every day to complain he hasn't been paid.

If all this leaks out, it will be a very public death for us, and undo
all the PR that we've bought. I talked to Ben. He said 1. he wasn't
paying the PR companies either and 2. he was writing a business
plan to secure another loan facility. 'For how much?' I asked.

'Two-fifty,' he said.

'Two hundred and fifty thou?' I said. 'Is that all? Ivo and I have got a loan facility for half a million!' (This is sadly true.) 'Why didn't you borrow money from me?'

The upshot of all this is I've had to write a segment of the business plan. Which I did. Here goes:

Editorial

When I took the editor's chair at *The Lady* I faced a delicate challenge – updating the editorial so that it reflected the concerns of the modern woman aged forty-five upwards, while not mortally insulting the sensibilities of the readership (average age seventy-eight). I decided there was no point in hanging back, and by Christmas root and branch changes to the way the magazine both looked and read were in place. We redesigned the cover, editorial and classifieds and returned to a more classic, nineteenth-century rubric. On the editorial side, I brought in top writers throughout the magazine, so that the journalism contained therein is now as good as, if not better than, anything else available on a fast-paced weekly basis.

Eight months in, the new design has stood the test of time, the readers are happier with it, and new ones – assisted by a blizzard of *Lady*-related publicity – are coming on board. I now intend to consolidate after a period of frantic change and build up our readership subscription base (essential to the magazine's survival) while maintaining newsstand appeal with fresh covers that tell existing and potential readers that even in a crowded, lowest-common-denominator market where all other women's weeklies are offering the same diet of sex and celebrity and gossip, the full-colour *Lady* stands alone in having a more distinguished and upmarket product to offer.

Drring drring outside the boudoir.

'Yes she is. Who shall I say is calling? Oh yes.' Slightly breathless pause. 'Does she know what it's about? Er, Rachel. There's a call from Jeremy Pax—' – to her credit, Gillian knew who was on the line, and can barely get the name out – 'Paxman. Shall I put him through?'

I was in the middle of shifting all the reviews – from opera, which currently sits with 'News & Reviews', to books and film and radio – into a cluster at the back of the magazine, to make a new, all-singing and dancing Review Section, ending with Alexander Chancellor's TV page on the side back. 'OK then,' I said.

'Do you want a 4,000-word piece on cobnuts?' Jeremy asked. After the doc – in which it was revealed that I nicknamed random nature articles that used to run in *The Lady* 'cobnuts' – I get jokes like this quite a lot. Indeed, on April Fool's Day, I added 'Cobnuts Editor – Helena Handbasket' to the masthead.

Jeremy told me he'd received an email from a hack called Sonia Purnell who is writing a book called *Boris. The Man. The Myth.* An attention-all-shipping went out yesterday from the Mayoral Glass Gonad, i.e., City Hall, saying we were by no accounts to talk to her.

'Don't talk to her,' I said. 'The air-raid warning has sounded.'

I wasn't going to, just checking,' he said. After that I asked him for 5,000 words on the history of the horse chestnut and he hung up.

Kath Hanley from Classifieds came up all excited. 'Nutter alert,' she said, as she petted Coco. Apparently a woman had come in and said her husband had written a song called 'The Lady' and wanted to serenade me with it. 'We get that sort of thing all the time,' said Kath. 'They're usually harmless.'

The in tray:

• a Rococo cherry-studded choccy egg (rather unseasonal, but at least it's not another Simnel cake).

- a short story about a haunted drawing room and a soldier and a gramophone.
- an angry letter from a reader in Edgbaston complaining that the author Juliet Nicolson was wearing jeans in her picture and demanding, 'Has she no pride in herself?'

Lembit Opik – who has lost his seat – is now following me on Twitter. Well, I suppose he has nothing better to do.

19 May 2010

Marco Pierre White has demanded to know why he's not been on the cover of *The Lady* yet and is offering his services – *gratis* – as a columnist. When I told the subs/art teams everyone had hot flushes and started fanning themselves. I got Carolyn to agree he could write a column about seasonal English food, which will go nicely with our nifty new column 'Britstop', all about English oddities like lollipop ladies and Pimm's, football and Wimbledon, etc., which I have introduced on the 'Diary' page.

Amanda Holden wants to be friends on Facebook. Why?

21 May 2010

Went into Tesco on Portobello Road and looked at *The Lady* versus the competition. It was immediately obvious that we were too decorous. Too discreet. Too *ladylike*. We are up against *Chat* and *Take a Break* and *Bella* and *Women's Weekly*, not to mention the thundering juggernaut of *People's Friend*. We have to amp up our cover lines. Get away from the curly old-fashioned font. Go all shouty and neon. Think about *cover mounts*. I called Ben to tell him that we had to go down Via Vulgaris and plunge downmarket visually.

He sounded pleased with me for the first time in ages, as if I was finally on message.

I'm finding the whole HR side nightmarish. I've never managed anyone in my life – nannies always left, or I sacked them, while my parenting 'skills' merely seemed to encourage my own children to sit around issuing me with Caligula-like demands. It all makes me feel very uneasy. When you are editor, I now realize, you are responsible for taking decisions that change people's lives. It is buck-stoppingly hair-raising.

Meanwhile, more bad news. The bankers have ratted on Ben. I listened in silence as he told me of their perfidy. I hereby take it all back about Ben getting his priorities arse about face. It turns out that today Coutts have pulled the plug on the loan (great vote of confidence in the product . . . my editorship . . . and my contribution to the business plan). It's been decided at the highest level that even after making Ben jump through endless hoops, come up with the biz plan, etc., they are not, after all, now going to extend him another tranche of credit of £250k to keep the magazine going, a sum that would enable us to pay contributors like David Jenkins and Drusilla Beyfus, and staff payroll.

It's been agony. I had a long chat with him this morning. I reminded him that Ivo and I had taken out a loan facility of half a million quid that he could tap. He said, 'That's very kind. But it's OK. Last night, I had a Damascene conversion. I really believe in this business. I don't need a penthouse apartment in Battersea. I'm going to mortgage it if necessary.'

And Helen, the new head of display ads – the one who has splashed logos all over 'Coco's Corner' – has also offered to dip into her pocket too. We all, it turns out, love *The Lady* so much we are prepared to spend our own money to keep her seaworthy.

So, for the moment, the Ladyship is still afloat. But – to continue the metaphor for a moment – the forecast is for squally showers and choppy waters.

For how much longer she is going to sail, Lord only knows.
I hope a very long time.

25 May 2010

Diana Athill has turned me down as a columnist. She has moved
into a home, and written 'movingly' about it for the *Guardian*.

As soon as I saw this, I wrote to her asking for a regular column
called – what else? – 'At Home'.

I got a nice card back. 'It just so happens I have screwed myself
up starting (touch wood) a new book and I haven't the writing
energy to do anything else.'

Nor have I found a cleaning lady of literary ability who could
contribute a column called 'The Daily'.

Am waiting to hear if *Shire Hell* has sold in France. I hope so – it
could pay for the new (i.e., reconditioned) Aga I've just had to
install at Nethercote, as the old one, installed in the 1940s, has finally
crumbled.

I went into the boardroom, as it was a Tuesday and the numbers
come in by 10 a.m., but no Ben. Claire said, 'He's at home sweating
and puking apparently.'

Finally, the sort of email I've been waiting for since I arrived. Email
of the day!

Dear Rachel, I have some great news! The Pudding Club is celebrat-
ing 25 years this year & in recognition of this amazing achievement
we are hosting a variety of events at The Home of The Pudding Club
in the Cotswold village of Mickleton, & in addition we have just
launched 3 new varieties of Pudding Club puddings into Waitrose
to join the 3 classic flavours launched last autumn – Sticky Toffee,
Treacle & Ginger Syrup Sponge Pudding.

A press release is attached, together with a couple of images to tempt you! If you would like to have some samples, please do let me know. If you could find a space to mention these delicious new puddings, I would be extremely grateful.

Jill of the Pudding Club – you got it.

Just bumped into Ben's PA Maureen in the ladies, where I was rinsing out my Her Ladyship mug prior to fresh infusion of a speciality tea.

She said Ben was poorly. She knew why.

'It got a bit hot in the boardroom yesterday. The chocolate biscuits were melting,' she said.

Then she said he hadn't had a proper holiday for eighteen months and it was getting to him. 'It's like my husband,' she said. 'He works in Aberdeen. I only see him when there's a Charlton football match.'

Nell Butler, of Granada, and an old chum, came in for peppermint tea and Extremely Chocolatey Chocolate Bites from M&S.

I introduced her to all and sundry as the inventor of *Come Dine With Me*, because she was the blinding genius who invented the format.

Everyone looked up from their screens (there is a bank hol. on Monday, so it's a pull-forward and we are losing a day from the production schedule) with beaming smiles. Finally, I'd got someone into the office they could all admire who had really done something!

Alain de Botton is following me on Twitter.

27 May 2010

Handed round copies of *The Lady* last night at a function with independent booksellers at Penguin. It was the latest issue, with

Mariella Frostrup on the cover, to time with the Hay-on-Wye litfest, at which she is much in evidence, as she presents daily programme called *Hay on Sky*.

To recap: in the interview, she generously said that the reason there was only one woman presenter on the *Today* programme was because BBC was run by 'a bunch of misogynists'. She went on to say that the search for a middle-aged female presenter wasn't exactly akin to looking for the Holy Grail as the 'streets of London were littered' with perfectly serviceable women past sell-by 'who'd been sacked by the BBC already'.

All this was gratifyingly picked up in *The Times* and *Daily Mail* this morning. '*Today* Programme run by Woman-Haters' was the half-pager in the *Mail*, crediting *The Lady*. She must have assumed that giving an interview to *The Lady* would be an essentially private experience limited to me and her, not knowing about the teams of PRs backstage. In the end, Mariella grovelled in a letter to BBC house mag *Ariel*, in which she took it all back. Quite unnecessarily, in my view.

Anyway, when I was handing round the magazine at Penguin, I noticed that everyone immediately turned to the back and started leafing through the classified and display ads, and started chuckling over the quarter-page ads for mare and foal sanctuaries, walk-in baths, and so on.

'Give your feet a treat,' tittered one top editor. 'Hand-made by a small family firm in Somerset who specialize in comfortable footwear . . .' Eleo Gordon was reading out one of our in-house *Lady* offers.

Now, I knew our classifieds for valets and underbutlers and live-in couples were a weekly treat savoured by many, but I had no idea that the display ads and special offers were also so keenly studied for entertainment value.

Ben has returned from his sickbed with red-rimmed eyes, looking puffy and cross. Claire went into the boardroom, to show him photographic proof of the Ruby Wax cover, in which she was sitting against a brown leather banquette, resting her elbows on a table, looking at the camera quizzically.

'We can't have that shit,' he exclaimed, after giving it a quick look. Then he ripped it in half, and handed it back to Claire. 'She looks as if she's in a pub.'

I went to interview Amanda 'Most Powerful Woman in Publishing' Ross. She has adopted two little boys, the younger brother only six months old. After a long struggle with IVF. And has two terriers. Perfect material for pick-up in the *Daily Mail*, in other words.

We've had a spew of angry letters from readers after we ran a full-page display ad from an Italian company on page 42. It showed a pregnant nun in a habit spooning ice-cream into her waiting mouth, by the words, 'Immaculately Conceived'. Honestly, readers will complain about anything!

> I write to complain in the strongest terms about the ad . . . the depiction of a pregnant nun holding ice-cream with the side-bar 'Immaculate Conception' is highly offensive to Christians in general and Catholics in particular. I am surprised the magazine accepts this type of ad, which clearly contravenes the ASA guidelines. I have informed them of this advertisement. I will not be renewing my subscription.

> Dear Sirs

> [another one wrote from North Lancing:] The advert for ice-cream is irritating and offensive. Not suitable for *The Lady* even if it pays a higher fee for space.

Email sent in by Gillian marked 'Reader Call':

Mrs Ryan from Enfield, subscriber for many years, rang to complain about the advertisement of a pregnant nun in the 25 May issue. It's absolutely disgusting, and if anyone rings her up to talk about it she will be very rude. Likes the new look of the magazine otherwise.

The in tray:

- Church Commissioners Annual Report.
- a copy of *Wolf Print*, the magazine of the UK Wolf Conservation Trust.

28 May 2010

George Osborne has written a personal note, handwritten from Number 11, to thank me for my crawly card.

Dear Rachel,

Thank you for your kind card.
I can confirm that no one else sent me tea-towels.
Surely the big news from the election is the arrival of Jo Johnson MP?

Best wishes,
George

The Lady

A Journal for Gentlewomen

25 MAY 2010   £1.80

Wedding belles
STEPHANIE CALMAN &
Mr Incompatible

LUCY MANGAN
The reluctant bride

Lunch with
MARIELLA
small, blonde & very cross

NICK VELCH
Dad-dinner in the mud

PHILIP MOULD
is the art detective

Dreamy
ENGLISH FASHION
by Katherine Hooker

FESTIVAL GUIDE

JEFFREY ARCHER'S DIARY   **GARDENING BOOKS**   **SPANISH COOKING COURSE**
ROBIN HOOD

JUNE

2 June 2010

I said to Ben, 'You're not going to see me much tomorrow ...'
I didn't want to go to Covent Garden – Oliver was going back to
school, all the children were in a half-term tennis camp and all
have exams (Oliver Common Entrance, Milly GCSEs, Ludo A
levels in the next fortnight). I've seen them so little that when I do
I have to restrain myself from exclaiming how much they've grown,
as if they are lesser-spotted godchildren.

I also have to write 2,000 words for the *Mail on Sunday* by
9 a.m. tomorrow – to big up a Radio 4 documentary I have made
about posh girls who were sent by their aristocratic fathers to
Munich in the mid- to late-thirties, in order to thicken blood ties
with Royal Houses of Europe, and bring back the good news about
the Third Reich. The documentary is in turn bigging up my new
novel *Winter Games*, which I was writing this time last year when I
got the fateful call from one B. Budworth. Articles, radio, telly,
novels – we authors have to be multi-platform pluggers now.

Ben cut in before I could explain why I wasn't going to be present and correct in the office. 'And you won't see me unless you're
coming to the mid-Suffolk Show, a day out with something for
everyone, where I'm doing an udder inspection.'

'What?' I said weakly.

He said he was judging the dairy goats.

3 June 2010

Drove to Wales. On the way to Hay-on-Wye we stopped at Tre-tower, run by Cadw (i.e., that's Welsh for Welsh Heritage). I was walking around the shell keep on the motte when Ben rang on Ivo's mobile (I'd left my iPhone in the car).

'Good news,' he said. Then he gave me some good news about a possible hire.

It dimly crossed my mind that I have bullied Ben into hiring my own replacement, but what the hell. Then Ivo and Ben talked about the bombshell news that Ivo's nephew David, a brilliant Classics student who knows every word of *Withnail & I* off by heart, went out with office beauty, our Bedford bloom, Edwina. During the course of this Ben said something that makes Ivo roar with laughter. 'What were you and Ben laughing about?' I asked.

'Oh nothing,' he said. 'Ben was just saying if they've done their mock GCSEs they're already FAR too old.'

'Very funny,' I snapped.

Got to Hay. The sun was shining, everyone was wandering round with punnets of small English strawberries and licking ice-cream cones made of goat's milk, clutching cloth bags emblazoned with Hay logos. If I had to write the 'Social Stereotype' of the average Hay punter, it would be: someone in their mid-fifties, in Birkenstocks and mauve cropped trousers, with long grey hair and a sunhat, read-ing the *Guardian* Review section. Both male and female.

Inside the 'Artists Only' area, a big green room with drinks, crisps and sofas, I saw the radio DJ Chris Evans, who kissed me hello. 'I love your column in the *Telegraph*,' he says. 'And I love your programme on Sky.' I blushed, even though I haven't written for the *Tel* for three years and don't have a programme on Sky. I wonder who he thinks I am? I texted Ben the glad tidings that I am schmoozing the biggest star in radio. He texts back, 'Ask Chris

Evans about when he put his advert in *The Lady* offering his services as a private detective.'

Blez is here in force, doing about a hundred events. Haven't
seen him since before his sacking. This is small cloud on horizon.
John Walsh, Carolyn's ex, tells me that Blez was doing an event for
a Burmese author in front of a mainly Burmese crowd of readers,
and instead of introducing himself he told the bemused audience,
'You'll all remember me. I'm the guy who was fired on live TV
from *The Lady* in that infamous documentary.'

Every time I glimpse his towering white-haired form and hear
his booming voice emanate from within a tented stage I run for
cover; meanwhile, he ignores me completely.

In the green room, Ivo introduced Ludo (now seventeen, doing
politics A level) to Alastair Campbell, lounging on a sofa before his
gig on the *Guardian* stage.

Naturally, I could not resist 'going in' (Ivo and Ludo cannot bear
my beelines for celebrity, and term it 'waggling'.) 'Who's this?' said
Alastair Campbell. 'The mother,' I said. 'Well, your son has just told
me he wishes you'd sent him to a state school, not Marlborough.'

Ludo has always rejected suggestions that we save 30k a year and
send him to our excellent state school down the road, Holland
Park Comp, alma mater of many successful West London media
creatives and Tony Benn's children.

'Did you, darling?' I said accusingly, whirling to face Ludo.

'Alastair's spinning you, you twit,' said Ivo, as Campbell grinned
at me from the sofa. Apparently Ludo, when Alastair dutifully asked
where my son was in education, had assured Campbell he was very
happy there. When I tipped up, Campbell had flipped this conversation 180 degrees so that the new line was that I, against my
firstborn's will and stated preference, was sending him to a posh
private school rather than the local state school. Ivo was right – I
was being spun like a roulette wheel. Course I was. It's what Alastair
Campbell does.

5 June 2010

Went into Hay to hear, first, Max Hastings give a masterclass on Churchill, introduced by Tom Stoppard. It was very hot, and as he talked – and my God he talked well – Max wiped the sweat from his forehead with a New & Lingwood shirtsleeve.

I fell in love with him. He is tall and soldierly and prodigiously clever and productive. And he has thick, dark, glossy boot-polish hair. Love object number two: Tom Stoppard. Rosie Boycott nudged me. 'Don't you think Tom looks more and more like Germaine Greer?' she whispered. No! He looks like a Roman emperor.

The best bit: it was the London Library lecture, and in his preamble about how wonderful the Library was, how it was the only club one needs, and how a day in the Library was never a wasted one, Max got going on the resource that was the archives in the basement. 'You can look up back copies of *The Times*, the *Illustrated London News*, even *The Lady*,' Max said. I almost expired from heat and pleasure.

Then at 7 p.m. we poured back under canvas again to hear David Remnick, the feted editor of *The New Yorker*, talk about his top-selling Obama book, *The Bridge*. He arrived straight off the plane in spotless Dad jeans (I guess Gap), Persil-white trainers, black T-shirt and black jacket, *à la* Steve Jobs. He talked about how Obama didn't learn how to become properly black until the project-days as a community organizer in Chicago, and was fluent and funny, as one would expect. I sat next to loony adman Robin Wight, who was looking more crazed than usual in a parti-coloured suit, purple suede loafers and stripey socks, in the front row.

'Ask a question,' Wight hissed in my ear at the end. He gestured to one of the roving mics. The session came to an end, and I was still holding the mic. My heart started going like the clappers, and

Remnick said, 'There's a woman in the front who'll be very disappointed if she doesn't get the floor,' so I got the nod. I stood up in
front of 1,200 people, and my flushed face filled the huge screen.

So I asked Remnick whether he had access to Obama, and whether
he reckoned that when Obama did authorize a biographer, it would
be a honky white boy ('I'm not white,' joked Remnick as I ploughed
on sweatily) or someone of his own race.

Remnick totally spanked me with his answer, pointing out that
there would be tons of books written about Obama, both author-
ized and unauthorized, now and for generations to come. As I sat
down, I didn't spot that my chair seat had flipped up to the verti-
cal, and I almost crashed to the ground.

I have been tormented by terrible *esprit d'escalier*. Instead of
asking such a clinker, I wish I'd said, 'Speaking as the editor of a
rival weekly publication . . .' (pause for laughter – *The Lady* v *The
New Yorker*! ho ho) and gone on to ask him whether he thought
that after a warrior leader, i.e., Bush/Blair, countries always went
for a weed, i.e., Obama/Cameron-Clegg-Miliband.

Too late now, of course.

Dinner with Rob Albert and Revel Guest, the King and Queen of
Hay, in their glorious crumbly Manderlay-style house on a green
hill. Sat next to Rob, who was all twinkly charm, my father's age,
and Ed Victor, super-agent to the stars. He called me Rebecca
throughout the evening as a tease, and we gossiped about Tina
Brown until we proceeded in convoy to another afterparty in
another mini-stately on another green hill, where there was a marquee and disco-dancing with Jamie Byng (founder of Canongate)
on the decks.

The next day I was so tormented that I sent Remnick an email
(address cadged from Ed Victor) making light of my awful question and sending him a little write-up of the Obama talk and the

Q&A from my POV. I get a slightly stiff response from him, telling me that, with respect, my 'entry was off'. I have displeased the editor of *The New Yorker*, the author of acclaimed tome on first black president, and probably the best journalist in the world.

Piercing agony!

6 June 2010

A perfect Hay weekend of walking and waggling in the Welsh sunshine was slightly spoilt at the end.

I felt terribly guilty whenever I saw the Blez – even though he is planning revenge novel *Saving Grace*. I do hope he gets a deal, then perhaps he'll cool down. Plus, when I did finally intersect with Peter Florence – who *is* Hay, and Paul's best friend for ever, he cold-shouldered me too. So my cunning plan to have a *Lady* tent here next year, with Lady Antonia Fraser interviewing David Walliams to the soundtrack of Lady Gaga's greatest hits, has already bitten the dust, I fear. Had to continuously dodge Blez in the green room aka the Hostility suite.

By the Sunday, I sensed it had been ten long, hot days on the Welsh borders and everyone – organizers, visitors, slebs, writers – seemed to be going on the turn, like a ripe Stilton sitting too long in the larder. Despite my idiocy with David Remnick, and getting the bum's rush from Peter Florence, it was still heavenly. The sun shone, the hills rolled, and there was that holiday mood that prevails whenever people who only ever see each other at London parties intersect in foreign lands, in this case, Wales. I've always noticed this. I think this explains the success of Hay much more than the embarrassment of choice when it comes to top speakers and gigs and crunchy debate.

Hay ho.

7 June 2010

Groaning in tray!

- three Yorkshire tea cakes from Betty's of Harrogate in three flavours: Moist and Tangy Marmalade, Moist & Rich Ginger & Treacle, and Moist & Fruity Tea Loaf. Most welcome! (Carolyn has also received the identical same three moist cakes so there are six cakes for tea today. It's getting like Test Match Special.)
- 4 x letters about the pregnant-nun advert from readers cancelling subs.
- a letter from Nottinghamshire from a woman who has been taking *The Lady* for fifteen years and not renewing because I have 'changed a perfectly agreeable magazine into one with a distinct air of being for a coterie of the rich well-connected from which I feel excluded' and ending, 'My real regret will be the loss of the Ladygram.'
- an invitation to Tea on the Lawn in Ashbourne, hosted by 'three passionate women supporting each other in their rural businesses', including a viewing of a 'scrumptious cut-flower collection in the edible water meadow.'
- two pairs of fold-up ballet pumps from CocoRose.
- an invitation to 'smile away the years' at a 3D natural face clinic run by a Finnish body-control teacher and a free massage to realign the overall balance between the facial muscles and head (a reminder that really not that much has changed since *The Lady* ran articles in the 1880s on how to preserve a youthful complexion, which was to 'avoid moving the face unduly').
- a press release from the Open Space Society, and their summer 2010 volume.
- a reader call, recorded by Gillian:

Mrs Rachel Hamilton from Coventry rang – been reading
The Lady since the Crimean War & thinks it's now absolutely
delightful! She doesn't subscribe because she loves the
fun of trying to buy it from Waitrose. Thinks we've had a really
difficult task to update it without losing its character, but
we've done it! She's 70 yrs old, and her London-based
daughter likes it too. Don't take any notice of the
complainers, she said!

Went off to the Royal Institution in Albemarle Street, to hear
John Sentamu, the Archbishop of York, give the memorial lecture
in the name of my great-grandfather Sir George Williams, who
was a hill farmer's son who left Ashwick farm on Exmoor, walked
to London and in due course founded the YMCA. At tea before-
hand, I am introduced to the twinkling, buoyant Sentamu. 'Are
you related to the mayor?' he asked. 'You must be, because when
you smile your eyes recede' – the Archbish. squinched at me – 'just
like his do.'

8 June 2010

Went to Highgrove to a lunch thing to celebrate Waitrose taking
over Duchy Originals. The Prince of Wales/Waitrose had invited
lots of foodie writers to bear witness and sample the extended new
range of delicious things to eat and drink. There was to be a tour
of the garden followed by lunch. Dress was lounge suit, which
meant all the women wore florals.

There were endless stiffy white cards, and passes, and name tags
to be brought with us. We mustered at the platform at Padding-
ton. It was drizzling. On the train I was reading a free copy of *The
Times* in First Class and I spotted an item that said the Prince

had a chest infection and was in bed somewhere called Birkhall. The train to Kemble started running slower and slower. It was now pouring with rain. Then I overheard a Waitrose PR say that 1. the Prince wasn't there and 2. there would be no garden tour. Great.

We decanted into taxis and drove in convoy to Highgrove. Tall estate walls. We gave our names to policewomen manning the gates at the back entrance, and drove in past signs painted a tastefully tubercular shade of palest green saying, 'You are now entering a GM-free zone.' We mingled in a clunky Tuscan new-build loggia called 'the Orchard Room', then formed up to go round the garden.

A handsome woman – a neighbour – called Amanda Hornby conducted the promised garden tour. Before we moved off, all the hacks were made to stand on lush Gloucestershire lawns under a bower created by dripping espaliered apple trees for her pre-amble (geddit?).

'The first question is, "How many gardeners does His Royal Highness have?"' (answer: eleven); 'the second is, "What does he do about slugs?"' she went on (answer: nothing) 'and the third is, "What was the Highgrove garden – about 20 acres, within a 1,000-acre estate – like before?"'

Then we went round the cottage and sundial gardens, the stumpery and kitchen garden at a gallop, taking care to keep on the right side of willow hoops placed in the ground to keep us from straying on to princely turf.

As HRH was in residence, we reptiles weren't allowed to sully the front of the house, where peons were raking gravel. Then we went back to the Orchard Room, where all the selected Duchy Original local producers, who trod lightly over their environment and loved their animals, stood smartly behind presentation tables laid out with tasting samples of their lines, wearing aprons.

And then lo, at the appointed hour, HRH/The Prince of Wales/ Prince Charles manifested and took endless trouble to meet and have a few words, and passed by every stall. He started with maple-cured ham and cheeses, proceeded past wine, apple juice, cakes, chocolates, scones, mueslis and granolas, lemon curds, preserves, ale, fizzy water; every item that had made the Duchy Original cut went into Royal mouth.

When he got to us – us being William Sitwell, editor of *Waitrose Kitchen* (who keeps telling me to have a 'Win a Stannah Stairlift' competition, not just once but every week), Lindsay Bareham, Allan Jenkins of *Observer Food Monthly* and Carolyn, i.e., a complete collection of reptiles – he beamed and said to me, 'Your brother's the only man I know who's made a speech in Latin. Do you speak Latin?'

Everyone looked at me expectantly. In fact, I had struggled with a Latin inscription carved on to a wooden sunhouse in the garden, by Horace, but wouldn't dream of admitting it.

'Yes, and Greek too of course,' I lied.

He was smaller than I expected. A slightly rumpled grey suit in a discreet Prince of Wales check hung off him. Despite his chest infection and weak voice – I could tell from his high colour he was running a fever – he made an expert speech in which he hailed the rain as a blessing from the gods without which none of the delicious foods we were eating could have been set before us, and thanked Waitrose for bailing out his Duchy Originals and setting it on a commercial footing. 'Thanks, Waitrose, for *showing such an interest*' were his exact words.

Only when I was leaving did I realize that I was so busy sampling all the blue cheese, ginger chocolate thins, etc., that I forgot to curtsey. I thought the Prince was bloody fantastic, took endless trouble to meet every single producer – in fact, every single person – in the Orchard Room, as well as chat to each and every hack. He does a jolly good oatcake too.

9 June 2010

The in tray:

- a care package from Tena Pants! I open it. 'TENA, the UK's leading bladder weakness brand, has launched two new products.' Which are without further ado 'TENA *Lady*' and 'TENA *Lady* with aloe vera'. There are samples – enclosed in a discreet rose-printed tin – plus other goodies. I am very grateful indeed for all this. Tena are big advertisers with us – without them, let's face it, the magazine would probably sink without trace, and we should retitle ourselves 'The TENA *Lady*' in honour of this lifesaving product.
- a letter from a reader in North Yorks asking me to advise her how many people read *The Lady* in Portugal.
- oooh this is nice. A bottle of Veuve Clicquot from JoJo Maman Bébé – the mumpreneur (bleugh) who brilliantly started this has won Veuve Clicqot Businesswoman of the Year.

I get a funny feeling in the building when I work late. Sometimes Janina appears at my door spectrally, but it's not that. I mentioned this to Claire – how jumpy I get – and we talked about the supposed *Lady* ghost. A previous editor called Jean Shepherd who'd been here ... actually, I know nothing about this. So I asked Edwina. And she said:

'An editor was halfway through an issue (two weeks before her retirement) when she tragically died of a stroke. Apparently, she haunts the building because she is desperate to finish the issue – some members of staff claim to have seen her. I remember Classified getting most cross with me when I went downstairs asking questions (so maybe not mention her name to anyone), but for your records, she was Editor from 1953 to 1971 (I think!).'

10 June 2010

Lunch with Marco Pierre White at Wheeler's in Jermyn Street. He was late, so I went to gents' hairdressers next door to stare at the shaving brushes and bottles. Barry Humphries was in there, buying cologne, wearing an ancient mac. I had a long chat with the manager of Truefitt & Hill about badger shaving brushes and the future of badger shaving brushes (he thinks they will soon, thanks to the cull, be banned; I wondered if that would make a good story for *The Lady* but decided it didn't as we are not called *The Gentleman*) then went back to see if Marco had arrived. He hadn't. I was shown to a corner booth, to await arrival.

When Marco did arrive, he was wearing a green faded polo; I was in jeans and trainers. He ordered for me – the egg mayonnaise, the crab, and the beetroot and goat's cheese and walnut salad; he had smoked salmon that had been cut very thin and spread out so it covered the whole plate like an oily orange lozenge. I took a photo of him sitting in front of the orange lozenge, staring moodily at me, on my iPhone and toyed with tweeting it, but managed to resist the urge.

I liked Marco a lot, even though he was the third person in a row that week who only appeared keen to chat to me (John Sentamu, Archbishop of York; Prince of Wales) because I was a blood-relation of Boris, which can be faintly pricking to the ego.

As we tucked in, he said the Tories had missed a trick by not grabbing 'working-class Tories' and using them as ambassadors for the party more, just as the Countryside Alliance had failed to see the PR value in the farriers and the whippers-in and the hunt followers, and focused on the toffs in the pink coats and black hats. 'But they didn't,' I pointed out (I seem to have read a million pieces about kennel keepers and stable lads in all publications). He is going to do a little column about dead-simple food such as we had been eating – no more than two ingredients – i.e., smoked salmon and lemon, quail's eggs and celery salt – and a bitty bit about his week in food.

He is mid-divorce and slightly crazed by it. Showed me a text from Mati, his wife. Said he was on the 'wealth diet'. Hates Blair, Labour – his line is that they are 'good for the working man but bad for the man who works'.

Not a bad line. Another Marcoism – 'Arrogance can breed success but only humility can breed greatness.' He puts his gift for the apophthegm down to early, undiagnosed dyspraxia. He worships the memory of his mother, who died when he was six, leaving a fourteen-day-old brother as well as his two older ones. He is the only one who has married. He went round all the tables after lunch, saying hello, and allowing diners to take pictures of him with them on their mobiles.

14 June 2010

Judy, our cosy production manager/den mother, who only wears M&S ('Marks'), was doing a key inventory. We realized that Janina still has the key to the Maiden Lane side entrance, as well as to the main entrance on Bedford Street. 'Why would she have that?' Judy asked Ben.

'Arline had it and presumably passed it down to her,' he said, in another terrible reminder of the *Wolf Hall* aspect of the Bedford Street HQ.

The in tray:

- a leaflet from Boots reminding me to stock up on flight socks and travel-sickness pills before I jet off on my 'exotic break abroad'.
- a letter from a reader decrying the Mary Killen and Penny Smith columns and saying the star of the magazine is, of course, Coco: 'and "Coco's Corner" is the first thing I turn to each week.'

- a letter from a man who wrote to Boris about the non-existence of a statue of Keats in London with a PS, 'I had an article published in *The Lady* a decade or so ago, "Pages of Pleasure".'
- one cancellation from Epsom, Surrey, from an 85-year-old reader who cites Mary Killen and Penny Smith, saying, 'I find so many empty articles, I read them and I wonder, "What was all that about?"'
- a cancellation (one of several) following Roger Lewis's review of the Jonathan King autobiography in which King says, 'Sex has been a huge and delightful part of my life.'
- a letter from a PR beginning, 'I rang to speak to you recently but you were not available and top marks to your PA for not letting me through.' (I offer up silent prayer of thanks to Gillian.) The letter wanted me to visit the Memorial Woodlands in Bristol. I read the whole letter. The PR invited me to come to see the Heirloom Tree. A family buys a tree, around which the entire family is buried over time, with relatives returning to visit, sit and picnic under their tree, and be with their loved ones, giving a whole new meaning to the phrase, 'family tree'.
- a letter from Mrs Budworth: 'Dear Rachel, Here we are, 5 June, and no answer from you to my letter of 29 May. Did it ever arrive? Julia Budworth.'

Email of the day:

> Good afternoon
>
> In view of the revamp of *The Lady*, I wondered if you would be interested in me writing an article on Cotswold sheep.

Feel like checking into the Memorial Woodlands, buying a *Lady* tree, and laying myself down underneath a spreading chestnut tree in the vestal glade, and waiting for the end to come quickly.

15 June 2010

Email of the day – received following yet another transmission of 'The Lady and the Revamp'.

> Hi Rachel,
>
> I have just watched the TV documentary on The Lady.
>
> It's obviously filmed some time ago, so no doubt you have had loads of HR people get in touch to offer assistance but if you or Ben ever need a lift with change management then give us a shout!

I must remember 'change management' for future ref. Change management is clearly central to editing. I henceforth intend to use the phrase all the time.

Runner-up email of the day from the oldest son of the Dowager Duchess of Bedford, who regularly advertises in The Lady.

> Good day to all at The Lady, the journal for gentlewomen read by Her Grace.
>
> Her Grace the Dowager Duchess of Bedford is celebrating her ninetieth birthday at her residence in Monte Carlo surrounded by all her children and grandchildren . . .

It is signed 'Didier, Her Grace's eldest son.' What does the family expect – a ten-gun salute?

Mrs Budworth has telephoned, in a bate about the fact that the word 'arsehole' appeared in the magazine. None of us can remember this and have been scratching our heads. It didn't appear in the Emin interview. Nor even in the Roger Lewis review of DJ Jonathan King's memoirs, in which he talks about his own penis and describes the appendage (a 'pink maggot') of a schoolboy he'd been intimate with (now a High Court judge). Jessica Lambert – a Cambridge undergrad, and our workie that week – was delegated to ring up Mrs B. in Suffolk.

'Well, I'm very glad indeed Ben is taking this seriously,' said Mrs B. 'I'm much too busy now in the garden of course to tell you which copy the word appeared in, but I definitely came across it. I thought, "Goodness gracious me! What is the dear girl Rachel doing?" Haven't we put our readers through enough already?'

So Jessica had to sit at a desk all morning, combing through the last few weeks' issues, but failed to spot the abhorrent item.

16 June 2010

Bad, bad news. The last two covers have tanked. Ben and I are trying to put brave face on. Ruby Wax only managed around 28,000 and then Mariella – I thought a slam dunk – not much better.

'Maybe the readers just didn't like the fifties-ish styling of the Ruby cover,' Ben mused. We chose a pic of Ruby lying in a bubble bath on the telephone. It was very Hollywood. 'Or maybe they just don't like Ruby.'

I pointed out that was unlikely, as our readers thought our cover star was not Ruby, anyway, but Gina Lollobrigida, born 1927, who was much more our speed (and demographic).

'How about a big fat sale to Condé Nast, or going down freebie alley?' I suggested to Ben. When I'm down, he props me up, and when he's down, I cheer him on. 'Why don't you sell to that chap from *The Dalesman*?' Apparently, Yorkshire-based *The Dalesman* is keen to walk up the isle with *The Lady* of Covent Garden, and it does sound like a match made in heaven.

*

I heard from Judy that, last week, Janina insisted that the loo window in the Ladies was kept closed. According to Judy, Janina once heard shouts from the street calling 'Lesbian, lesbian,' when the window was left open.

As I lay in bed I remembered – the Mariella and Ruby covers were published over half-term – maybe that explains it.

Or maybe it doesn't.

The in tray:

- an adorable stiffy card from Sam Cam in sumptuous Smythson stationery – white, tissue-lined in bright orange, and laid with matching orange lettering – thanking me for lovely note and tea-towels. It is signed 'Love Sam x'. She must have written it while moving house. I am hers, for ever.
- a card from a writer called Christine Webber who has written a book called *Too Young to Get Old*. She boldly asks for a column about being an over-fifty and adds, 'You'd probably have to shut Ben in the cupboard permanently' if I wanted to publish it in *The Lady*.

17 June 2010

Gave dinner party in our communal garden for eight. It should have been ten, but Toby Young jacks at last minute and his wife Caroline is, he proudly told me, 'also unavailable as she is at a reunion for her year at Cheltenham Ladies' College', as if that was all right then, because his lady wife went to posh girls' boarding school.

The Bodens (the mail-order moleskin magnate and his wife, Sophie, whom Ivo finds v. attractive in a dark Mitteleuropean way), the Bazalgettes (of Endemol fame) and filmmaker Gaby Dellal were attending.

Nicky Haslam came late, wearing punk TV shirt and Liam Gallagher jacket with his hair rising in a quiff. He was sweet to come, as he'd done Stephen Fry dins to benefit the Terrence Higgins Trust. We sat around a table in the garden, surrounded by flares (i.e., oil lamps not wide-bottomed trousers). My favourite bit was when Ivo offered him some Duchy Originals wine (I should in the interests of full disclosure point out that Waitrose, who is now in charge of Duchy Originals, comped and cooked the whole dinner and also socked me the chef) and Nicky said, 'I never drink wine,' as if it was vulgar. Red wine is 'wine' and rosé is called 'pink wine', and only white wine can be called 'white wine' according to Nicky (because, as above, red wine is 'wine').

Then he said – apropos a tidbit about a mutual married friend parading about with his gay lover – 'Being gay is terribly common,' which made us all scream with laughter, not merely because he has described himself as a living link to 'post-war faggotry' but because he ritually describes everything as 'common', from loving one's parents to water and saying please.

21 June 2010

Roger Lewis did not win the Oxford Professorship of Poetry. In fact, he only got 167 votes. He emailed me in despair.

> Oh, what a weekend. The Oxon thing was a disaster – the dopey buggers wanted Geoffrey Hill from the start. But *where were my troops*? I polled so few votes (167!) – I felt like Antony at Alexandria, all alone in the field of battle. Even my sworn enemy Michael Horovitz got twice my votes, and he's a well-known twat. I was only a handful of votes better off than a *busker*! Boris evidently succeeded handsomely in making me into *toast*. Then I did a piece

in the *Mail on Sunday* that was cut by a half. I had a much funnier
para about 'The Johnsons At Home', these brilliant blond Turkish
brigands with scimitars. But worst of all – the online version was
sub-edited by a madman who made it look like I'd won! Thank God
for my insomnia – at 2.30 a.m. I was on the phone to the night
watchman/editor getting a rectification. Scandal only very narrowly
averted.

Is Rules your office canteen? Because you can take me there if yes.

Shall I stand again in 2045, when I am more Geoffrey Hill's age?

Merrily rolling along,
Roger

In the evening, I went to Paul Johnson and Marigold Johnson
summer party. Asked Princess Michael if she'd write a 'Diary'. She
agreed to immediately. Then I turned to Prince Michael and said
that any time he needed to advertise for a new valet or HRH
needed a new lady's maid, he just had to say the word, as if I would
pay them in kind. Then I winked.

22 *June 2010*

A Tuesday. Circulation figures up, but only up a bit. The problem
is, we pop two copies of *The Lady* in 11,000 newsagents, and we
either sell one or two (and then we don't have a presence on the
shelf) or none, and at £1.80, of that, 80p goes to the distributor.
The answer is to go fortnightly, but then that mucks up the reve-
nue stream that is the classified.

Lunch with Ben at Leon. He wants me to dream up things that
will make *The Lady* unmissable, something you just have to have
each week. Like *Country Life* has country houses, and *The Week* has

a digest of the week. The only thing that he regards as unmissable is 'Coco's Corner'. I wondered out loud whether to have a column by Nicky Haslam on what was common this week (Wimbledon, Glastonbury, glamping, barbecues, etc.) and what was not common (pink wine, sweet peas, chintz, etc.) and call it 'Common or Garden'.

On the money front, Ben has abandoned hope that Coutts will reverse their decision not to stump up the next tranche of money. He has announced he'll tap a different, even more exclusive private bank, which charges like the Light Brigade. I know this because I bank there myself – thanks to having high-born husband, I hasten to add.

'At least then I'll be able to boast that we've got Hoare's at *The Lady*,' he said.

I think the answer to all these intractable problems of identity, of circulation, unmissable columns, hooks, etc., is that there is probably no answer. We have to carry on producing a magazine people enjoy reading, and do it every week. Ben has a very difficult job, and I would not trade places with him for all the tea in China.

I asked about the board meeting on 4 July which Willy, Adam, Richard and Ben Budworth, plus of course Mrs Julia Budworth, will be attending in the boardroom.

Ben was non-committal as to what will be on the agenda.

'Is it my sacking?' I asked over Leon chicken superfood salad. Boiling-hot day on the Strand. Coco panting under the table.

'Well, I think it's safe to say that Mum's not your biggest fan,' he said.

'Well, tell Maureen to keep a note of what she says so you can tell me after,' I said.

'I will, but at the board meeting this time last year, Maureen appeared to take a careful note of every word and only admitted later that she hadn't heard a thing because they were drilling in Bedford Street,' Ben said.

23 June 2010

Lots to report! Apparently not only Blez is hawking a book about his time at *The Lady* around publishers, but Lindsay is too!

Mrs Budworth – who has been talking to Lindsay and Janina about their time here, which doesn't exactly make the heart sing with happiness – has submitted a six-page document of things to be discussed at the board meeting in July. I was allowed a quick look.

She has formally asked Ben, as chief executive ('What a pomp-ous title,' she added), to supply the four other directors (i.e., his brothers and mother) a comprehensive dossier explaining who everyone is and how much they get paid relative to the Golden Age, i.e., Arline's editorship. There are suggestions from Mrs B. about having a country-life column, and using the Fromenti fash-ion drawings from the archive more (not a bad idea) and lots of pointed queries about the editorial process. For example, 'Who is reading the proofs?' one item demands to know. This is, presum-ably, so she knows who to dress down over further appearances of words like 'arsehole'. There is one item specifically concerning me. 'What do we think of the new editor?' The note goes on. 'I expect this meeting to take longer than usual and suggest we break for coffee and sandwiches at 1 p.m.'

24 June 2010

The comedienne and author Annabel Giles came in – to talk about doing a series of interviews – women and their dogs. She was beau-tiful. And single. And Ben is single.

Annabel gamely quizzed Ben in the boardroom. 'Are you enjoy-ing it?' she asked.

'When I think I could be flying hairy-arsed, foul-mouthed Scots-men to oil rigs,' he sighed wistfully. He checked her out, before adding, 'Why don't we do something about biscuits? Everyone likes biscuits.'

We all agreed on that, then he told us a long anecdote about when he'd come back from flying helicopters in Florida to take over the old girl, and making desperate efforts to get rid of a tea cosy that kept appearing on the pot every time the tea service from Ros, who also multi-tasks as our dulcet-toned telephonist, came round.

He'd tried throwing it out of the window, burying it at the bot-tom of bins wrapped in plastic bags, but whatever he did, it would reappear the next day, laundered, over the pot, which Ros would bring in, pursed of lip. 'They still give me dirty looks if I try to make my own tea,' he finished.

'So, is it a bit like a girls' school here?' continued Annabel.

She'd just witnessed a scene in my office when Judy, the pro-duction manager, made me put cortisol cream on an insect bite on my ankle – an injury sustained during my father's seventieth birth-day party in Regent's Park on Tuesday – while Gillian bustled about with TCP and cotton wool. It was a scene from Matron's landing in a prep school *circa* 1956.

'Yes it is, apart from the fact there's never lights out,' he said.

25 June 2010

So ... speaking of lights out, it has come to my attention that I started this diary on 9 June 2009, I was announced editor in July, and I became editor at the beginning of September.

It's Friday, and am shirking from home. About to go to Nicky Haslam's in Hampshire for the weekend bearing a tray of figs (they surely can't be common?). I asked him for the dress code. 'A wisp of chiffon,' he replied.

Now, not wanting to be too pedantic about the subtitle, 'My first year as editor', and all that (Ben wearily knows, because I tell him all the time, I worked *pro bono* from the second I got the gig. I commissioned, for example, Charlie Glass's now-legendary article on humping the help exactly a year ago), it strikes me that this might be a good time to stop.

To date, I've commissioned and edited around forty-four editions of the magazine, and shifted around 1.3 million copies. That's about half as many as I was expected to sell. On the plus side, I've personally soiled around 323 tea-towels, and according to *Campaign*, '*The Lady* magazine has had more media attention in the past six months than in its entire 125-year existence. And it's all down to Rachel Johnson.'

(Their words, not mine. When I put the words 'Arline Usden' and '*The Lady*' into Google, it returned 323 results. When I put my own and '*The Lady*', it returned 995,000, and when Edwina did it, she got more than 3 million.)

Not that it matters much.

I fear that all the buzz in the world is not going to persuade new readers in their forties to pick up a magazine they last spotted in their great-grandmother's care home – not in a tearing hurry, anyway. The magazine has masses for them to read, but it's still an impossible gig, doubling the circulation. While my old readers are still being gathered (that's trendy vicar-speak for 'dying'), any new ones are still going online. The rats!

Another problem: the 'brand association' between *The Lady* with nannies, carers, holiday cottages and housekeepers for country piles – an association that keeps the business going – is not going to change quickly either.

But still. Whatever the old guard think, and I dread to imagine sometimes, I am proud of the magazine, and pleased with the quality of the writing contained within the curiously slimy, shiny covers (carry a bunch of copies, and they always slither out of your

arms to the floor – we get Basildon Bond about it, as we do everything else).

I'm pleased I restored the subtitle, 'A Journal for Gentlewomen',
in wiggly, toothpaste writing on the front cover, because I want to
reassure everyone that I'm not going to turn the old girl into a
fallen woman, Lady-to-Ladette-style, even if I did put Tracey Emin
on the cover and have probably perpetrated many other sundry
crimes against gentility.

So, I think this is the time to stop. Even though I don't know the
outcome of the Mail on Sunday potato-growing contest; even
though I haven't quite sat in the editor's chair a year; and even
though the board meeting in which at least one director has called
for my sacking hasn't yet taken place.

And even though I can't claim I've doubled circulation, or made
The Lady cool, or pleased Mrs Budworth. But I don't rule either of
those things out . . . oh, in the next 125 years or so.

Until that time, as Lady Thatcher once said, we fight on.

To be honest, I don't really want to return to my old life of
strolling around the Portobello Road in yogawear, dipping into
Gail's for their no-dairy, no-sugar bran muffin, and the Grocer on
Elgin for a £4 packet of assorted, organic, hand-picked leaves. It
was actually quite dull, even if I do miss those lunches in the raw
bar at Daylesford, and those power naps after. To paraphrase that
BP chap, I don't want my life back.

So, as I said, we fight on! We will fight them on the beaches, we
will fight them on the landing grounds, we will fight them in
WHSmith and John Menzies and in R. S. McColl, and in newsagents up and down the land, we will fight them in Martins with
doilies and glass cloths and tea cosies. We fight on wearing Tena
pants, and we fight to win.

And if we fail, I will always hold my head up high to have served
my time as the ninth editor of the first and finest women's weekly
in the land, the longest continuously published women's maga-

zine in the world, the journal for gentlewomen, *The Lady*, 39/40 Bedford Street, The Strand, WC2 9ER, est. 1885.

It's been the best year of my life so far.

Postscript

Ten random things I have learnt about being an editor in one short year:

1. A full-colour, hand-tooled, weekly magazine containing 50 pages of glistening editorial must sell more than 35,000 copies at £1.80 at the newsstand to break even, and a weekly magazine must sell more than 45,000 copies before advertisers – I mean, real advertisers, i.e., those that do not advertise donkey sanctuaries in the Holy Land or surgery for poor, hare-lipped children, walk-in baths and pill dispensers – will even consider buying space. Remember – I couldn't even *give* away space to Burberry.

2. Never underestimate how difficult it is to get anyone to buy anything. I am now like a politician needing voters to stay in office – so this is what I say to my valued readers and subscribers and advertisers, past, present and future: *with my body, I thee worship.*

3. Even so, I feel like killing with my bare hands contributors who send me emails asking me when their piece entitled 'Amazing Mazes' or 'Scents & Sensibility', commissioned by the previous editor sometime in 2008, will run. When travel PRs call to ask me when a freelancer's piece on the cuisine of Tunisia following a three-week-long freebie in 2007 will be published, I want to order a massacre of the firstborns, followed by Gillian for putting them through. This is normal.

4. I have to restrain myself when journo friends email me directly complaining they haven't been paid. Invoicing is *so*

beneath my pay grade! Instead, I respond instantly with icy politeness, and call Tracey, in Accounts.

5.   I have learnt that Ben, far from needing to 'grow a pair of balls', is a dynamic, kind, nay inspirational publisher and supreme commander, with rock-hard *cojones* you can see from space, who responds to my diva-ish strops with superhuman tolerance. I couldn't begin to control the operation that is *The Lady*, talk to distributors, advertisers – both display and classified – marketers, brand agents, PRs, printers, and so on. In fact, I barely know what the moving parts are, let alone have the ability to control them. I can barely keep myself in running order, get from A to B, etc.

6.   Despite the fact that running a weekly magazine is like continuously standing on a beach in North Cornwall and feeling wave after wave hit you and then, just as you catch your breath, a really BIG wave (press day) smashes you and drags you under into the riptide, I quite like it, on the whole. This has been funner than anything else I've ever done, but is, it has to be admitted, quite ageing. I feel about 125 now, and no longer look in the mirror apart from to check for overnight apparition of rogue hairs on chin and inspect deepening of nasolabial lines, as if watching my face in time-lapse, speeded-up time.

7.   It really matters what you put on the cover. Don't put Mark Thatcher (a mummy's boy of the first order) or Sharon Osbourne (a woman who has admitted to sending people excrement in the post) on the cover of a magazine called *The Lady* unless you want to offend virtually all your loyal readers of forty years' standing, who regard the magazine as the last remaining bastion of gentility in a thoroughly depraved universe.

8.   Changes will offend most of your existing readers all the time, and new ones will clamber on board very slowly. Every time you replace a long-standing theatre critic or gardening column with someone dewier and fresher, your long-standing

readers will react as if you have taken a chainsaw to the Crown Jewels. You just have to be brave and take it on the chin because, after six months, they react even more furiously if you bin any of your own, initially unpopular, innovations. I got heaps of letters complaining about my column for chaps called 'The Gents'. And I got just as many after I canned it.

9. Online really matters. Online is our only hope. My children have never bought a newspaper. Magazines will not be around in twenty years. Nor will newspapers. This is what the doomsayers are saying, anyway, and it would be foolish to ignore them.

10. The magazine – especially a national institution, whose mere existence transmits 'something benign into the ether' (as the journalist from the *Khaleej Times* put it, as if the weekly magazine is like a Glade 'Sense and Spray'™ that spritzes the country, once a week, with deodorizing fragrance) – does not belong to me. It doesn't even belong to the Budworths. It belongs to the readers. All magazines do.

An editor forgets that at her peril. That's about it.